InterViews

Steinar Kvale

InterViews

An Introduction to Qualitative Research Interviewing

SAGE Publications
International Educational and Professional Publisher
Thousand Oaks   London   New Delhi

For information address:

SAGE Publications, Inc.
2455 Teller Road
Thousand Oaks, California 91320
E-mail: order@sagepub.com

SAGE Publications Ltd.
6 Bonhill Street
London EC2A 4PU
United Kingdom

SAGE Publications India Pvt. Ltd.
M-32 Market
Greater Kailash I
New Delhi 110 048 India

Printed in the United States of America

Library of Congress Cataloging-in-Publication Data

Kvale, Steinar, 1938-
    InterViews: An introduction to qualitative research interviewing / author, Steinar Kvale.
        p.   cm.
    "Originally published by Studentlitteratur. © Steinar Kvale and Studentlitteratur, Lund, Sweden, 1994"—Verso t.p.
    Includes bibliographical references and index.
    ISBN 0-8039-5819-6 (cloth: acid-free paper). —
ISBN 0-8039-5820-X (pbk.: acid-free papr).
    1. Interviewing in sociology. 2. Interviewing. 3. Sociology—Research—Methodology. I. Title.
HM48.K9   1996
301′.01—dc2   95-50205

This book is printed on acid-free paper.

    97 98 99 10 9 8 7 6 5 4

Sage Production Editor: Astrid Virding
Sage Typesetter: Janelle LeMaster

Contents

List of Boxes,
Figures, and Tables

Boxes

Figures

Tables

Acknowledgments

Earlier versions of parts of the present book have been published in the following journals and books:

Kvale, S. (1983a). The qualitative research interview—A phenomenological and a hermeneutical mode of understanding. *Journal of Phenomenological Psychology*, *14*, 171-196. [Reprinted from: Kvale, S. (1979). Det kvalitative forskningsinterview—Ansatser til en fænomenologisk-hermeneutisk forståelsesform. In T. Broch, K. Krarup, P. K. Larsen, & O. Rieper (Eds.), *Kvalitative metoder i dansk samfundsforskning* (pp. 160-185). København: Nyt fra Samfundsvidenskaberne.]

Kvale, S. (1983b). The quantification of knowledge in education: On resistance toward qualitative evaluation and research. In B. Bain (Ed.), *The sociogenesis of language and human conduct* (pp. 433-447). New York: Plenum.

Kvale, S. (1986). Psychoanalytic therapy as qualitative research. In P. Ashworth, A. Giorgi, & A. de Koning (Eds.), *Qualitative research in psychology* (pp. 155-184). Pittsburgh: Duquesne University Press.

Kvale, S. (1987). Interpretation of the qualitative research interview. In B. Mook, F. Wertz, & F. van Zuuren (Eds.), *Advances in qualitative psychology* (pp. 25-40). Lisse, The Netherlands: Swets & Zeitlinger.

Kvale, S. (1988). The 1000 page question. *Phenomenology + Pedagogy*, *6*, 90-106.

Kvale, S. (1989). The primacy of the interview. *Methods,* No. 1, pp. 3-37.

Kvale, S. (1989). To validate is to question. In S. Kvale (Ed.), *Issues of validity in qualitative research* (pp. 73-92). Lund, Sweden: Studentlitteratur.

Kvale, S. (1994). Ten standard objections to qualitative research interviews. *Journal of Phenomenological Psychology, 25,* 147-173.

Kvale, S. (1995). The social construction of validity. *Qualitative Inquiry, 1,* 19-40.

The topics of these articles and chapters are, with the exception of those from 1986 and 1995, treated more extensively in this book.

Preface

This book has two purposes. First, it provides new interview researchers with practical guidelines for "how to do" research interviews. Second, it suggests—for novice and experienced interview researchers alike—conceptual frames of reference for "how to think about" interview research.

The book arose from my own use of interviews in a study on the educational effects of grading in Denmark in 1978. The experiences with what was then a new form of research instigated reflection on methodical and theoretical issues. At that time, there was an awakening interest in qualitative research, which led to lectures and courses on qualitative methods, which led again to a Center of Qualitative Research at the Institute of Psychology in Aarhus—as well as courses elsewhere, in particular at the University of Oslo and the Saybrook Institute in San Francisco.

There was little literature on interview research in the early 1980s, and a demand for writings on the topic resulted in several articles and book chapters (see the Acknowledgments). They originated as preparations for research courses and were further developed in dialogues with the participating students. The students' insightful comments, and their often difficult questions, stimulated and contributed significantly to the present work. These earlier articles and chapters have now been rewritten and extended as the present book.

I am indebted to Scandinavian co-teachers and organizers in the qualitative research courses, such as Erle Bryn, Jette Fog, and Tove Arendt Rasmussen; colleagues in the Danish network of qualitative research Klaus Bruhn Jensen, Grethe Skylv, and Jan Helge Larsen, and Biørn Hasselgren at the Nordic courses. By teaching together with quantitative researchers such as Finn Tschudi, Bo Sommerlund, and Ole Steen Kristensen—the first two are mathematicians—I learned that quantitative research need not be understood in a positivist frame and to regard the qualitative versus quantitative controversy as a pseudo-issue.

In the mid-1980s there was a marked increase in public investment in Ph.D. education in Denmark. This included the financing of courses on qualitative methods by the Danish Research Council for the Social Sciences, the Danish Research Academy, and Nordic Research Courses. The financial support made it possible to invite foreign scholars to promote and inspire qualitative research in Denmark, including the present work. These guests include Hubert Dreyfus, Stuart Dreyfus, Elliot Eisner, Regi Enerstvedt, K. Anders Ericson, Amedeo Giorgi, Ken Gergen, Mary Gergen, David Goode, Hanne Haavind, Patti Lather, Jean Lave, Lasse Løvlie, Ference Marton, Elliot Mishler, Martin Packer, Bryan Pfaffenberger, Donald Polkinghorne, Marcia Salner, Renata Tesch, Finn Tschudi, and John Van Maanen.

For critical readings of the manuscript I am indebted to Ulla Bøwadt, Henrik Brogaard, Marsha Hammond, Mary Ann McGuire, Klaus Nielsen, Tone Saugstad, and Carsten Østerlund. Knud-Erik Sabroe has kindly provided the example of the ethical complaint reported in Chapter 6. Mitch Allen at Sage has encouraged the book project and given valuable comments, and Peter Labella has helpfully kept the manuscript on track during final editing. I am further indebted to David Morgan, Lynn Schlesinger, and an anonymous reviewer for their suggestions for improving the manuscript.

I am grateful to Birgit Wenzel, who assisted by compiling the literature used in the book; to Annie Dolmer Kristensen and Lone Hansen, who have patiently written and edited the many versions of the journal articles and the book; and to Kristin Bergstad who has worked to transform my Norwegian-Danish English into readable English.

Interviews are conversations where the outcome is a coproduction of the interviewer and the subject. This book is the result of the variety of conversations about interview conversations with the persons mentioned above. They do not, however, share all of the views presented here. I am thankful for their significant contributions to the present book.

—Steinar Kvale

PART

I

Introduction

If you want to know how people understand their world and their life, why not talk with them? In an interview conversation, the researcher listens to what people themselves tell about their lived world, hears them express their views and opinions in their own words, learns about their views on their work situation and family life, their dreams and hopes. The qualitative research interview attempts to understand the world from the subjects' points of view, to unfold the meaning of peoples' experiences, to uncover their lived world prior to scientific explanations.

The qualitative research interview is a construction site of knowledge. An interview is literally an *inter view,* an inter change of views between two persons conversing about a theme of mutual interest. This book attempts to lay out the richness and the scope of qualitative interviews in social science research. It tries to link methods of—and ideas about—interviews, continually drawing attention to the interplay of practical and theoretical issues of interview research.

1

Interviewing as Research

In this chapter I first present two alternative metaphors for the research interviewer's role—as a miner or as a traveler. I then turn to the interview as a conversation and give a few examples before addressing the position of qualitative interviews in social science research. Thereafter some theoretical and methodological issues raised by employing interviews as a research method are introduced. The chapter concludes with a model of interviews as literally *inter views,* followed by an overview of the book's chapters.

The Interviewer as a Miner or as a Traveler

Two contrasting metaphors of the interviewer—as a miner or as a traveler—can illustrate the implications of different theoretical understandings of interview research.

In the *miner metaphor,* knowledge is understood as buried metal and the interviewer is a miner who unearths the valuable metal. Some miners seek objective facts to be quantified, others seek nuggets of essential meaning. In both conceptions the knowledge is waiting in the subjects' interior to be uncovered, uncontaminated by the miner. The interviewer digs nuggets of data or meanings out of a subject's pure experiences, unpolluted by any leading questions. The interview researcher strips the surface of conscious experiences, the therapeutic interviewer mines the deeper unconscious layers. The precious facts and meanings are purified by transcribing them from the oral to the written mode. The knowledge nuggets remain constant through the transformations of appearances on the conveyor belt from the oral stage to the written storage. By analysis, the objective facts and the essential meanings are drawn out by various techniques and molded into their definitive form. Finally the value of the end product, its degree of purity, is determined by correlating it with an objective, external, real world or to a realm of subjective, inner, authentic experiences.

The alternative *traveler metaphor* understands the interviewer as a traveler on a journey that leads to a tale to be told upon returning home. The interviewer-traveler wanders through the landscape and enters into conversations with the people encountered. The traveler explores the many domains of the country, as unknown territory or with maps, roaming freely around the territory. The traveler may also deliberately seek specific sites or topics by following a *method,* with the original Greek meaning of "a route that leads to the goal." The interviewer wanders along with the local inhabitants, asks questions that lead the subjects to tell their own stories of their lived world, and converses with them in the original Latin meaning of *conversation* as "wandering together with."

What the traveling reporter hears and sees is described qualitatively and is reconstructed as stories to be told to the people of the interviewer's own country, and possibly also to those with whom the interviewer wandered. The potentialities of meanings in the original stories are differentiated and unfolded through the traveler's interpretations; the tales are remolded into new narratives, which are convincing in their aesthetic form and are validated through their impact upon the listeners.

The journey may not only lead to new knowledge; the traveler might change as well. The journey might instigate a process of reflection that leads the interviewer to new ways of self-understanding, as well as uncovering previously taken-for-granted values and customs in the traveler's home country. The transformative effects of traveling are expressed in the German term *Bildungsreise*—a scholarly, formative journey. Through conversations, the traveler can also lead others to new understanding and insight as they, through their own storytelling, may come to reflect on previously natural-seeming matters of course in their culture. Rorty's (1992) picture of inspired criticism pertains to a transformative conversation that is "the result of an encounter with an author, character, plot, stanza, line, or archaic torso which has made a difference to the critic's conception of who she is, what she is good for, what she wants to do with herself; an encounter which has re-arranged her priorities and purposes" (p. 107).

The two metaphors—of the interviewer as a miner or as a traveler—represent different concepts of knowledge formation. Each metaphor stands for alternative genres and has different rules of the game. In a broad sense, the miner metaphor pictures a common understanding in modern social sciences of knowledge as "given." The traveler metaphor refers to a postmodern constructive understanding that involves a conversational approach to social research. The miner metaphor brings interviews into the vicinity of human engineering; the traveler metaphor into the vicinity of the humanities and art.

Conversation as Research

Conversation is a basic mode of human interaction. Human beings talk with each other—they interact, pose questions, and answer questions. Through conversations we get to know other people, get to learn about their experiences, feelings, and hopes and the world they live in.

There are multiple forms of conversations—in everyday life, in literature, and in the professions. Everyday conversations may range from chat and small talk, through exchanges of news, disputes, or formal negotiations, to deep personal interchanges. Within literature, the varieties of conversation span drama to novels to short stories, which may contain longer or shorter passages of conversations. Professional conversations include journalistic interviews, legal interrogations, academic oral examinations, religious confessions, therapeutic dialogues, and—to be discussed here—qualitative research interviews. Each of these conversational genres uses different rules and techniques.

The research interview is based on the conversations of daily life and is a professional conversation. One form of research interview—a semistructured life world interview—will be treated in this book. It is defined as *an interview whose purpose is to obtain descriptions of the*

*life world of the interviewee with respect to interpreting the meaning
of the described phenomena.*

The use of the interview as a research method is nothing mysterious: An interview is a conversation that has a structure and a purpose. It goes beyond the spontaneous exchange of views as in everyday conversation, and becomes a careful questioning and listening approach with the purpose of obtaining thoroughly tested knowledge. The research interview is not a conversation between equal partners, because the researcher defines and controls the situation. The topic of the interview is introduced by the researcher, who also critically follows up on the subject's answers to his or her questions.

Examples of interviews will be given throughout this book (particularly in Chapters 2 & 7). To illustrate this form of inquiry, I will present interview passages taken from a study of the effects of grading in Danish high schools (Kvale, 1980):

Interviewer: You mentioned previously something about grades, would you please try and say more about that?

Pupil: Grades are often unjust, because very often—very often—they are only a measure of how much you talk, and how much you agree with the teacher's opinion. For instance, I may state an opinion on the basis of a tested ideology, and which is against the teacher's ideology. The teacher will then, because it is his ideology, which he finds to be the best one, of course say that what he is saying is right and what I am saying is wrong.

Interviewer: How should that influence the grade?

Pupil: Well, because he would then think that I was an idiot—who comes up with the wrong answers.

Interviewer: Is this not only your postulate?

Pupil: No, there are lots of concrete examples.

In response to an open question from the interviewer, the pupil himself introduces a dimension of his experience of grades—they are unfair—and he spontaneously gives his reasons for why they are unfair. The interviewer critically follows up the answers, asks for specifics, and tests the strength of the pupil's belief by doubting it.

Interview inquiries may include multiple actors in a social scene. Two further views on the fairness of grades—from a fellow pupil and from a teacher—follow:

Pupil: I find that the teachers actually evaluate in a rather fair way. It is not possible to cheat them either, which many believe they can. If you sit there—and as soon as someone has raised his hand, and the teacher has asked him and then—(raises his hand). Well, I don't think it will work. I don't think they are that stupid.

*   *   *   *   *

Interviewer: Do you think that there are some pupils who want to bluff by raising their hands?

Teacher: Well, I don't think so, I don't think they are particularly sly in that respect—in some way or another—to give the impression that they know more than they do. That is not my impression—at least not in my classes.

These later statements contradict the first pupil; the second pupil finds the grading fair and believes that teachers see through other pupils' attempts to raise their grades by bluffing, and this view is confirmed by the teacher interviewed. With such contradictory information obtained from these three actors in the classroom scene, one might be tempted to discard the qualitative interview as a research method—the knowledge obtained is not objective, but subjective in the sense that it depends too much on the subjects interviewed. Throughout this book I will argue that, on the contrary, it is in fact a strength of the interview conversation to capture the multitude of subjects' views of a theme and to picture a manifold and controversial human world. A main issue will be how to obtain reliable and valid knowledge of the social world through the various views of the interacting subjects. In later chapters (Chapter 12, Questions Posed to an Interview Text, and Chapter 13, Validity as Quality of Craftsmanship) I will return to the interpretation and validation of the statements above and also discuss their representativity (Chapter 5, Interviews About Grades).

Interview Research in the Social Sciences

If conversations did not exist, there would hardly be any shared knowledge about the social scene. As a thought experiment we might imagine that human conversation did not exist, and therefore that the knowledge acquired through conversations—as personal knowledge for the reader and as general knowledge for humankind—was nonexistent. Yet in the social sciences, conversation as a method of obtaining knowledge has—until recently—rarely been mentioned in method textbooks.

Conversation is an ancient form of obtaining knowledge. Thucydides interviewed participants from the Peloponnesian Wars to write the history of the wars, and Socrates used dialogue to obtain philosophical knowledge. Within the modern social sciences, which originated in the 19th century, systematic interview research is, however, a new phenomenon of the past decades. Conversations have belonged to the realm of the humanities and philosophy, whereas social science methodology has long been modeled on the natural sciences. The present emphasis on the interview as conversation and on the interpretation of its meanings brings interview research closer to the domain of the humanities.

Interviews have, however, been previously employed in the social sciences. Anthropologists and sociologists have long used informal interviews to obtain knowledge from their informants. Sociologists and psychologists have talked with their human subjects in order to obtain necessary background knowledge for conducting questionnaire studies and laboratory experiments. What is new in recent decades is that qualitative interviews are increasingly employed as a research method in their own right, with an expanding methodological literature on how to carry out interview research systematically.

Technical as well as theoretical reasons might be suggested for today's growing research use of qualitative interviews. The development in the 1950s of small portable tape recorders made the exact recording of interviews easy. In the 1980s, computer programs facilitated the qualitative analyses of transcribed interviews. Broad changes in current thought, reflected in philosophy, emphasize themes such as the everyday lived world and its common language, meaning, and interrelations. Narratives and conversations are today regarded as essential for obtaining knowledge of the social world, including scientific knowledge.

Until recently, the field of qualitative inquiry was fragmented into different disciplines with communication gaps across interpretative communities. With an absence of common literature, procedures, and criteria, interviewers have to a large extent had to rely on their individual creativity. One consequence is that isolated researchers have invented small qualitative wheels over and over again.

This state of affairs is now changing with the increasing number of books, journals, and conferences in the field of qualitative research. Cross-disciplinary works have been published, such as *Handbook of Qualitative Research* edited by Denzin and Lincoln (1994) and *Handbuch Qualitative Sozialforschung* edited by Flick, Kardoff, Keupp, Rosenstiel, and Wolff (1991). Several journals dedicated to qualitative research have appeared in the past decades: *Qualitative Sociology* (first published in 1978), *Qualitative Studies in Education* (first published in 1988), *Qualitative Health Research* (first published in 1991), and the cross-disciplinary *Qualitative Inquiry* (first published in 1995). With the new literature, a common knowledge base is available for methodological and theoretical development of qualitative research.

Sophistication in qualitative research is today rather unevenly distributed in the social sciences. Although much of what is said here may be old news within anthropology and sociology, it can be relatively new, and perhaps shockingly unscientific, within some departments of psychology. One might have assumed that the production of knowledge through the human interaction of the interview might be a central concern in psychology. In the psychological profession, the interview is an essential tool—for example, in personnel selection, in counseling, and in therapy. A scientific psychology leaning heavily on natural sciences has, however, generally neglected the human aspects of knowledge production, including the knowledge potentials of the human conversation. Throughout this book I will draw on insights from the use of interviews in psychological practice, in particular the psychoanalytic interview (Chapter 4, Psychoanalytical Knowledge Production).

That there has been little systematic reflection on the practical and conceptual issues of using interviews as a research method may also be due to the closeness of the research interview to the conversations of daily life. This may have implied that it was superfluous to reflect on the interview methodologically. To contemplate the nearness of the research interview to everyday conversations may also have been threatening to the scientific legitimacy of the "young" social sciences. A further reason for the lack of conceptualization and of common frames for understanding qualitative research may be that its proximity to the human sciences has been at odds with dominating conceptions of social science as a natural science. The somewhat controversial position of interview research in the social sciences will be taken up again in Chapter 4.

Theoretical Issues

Developing the interview as a research method involves a challenge to renew, broaden, and enrich the conceptions of knowledge and research in the social sciences. The research interview is not merely a new method, yielding qualitative texts rather than quantitative data, but reflects alternative conceptions of the subject matter of the social sciences. Many apparently methodological problems do not stem from the relative newness of the interview method or from insufficiently developed techniques, but are the consequences of unclarified theoretical assumptions.

Some authors have pointed out a neglect of theory in current qualitative research. Strauss (1995) thus criticizes the absence of theoretical discussions in the large majority of the chapters in Denzin and Lincoln's *Handbook of Qualitative Research* (1994), mentioned above. Giorgi (1994) concludes a review of recent literature on qualitative methods in this way: "Thus, greater theoretical clarity and consistency as well as deeper reflection or better utilization of imaginative possibilities still seem to be called for in order to bring better theoretical conceptualization and more consistent practices to qualitative research" (p. 190).

Addressing the methodological questions of conducting an interview leads to theoretical issues—conceptions of the specific themes investigated, as well as of the nature of the social world. Qualitative methods are not merely some new, soft technology added to the existing hard-core quantitative arsenal of the social sciences. Rather, the mode of understanding implied by qualitative research involves alternative conceptions of social knowledge, of meaning, reality, and truth in social science research. The basic subject matter is no longer objective data to be quantified, but meaningful relations to be interpreted. The transition from the miner metaphor of interviewing as digging up nuggets of meaningful data to the traveler metaphor of interviewing as the construction of stories was discussed in this chapter's introduction.

There is a move away from obtaining knowledge primarily through external observation and experimental manipulation of human subjects, toward an understanding by means of conversations with the human beings to be understood. The subjects not only answer questions prepared by an expert, but themselves formulate in a dialogue their own conceptions of their lived world. The sensitivity of the interview and its closeness to the subjects' lived world can lead to knowledge that can be used to enhance the human condition. The interview as such is, however, neither a progressive nor an oppressive method. As will be discussed later, the knowledge produced can be used either to enhance the investigated subjects' condition or to manipulate their behavior more efficiently (see Chapter 4).

Within philosophy in the past half century the positivist philosophy of science has declined. Positivism conceived of the social sciences as natural sciences, to be based on objective quantifiable data, with the prediction and control of the behavior of others as a goal. Today there is a shift toward philosophical lines of thought closer to the humanities. These include a postmodern social construction of reality, hermeneutical interpretations of the meanings of texts, phenomenological descriptions of consciousness, and the dialectical situating of human activity in social and historical contexts. That the qualitative interview is being focused on today, may in part be due to the correspondence of themes central to current philosophy and to the qualitative interview, such as experience, meaning, life world, conversation, dialogue, narrative, and language (see Chapters 2 & 3). Thus a postmodern approach will, in line with the traveler metaphor of the interviewer, emphasize the constructive nature of the knowledge created through the interaction of the partners in the interview conversation.

Throughout this book I will attempt to spell out the implications of these philosophical analyses for the understanding of interview research. I am not offering a comprehensive theory of the research interview. Rather, different philosophical conceptions of conversation and its use as a research method will be presented. They will provide theoretical contexts for conceptualizing the methodological and theoretical issues that arise when using interview conversations as a research method and they will be addressed in Part II of this book, Conceptualizing the Research Interview.

Methodological Issues

Research using interviews involves a deceptive simplicity; it is easy to start interviewing without any advance preparation or reflection. The novice researcher may have a good idea, grab a tape recorder, go out and find some subjects, and start questioning them. The recorded interviews are transcribed and then—during analysis of the many pages of transcripts—questions about the purpose and content of the study start to come up. This kind of theoretical naïveté and methodological spontaneity may in part be counterreactions to the abstract theories and formalized methodology taught in some social science departments.

A novice researcher who is more methodologically oriented may have a host of questions about the methodological and practical issues in an interview project. For example: How do I begin an interview project? How many subjects will I need? Could the interviews harm the subjects? How can I avoid influencing the subjects with leading questions? Can I be sure that I get to know what the subjects really mean? Is transcription of the interviews necessary? How do I analyze the interviews? Will the interpretations be subjective? How do I report my extensive interviews?

If corresponding questions were raised about, for example, questionnaire surveys, they would be fairly easy to answer. Standard techniques exist for conducting surveys, and there are a multitude of textbooks that provide generally accepted rules and guidelines for necessary sample sizes, formulation of questions and of response alternatives, coding of answers, statistical methods of analysis with levels of significance for acceptable evidence, and so forth. Standard forms of tables and figures are also available for presenting the quantitative data.

The situation is quite the contrary for qualitative research in two senses: First, there are few standard rules or common methodological conventions in qualitative research communities; and second, hardly any general texts have existed in which questions of method, such as those raised above, were discussed. This second problem is being quickly resolved, and the task today is rather to find one's way in the expanding literature on qualitative research. An overview of literature pertaining to interviewing is given later, in Box 5.3 in Chapter 5.

The first issue—standard rules for qualitative interviewing—is more complex. There is no common procedure for interview research. Interview research is a craft that, if well carried out, can become an art. The varieties of research interviews approach the spectrum of human conversations. The forms of interview analysis can differ as widely as there are ways of reading a text. The qualitative interview is sometimes called an *unstructured* or a *nonstandardized* interview. Because there are few prestructured or standardized procedures for conducting these forms of interview, many analyses of the methodical decisions have to be made on the spot, during the interview. This requires a high level of skill in the interviewer, who needs to be knowledgeable about the interview topic and to be familiar with the methodological options available, as well as having a grasp of the conceptual issues of producing knowledge through conversation.

In this book I will attempt to steer between the free spontaneity of a no-method approach and the rigid structures of an all-method approach by focusing on the expertise, skills, and craftsmanship of the interview researcher. Some of the decisions that will have to be made on the way through the stages of an interview inquiry, and the methodological options available, are outlined in Part III: The Seven Stages of an Interview Investigation.

Overview of the Book

My aim in this book is to provide an overview and some guidelines for doing interview research, and to present philosophical perspectives that will be helpful for thinking about interviews. On a horizontal *methodological* level, the chapters in Part III take the reader through the methodological stages of an investigation with an emphasis on interviewing as a craft and on the techniques that that involves, providing practical guidelines for conducting research interviews. An interview investigation will be outlined in seven method stages, from the original idea to the final report: (1) thematizing, with a conceptualization of the research topic and formulation of the research questions; through (2) designing the study so it addresses the research questions, treating both knowledge construction and moral implications; to (3) the interviewing itself; (4) transcribing; (5) analyzing; (6) verification; and (7) reporting. The chapters take issue with the apparently mystical skills of interviewing, breaking them down in discrete steps, giving examples, and pointing out the practical and conceptual complexities involved.

On a vertical *epistemological* level, the chapters in Part II suggest theoretical frames of reference for conceptual clarification of the methodological issues, providing contexts for how to think about interview research. *Epistemology* here refers to theories of knowledge. One of the book's main themes is the interconnectedness of the practical issues of the interview method and the theoretical issues of the nature of interview knowledge.

Because the use of qualitative interviews as a systematic research method is not only relatively new but controversial as well, I first treat the epistemological themes in Part II, Conceptualizing the Research Interview, and then turn to the methodological issues in Part III, The Seven Stages of an Interview Investigation. Novice readers who are primarily interested in the practice of interviewing can turn directly to Chapter 7, The Interview Situation, to get "a sense of the trade" and then continue through the concrete methodological steps in an interview investigation. They can then return to the conceptual discussions in Part II and the overall method design in the first two chapters of Part III.

The qualitative research interview is a construction site for knowledge. An interview is literally an *inter view,* an inter-change of views between two persons conversing about a theme of mutual interest. The interdependence of human interaction and knowledge production is a main theme throughout this book.

Figure 1.1. The Research Interview Seen as InterViews

The ambiguous drawing in Figure 1.1 was introduced by the Danish psychologist Rubin as an example of the figure/ground phenomenon in visual Gestalt perception—it can be seen alternatively as two faces or as a vase, but not as both at the same time. I use the figure to illustrate the present perspective on the interview conversation as *inter views*. We can focus on the two faces of the ambiguous figure, see them as the interviewer and the interviewee, and conceive of the interview as the interaction between the two persons. Or we can focus on the vase between the two faces, see it as containing the knowledge constructed *inter* the *views* of the interviewer and the interviewee. There is an alternation between the knowers and the known, between the constructors of knowledge and the knowledge constructed. This dual aspect of the interview—the personal interrelation and the inter-view knowledge that it leads to—will run through the chapters of this book, which alternate between focusing on the personal inter-action and on the knowledge constructed through the interaction.

I emphasize the *human inter action of the inter view* as producing scientific knowledge. The interrelation of the interviewer and his or her subjects is treated in Chapter 2, The Interview as Conversation, and the moral implications of this human interaction are taken up in Chapter 6, on ethics. The situational interaction of interviewer and interviewee is the main emphasis of Chapters 7 and 8, on the interview situation. The conversation between the reader and the texts produced from the interviews goes through the chapters on analysis (Chapters 10, 11, & 12). In the last three chapters (Chapters 13, 14, & 15), the focus on the inter views of researcher and subject is extended to encompass the inter views of the interview researcher and his or her audience. This extension of the inter views is illustrated in Figure 15.1, which extends Figure 1.1. Chapter 15, the final chapter, addresses different conversations about the value and validity of the knowledge produced by research interviews, concluding with their potentials for increasing our understanding of the human conversation.

The nature of the *knowledge constructed inter the views* of subject and researcher is discussed in relation to conversations in Chapter 2 and to philosophical conceptions of knowledge in Chapter 3, and followed up in Chapter 4 with different views on science and research. Chapter 13, on validation, focuses on the truth value of the knowledge produced and the constitution of true knowledge in a dialogue, and Chapter 15 pictures the conversation as a privileged access to a human world understood as a conversational reality.

PART

II

Conceptualizing
the Research Interview

The meaning of the three key terms of the subtitle—*interviewing, research,* and *qualitative*—are addressed in this epistemological second part of the book. The mode of understanding in a qualitative research interview is outlined, discussed in relevant philosophical contexts, and related to conceptions of scientific research in the social sciences. The conceptual understanding of the interview that is developed will serve as a framework for clarifying the methodological and theoretical issues arising during the stages of an interview investigation.

17

In Chapter 2, the qualitative research *interview* is regarded as a one form of conversation and related to other forms of conversation, such as a philosophical discourse or a therapeutic interview. The chapter concludes with an outline of the mode of understanding of the qualitative research interview and a discussion of the interview in relation to different conversational contexts.

Philosophical traditions congenial to the nature of qualitative research interviewing are presented in Chapter 3. They involve postmodern linguistic constructions of reality, hermeneutical interpretations of the meaning of texts, phenomenological descriptions of consciousness, and dialectical development through contradictions.

The meaning of *research* is discussed in Chapter 4 with regard to conceptions of science, including a positivist conception of science hardly compatible with qualitative interviewing. The meaning of *qualitative* is treated in relation to a common quantitative versus qualitative controversy. The issue of objectivity and subjectivity in qualitative interviews is also addressed and, finally, examples of qualitative research in practice are included: market research, feminist research, and psychoanalysis.

Readers who are unfamiliar with social science methodology and philosophy may, as suggested in the first chapter, go directly to the depiction of the interview situation in Chapter 7 and subsequent chapters on the interview stages and then return to the following conceptual discussions.

2

The Interview as a Conversation

The research interview is a specific form of conversation. In order to clarify the nature of the research interview I will compare it to other forms of conversation. Excerpts from three different conversations are presented here: first, Socrates teaching Agathon the conceptual nature of love; then, a patient learning about her own feelings of hate in a therapeutic session as presented by Rogers; and finally, a research interview on the experience of learning about interior architecture as reported by Giorgi. These different interviews invoke different forms of interaction that produce different kinds of knowledge. The chapter concludes with an outline of the mode of understanding of the qualitative research interview, followed by a discussion of the interview in relation to different conversational contexts.

Knowledge as Conversation

In Chapter 1 a traveler metaphor of interview research was introduced, emphasizing conversation. I will distinguish among the use of conversation as part of everyday interactions, as a professional interchange, and as a philosophical dialogue. These three uses may be seen as specific forms of a common language understanding of conversation as an "oral exchange of sentiments, observations, ideas, opinions" (*Webster's*, 1967); they involve different forms of interaction and levels of reflection on the form and the content of the conversation.

In the spontaneous *conversations of daily life* attention will tend to be on the conversation topic, whereas the purpose and the structure of the conversation remain unproblematized. If, however, some kind of break occurs, there may be a change from a spontaneous level to a meta-level where the aim and form of the talk is reflected. This may be the case if, for example, one of the participants asks, "Why are you asking me about this?"

Professional interviews take a variety of forms, such as a legal interrogation, a job interview, a therapeutic interview, or a research interview. They each have their different purposes and structures, with less or more systematic questioning techniques, as well as a reflection upon the aim and mode of questioning. In relation to conversations in everyday life, the research interview is characterized by a methodological awareness of question forms, a focus on the dynamics of interaction between interviewer and interviewee, and a critical attention to what is said. In professional interviews there is usually an asymmetry of power: The professional is in charge of the questioning of a more or less voluntary and naive subject. In contrast to the reciprocal interchanges of everyday and philosophical conversations, there tends to be a one-sided questioning of the subject by the professional.

In a *philosophical discourse* the partners are on an equal level and there is a reciprocal questioning of the logic of the participants' questions and answers, as well as of the true nature of the knowledge being debated. The discourse rests on a joint commitment of the participants to seek truth—it is an attempt to get beyond mere opinion to true knowledge. It is guided by a questioning of the conversation's subject matter, with the partners in the dialogue following mutually binding rules for argumentation (see Bernstein, 1983).

The hermeneutical philosopher Gadamer (1975) describes a genuine conversation on the basis of Plato's dialogues:

> A conversation is a process of two people understanding each other. Thus it is characteristic of every true conversation that each opens himself to the other person, truly accepts his point of view as worthy of consideration and gets inside the other to such an extent that he understands not a particular individual, but what he says. The thing that has to be grasped is the objective rightness or otherwise of his opinion, so that they can agree with each other on the subject. (p. 347)

The intentions of the conversing partners give way to what Gadamer calls "the law of the subject matter." When one enters into a dialogue with another person and is then carried further by the dialogue, it is no longer the will of the individual person that is determinative. Rather, the law of the subject matter is at issue, and it elicits statement and counterstatement and in the end plays these into each other.

This ideal description of a conversation pertains to a philosophical discourse, and may in some cases also apply to the interactions of daily life. In professional conversations, however, there is usually an asymmetry of power with specific, and sometimes contradictory, underlying purposes.

I now give an example of a philosophical conversation and examples of two professional conversations, a therapeutic interview and a research interview. The philosophical conversation seeks truth through an argumentative discourse; the therapeutic interview aims to instigate changes in the patient's personality and self-understanding through interpretations in an emotional interaction; and the research interview seeks through questioning to obtain knowledge of the subject's world. The nature of the knowledge constituted through the interactions of the three conversations differs: logical conceptual knowledge, emotional personal knowledge, and empirical knowledge of the everyday world.

Socrates' Philosophical Dialogue on Love

Plato's "Symposion" is a philosophical dialogue in a dramatic form. A party has been cast in honor of the poet Agathon, who in the year 416 B.C. had received a prize for one of his plays. The guests, each in their turn, give speeches in honor of Eros, the god of love. Their talks are accompanied by plenty of wine: Aristophanes has to miss his turn because of severe hiccups, but does give his speech; a drunken Alcibiades crashes into the party with a speech of love to Socrates, who—as dawn arrives—is the only one still seated at the table.

The "Symposion" consists of monologues and dialogues, alternating among rhetorical speeches, rigorous argumentation, and humor. Plato's form of communication is indirect: Socrates' assumed ignorance and his ironical style neither confirm nor disconfirm the many knowledge claims put forth. His uncovering of contradictions in his opponent's arguments offers indications to those who will listen.

In his own speech, Socrates depicts Eros as desire for beauty, good, and truth. He starts by questioning the preceding speaker, Agathon, who has given a rather pompous talk in the rhetorical tradition of the Sophists. The introduction and the conclusion of this passage of the dialogue follow:

"I must say, my dear Agathon, you gave your speech an excellent introduction, by stating that your duty was first to display the character of Love, and then to treat of his acts. Those opening words I thoroughly admire. So come now, complete your beautiful and magnificent description of Love, and tell me this: Are we so to view his character as to take Love to be love of some object, or of none? My question is not whether he is love of a mother or a father—how absurd it would be to ask whether Love is love of mother or father—but as though I were asking about our notion of "father," whether one's father is a father of somebody or not. Surely you would say, if you wished to give the proper answer, that the father is father of son or of daughter, would you not?"

"Yes, of course," said Agathon.

*   *   *   *   *

"Now then," said Socrates, "let us agree to what we have so far concluded. First, is not Love directed to certain things; of which, in the second place, he has a want?"

"Yes," he said.

"Then, granting this, recollect what things you named in our discussion as the objects of Love: if you like, I will remind you. What you said, I believe, was to the effect that the gods contrived the world from a love of beautiful things, for of ugly there was no love. Did you not say something of the sort?"

"Yes, I did," said Agathon.

"And quite properly, my friend," said Socrates; "then, such being the case, must not Love be only love of beauty, and not of ugliness?" He assented.

"Well then, we have agreed that he loves what he lacks and has not?"

"Yes," he replied.

"And what Love lacks and has not is beauty?"

"That needs must be," he said.

"Well now, will you say that what lacks beauty, and in no wise possesses it, is beautiful?"

"Surely not."

"So can you still allow Love to be beautiful, if this is the case?"
Whereupon Agathon said, "I greatly fear, Socrates, I know nothing
of what I was talking about." (Plato, 1953, pp. 167-173)

In this passage, Socrates takes Agathon's speech on love as his point
of departure. He repeats it in a condensed form and interprets what
Agathon has said and then asks for his opponent's confirmations or
disconfirmations of the interpretations. Socrates starts out by appear-
ing naive and innocent, he praises Agathon's views on Eros, then
follows up by uncovering one contradiction after another in Agathon's
position. Several of the arguments end with a question leading to a
given answer, which Agathon then accepts. In the end Agathon is led
to retract his views completely and to agree with Socrates' position.

This dialogue on the nature of love is open to several readings. In one
interpretation, the dialogue is a genuine conversation in Gadamer's
(1975) sense, here as an open philosophical inquiry seeking true
knowledge about the nature of love through a discursive argumentation. It is not the understanding of a particular individual, but of the
objective rightness of what he says, so that the two of them can agree
on the subject matter. In another reading, Socrates already has a true
knowledge of the nature of love, and the purpose of the conversation
is educational, through a critical questioning of Agathon to lead him
and the other participants in the symposium toward an insight into
the nature of love that Socrates already possesses. At the basis of his
questioning there is a fundamental belief that Agathon already possesses true knowledge of the nature of love but needs help to uncover
this truth, and Socrates takes the role of midwife, delivering the truth.
His questioning is not open, nor is it neutral on the content of the
dispute, but presupposes a specific theory of knowledge—the belief
in man as an immortal and reborn soul, where learning is recognition
of what the soul has already known.

The philosophical discourse is a harsh form of interaction—
Socrates likens himself to a legal interrogator—that aims at gaining
theoretical knowledge through the unrelenting rigor of a discursive
argumentation. Research interviews generally have a milder form; the
interviewee is an informant, not a philosophical opponent. The interviewer asks questions of the interview subject in order to obtain
knowledge about his or her life situation, and rarely enters into

tenacious arguments with the subject about the logic and truth of his or her statements. It is beyond the scope of the research interview for the interviewer to argue the strength of his or her own conception of the topic investigated or to try to change the subject's convictions. In contrast, the therapeutic interview aims at changes—through personal interaction rather than through logical argumentation—and the changes sought are not primarily conceptual, but emotional and personal.

A Therapeutic Interview on Hate

Since Freud's invention of psychoanalysis at the turn of the century, a large body of experience has been gathered about the use of therapeutic interviews. The presentation below of a passage from a therapeutic interview has a twofold purpose: to indicate the possibilities for research interviewers to learn from the techniques developed within the therapeutic profession, and to demonstrate some of the differences between therapeutic and research interviews.

Rogers was a pioneer in developing an open, client-centered interview form, originally termed *non-directive* and later changed to *client-centered,* with the insight that all interviewing implies a sense of direction. Rogers also pioneered the use of tape recorders and the transcription of entire therapy sessions, making the therapeutic interaction and questioning techniques available for public scrutiny. Rogers's writings on therapeutic interviews have been a source of inspiration for the development of qualitative interviews for research purposes.

The following sequence is taken from *Client-Centered Therapy* (Rogers, 1965). It was conducted by a counselor applying Rogers's approach, and in this case it is reproduced from notes the therapist took during the interview.

S (Subject): (*Silent for two minutes. Then begins to talk in a hard flat voice, quite unlike her usual tone. Does not look at counselor. There was much repetition, but the following excerpts give the major thoughts.*) You feel I want to come, but I *don't!* I'm not coming any more. It doesn't do any good. I don't like you. I hate you! I wish you never were born.

C (Counselor): You just hate me very bitterly.

3. I think I'll throw you in the lake. I'll cut you up! You think people like you, but they don't. . . . You think you can attract women, but you *can't.*. . . I wish you were *dead.*

C: You *detest* me and you'd really like to get rid of me.

S: You think my father did bad things with me, but he didn't! You think he wasn't a good man, but he *was.* You think I want intercourse, but I *don't.*

C: You feel I *absolutely misrepresent* all your thoughts.

S: .. You think you can get people to come in and tell you everything, and they'll think they're being helped, but they're *not!* You just like to make 'em suffer. You think you can hypnotize them, but you can't! You think you're good, but you ain't. I hate you, I hate you, I *hate* you!

C: You feel I really like to make 'em suffer, but that I *don't* help them.

S: You think I haven't been straight, but I have. I *hate* you. All I've had is pain, pain, pain. You think I can't direct my own life, but I can. You think I can't get well, but I can. You think I had hallucinations, but I didn't. I hate you. (*Long pause. Leans on desk in strained, exhausted pose.*) You think I'm crazy, but I'm not.

C: You're sure I think you're crazy.

S: (*Pause.*) I'm tied, and I just can't get loose! (*Despairing tone of voice, and tears. Pause.*) I had a hallucination and I've *got* to get it out!

*   *   *   *   *

S: I knew at the office I had to get rid of this somewhere. I felt I could come down and tell you. I knew you'd understand. I couldn't say I hated myself. That's true but I couldn't say it. So I just thought of all the ugly things I could say to you instead.

C: The things you felt about yourself you couldn't say, but you could say them about me.

S: I know we're getting to rock bottom . . . (pp. 211-213)

The emotional tone of this counseling session was described as follows:

> Just as it is impossible to convey on paper the venom and hatred in the client's voice, so it is utterly impossible to convey the depth of empathy in the counselor's responses. The counselor states, "I tried to enter into and to express in my voice the full degree of the soul-consuming anger which she was pouring out. The written words look incredibly pale, but in the situation they were full of the same feeling she was so coldly and deeply expressing." (p. 212)

In this therapeutic session the subject takes the lead right from the start, introduces the focal topic—the detestable counselor—and tells how much she hates him. He responds by reflecting and rephrasing her statements, emphasizing their emotional aspects. He does not, as would be likely in a normal conversation, take issue with the many accusations against him. In this specific sequence the counselor neither asks questions for clarification, nor does he offer interpretations. At the end, after "she has gotten it all out," the subject acknowledges the counselor's ability to understand her, and she herself offers an interpretation: I couldn't say I hated myself, so I just thought of all the ugly things I could say to you instead.

The purpose of the counseling interview was to help the patient with her emotional problems, and the counselor consistently reflected the emotional aspects of the patient's statements about his relationship to her, which in this case led to the subject interpreting her own behavior. In psychoanalytical terminology, the topic of this session was *transference,* the patient's intense emotional relationship with the therapist. It is difficult to draw any strong line of demarcation between a therapeutic and a research interview. Both may lead to increased understanding and change, but with the emphasis on personal change in a therapeutic interview and on intellectual understanding in a research interview. Although the main purpose of therapeutic interviews is to assist patients to overcome their suffering, a side effect is general knowledge about the human situation. This will be discussed later in relation to psychoanalysis as a research method (see Chapter 4, Psychoanalytical Knowledge Production).

A Research Interview on Learning

The purpose of the qualitative research interview discussed here is to understand themes of the lived daily world from the subjects' own perspectives. The structure of the research interview comes close to an everyday conversation, but as a professional interview it involves a specific approach and technique of questioning. Technically, the qualitative research interview is semistructured: It is neither an open conversation nor a highly structured questionnaire. It is conducted according to an interview guide that focuses on certain themes and that may include suggested questions. The interview is usually transcribed, and the written text together with the tape recording are the material for the subsequent interpretation of meaning.

The following interview passage is taken from the article "An Application of Phenomenological Method in Psychology" by Giorgi (1975). The research question guiding the interview was: What constitutes learning in the everyday world? The first half of the interview, conducted by a student, is reproduced here.

R (Researcher): Could you describe in as much detail as possible a situation in which learning occurred for you?

S (Subject: E. W., 24 year-old female, housewife and educational researcher): The first thing that comes to mind is what I learned about interior decorating from Myrtis. She was telling me about the way you see things. Her view of looking at different rooms has been altered. She told me that when you come into a room you don't usually notice how many vertical and horizontal lines there are, at least consciously, you don't notice. And yet, if you were to take someone who knows what's going on in the field of interior decorating, they would intuitively feel if there were the right number of vertical and horizontal lines. So, I went home, and I started looking at the lines in our living room, and I counted the number of horizontal and vertical lines, many of which I had never realized were lines before. A beam . . . I had never really thought of that as vertical before, just as a protrusion from the wall. (Laughs) I found out what was wrong with our living room design: many, too many, horizontal lines and not enough vertical. So I started trying to move things around and change the way it looked. I did this by moving several pieces of furniture and taking out several knick-knacks, de-emphasizing certain lines, and . . . it really looked differently to me. It's interesting because my husband came home several hours later and I said, "Look at the living room; it's all different." Not knowing this, that I had picked up, he didn't look at it in the same way I did. He saw things were different, he saw things were moved, but he wasn't able to verbalize that there was a de-emphasis on the horizontal lines and more of an emphasis on the vertical. So I felt I had learned something.

R: What part of that experience would you consider learning?

S: The knowledge part that a room is made up of horizontal and vertical lines. The application of that to another room; applying it to something that had been bothering me for quite a long time and I could never put my finger on it. I think the actual learning was what was horizontal and vertical about a room. The learning that was left with me was a way of looking at rooms.

R: Are you saying then that the learning was what you learned from Myrtis, what you learned when you tried to apply . . . ?

S: Since I did apply it, I feel that I learned when I did apply it. I would have *thought* that I learned it only by having that knowledge, *but* having gone through the act of application, I really don't feel I would have learned it. I could honestly say, I had learned it at that time. (pp. 84-86)

This interview investigated what constitutes learning for a woman in her everyday world. It began with an open request to describe a situation where learning occurred. The woman chose the learning situation she would talk about—interior decorating; she described this freely and extensively in her own words. The answer spontaneously took the form of a story, a narrative of one learning episode. The interviewer's first question introduced learning as the theme of the interview; her remaining questions depart from the subject's answers in order to keep learning in focus and to ask for clarification of the different aspects of the subject's learning story.

This interview gives a good picture of a semistructured research interview focusing on the subject's experience of a theme. The purpose was to investigate the subject's experience of learning, and the interviewer's questions aimed at a cognitive clarification of the subject's story of learning. The mode of interviewing was inspired by a phenomenological philosophy, which is based on a descriptive study of consciousness to be discussed in the next chapter (Chapter 3, Phenomenological Description); the analysis of this interview will be treated later (Chapter 11, Meaning Condensation).

The Mode of Understanding in the Qualitative Research Interview

I now outline the mode of understanding in the qualitative research interview, of which the above interview on learning is one example.

In Box 2.1, 12 aspects of the mode of understanding in the qualitative research interview are depicted in a condensed form. They may be found more or less explicitly formulated in descriptions of research interviews. As brought together here, they represent an attempt to describe the main structures of the qualitative research interview. They will now be discussed in greater detail, with examples from the interview on learning reported by Giorgi and from my own interviews on grading in high schools (see Chapter 1, Conversation as Research; Chapter 5, Interviews About Grades; & Chapter 7, An Interview About Grades).

1. Life World. The topic of the qualitative research interview is the lived world of the subjects and their relation to it. The purpose is to describe and understand the central themes the subjects experience and live toward. In the interview reported by Giorgi, the topic of learning was introduced by the interviewer, whereas the subject herself chose the specific instance of learning from her everyday world to talk about. In my own investigation, grades were a central theme in the life world of the high school pupils, and the interviews sought to describe and reflect the meanings that grades had for the pupils.

The qualitative research interview is theme oriented. Two persons talk together about a theme that is of interest to both. The resulting interview can then be analyzed primarily with respect to the life world that is described by the person, or the subject describing his or her life world. The interviews about grades were analyzed with regard to the common social situation constituted by the grades, such as submissiveness to teachers, competition with peers, and instrumentalization of learning. The interviews could also have been analyzed with respect to the personality structures of the individual pupils in relation to grading. In this study, however, it was the common structures of the school situation constituted by the grades that were of interest and not individual differences among the pupils.

Box 2.1

Aspects of Qualitative Research Interviews

The purpose of the qualitative research interview treated here is to obtain descriptions of the lived world of the interviewees with respect to interpretations of the meaning of the described phenomena.

Life World. The topic of qualitative interviews is the everyday lived world of the interviewee and his or her relation to it.

Meaning. The interview seeks to interpret the meaning of central themes in the life world of the subject. The interviewer registers and interprets the meaning of what is said as well as how it is said.

Qualitative. The interview seeks qualitative knowledge expressed in normal language, it does not aim at quantification.

Descriptive. The interview attempts to obtain open nuanced descriptions of different aspects of the subjects' life worlds.

Specificity. Descriptions of specific situations and action sequences are elicited, not general opinions.

---

2. *Meaning.* The qualitative research interview seeks to describe and understand the meanings of central themes in the life world of the subjects. The main task in interviewing is to understand the meaning of what the interviewees say. Recall the several questions in the interview reported by Giorgi (1975), which sought to clarify the precise meanings of the subject's descriptions.

The interviewer registers and interprets what is said as well as how it is said; he or she must be observant of—and able to interpret—

Box 2.1 Continued

Deliberate Naïveté. The interviewer exhibits an openness to new and unexpected phenomena, rather than having ready-made categories and schemes of interpretation.

Focused. The interview is focused on particular themes; it is neither strictly structured with standardized questions, nor entirely "non-directive."

Ambiguity. Interviewee statements can sometimes be ambiguous, reflecting contradictions in the world the subject lives in.

Change. The process of being interviewed may produce new insights and awareness, and the subject may in the course of the interview come to change his or her descriptions and meanings about a theme.

Sensitivity. Different interviewers can produce different statements on the same themes, depending on their sensitivity to and knowledge of the interview topic.

Interpersonal Situation. The knowledge obtained is produced through the interpersonal interaction in the interview.

Positive Experience. A well carried out research interview can be a rare and enriching experience for the interviewee, who may obtain new insights into his or her life situation.

vocalization, facial expressions, and other bodily gestures. An every-day conversation often takes place on a factual level. A pupil may state: "I am not as stupid as my grades at the examinations showed, but I have bad study habits." Common reactions could then be on a factual level: "What grades did you get?" or "What are your study habits?"—questions that also may yield important information. A meaning-oriented reply would, in contrast, be something like, "You feel that the grades are not an adequate measure of your competence?" Recall the consistent rephrasings of the emotional messages in the client's statements by the counselor in the interview reported by Rogers (1965).

A qualitative research interview seeks to cover both a factual and a meaning level, though it is usually more difficult to interview on a meaning level. It is necessary to listen to the explicit descriptions and meanings as well as to what is "said between the lines." The inter-viewer may seek to formulate the "implicit message," "send it back" to the subject, and obtain an immediate confirmation or disconfirmation of the interviewer's interpretation of what the interviewee is saying.

3. Qualitative. The qualitative research interview aims at obtain-ing nuanced descriptions from the different qualitative aspects of the interviewee's life world; it works with words and not with num-bers. Precision in description and stringency in meaning interpreta-tion correspond in qualitative interviews to exactness in quantitative measurements.

4. Descriptive. The qualitative research interview aims at obtaining uninterpreted descriptions. The subjects describe as precisely as pos-sible what they experience and feel, and how they act. Recall the interview reported by Giorgi (1975) in which the introductory ques-tion asked the subject for a detailed description of a situation in which learning occurred. The focus is on nuanced descriptions that depict the qualitative diversity, the many differences and varieties of a phe-nomenon, rather than on ending up with fixed categorizations.

The question of why the subjects experience and act as they do is primarily a task for the researcher to evaluate. An analogy to a doctor's diagnosis may be clarifying. The doctor does not start by asking the patient why he is sick, but rather asks the patient what is wrong, what he is feeling, and what the symptoms are. On the basis of the information obtained, the doctor may then formulate a hypothesis of which illness may be likely. Further questioning proceeds from this hypothesis, and on the basis of the patient's answers and results from other methods of investigation, the doctor then makes the diagnosis. For both the doctor and the researcher there are cases where it is important to know the subject's own explanations of his or her condition and to ask questions about why. The primary task for both the doctor and the researcher, however, remains that of obtaining descriptions so they will have relevant and precise material from which to draw their interpretations.

5. Specificity. The qualitative research interview seeks to describe specific situations and action sequences from the subject's world. It is not general opinions that are asked for. Knowing the opinions, for example, of a pupil about the grading system, is subordinated in a research interview to obtaining concrete descriptions from the pupils —how they experience the grading, how they and the other pupils react to it. On the basis of extensive and rich descriptions of specific grading situations, the interviewer will be able to arrive at meanings on another level, instead of posing such questions as "What is your opinion of grading?" Still, it should be recognized that this type of general opinion question may be relevant, yielding information that is of interest in itself and that may also be compared with the understanding of grades expressed in the spontaneous descriptions of grading situations.

6. Deliberate Naïveté. The qualitative interview attempts to gather descriptions of the relevant themes of the interviewee's life world that are as rich and presuppositionless as possible. Rather than the interviewer having preformulated questions and ready-made categories for analysis, the deliberate naïveté and absence of presuppositions advocated here implies an openness to new and unexpected phenomena. The interviewer should be curious, sensitive to what is said—as well as to what is not said—and critical of his or her own presuppositions and hypotheses during the interview. Presuppositionlessness thus also implies a critical consciousness of the interviewer's own presuppositions.

7. *Focus.* The qualitative research interview is focused on certain themes in the interviewee's life world. It is neither strictly structured with standardized questions, nor entirely "nondirective," but is focused on certain themes. The task of the interviewers in the grading study was to keep the grades at the focus of the interview, but within different perspectives or contexts—such as social milieu in school, examinations, and the pupils' plans for the future. It is then up to the subjects to bring forth the dimensions they find important within the focus area. The interviewer leads the subject toward certain themes, but not to certain opinions about these themes.

8. *Ambiguity.* A subject's statements are sometimes ambiguous. An expression can imply several possibilities of interpretation, and the subject may also give apparently contradictory statements during an interview. It becomes the task of the interviewer to clarify, as far as possible, whether the ambiguities and contradictory statements are due to a failure of communication in the interview situation, or whether they reflect real inconsistencies, ambivalences, and contradictions in the interviewee. The aim of the qualitative research interview is not to end up with unequivocal and quantifiable meanings on the themes in focus. What matters is rather to describe precisely the possibly ambiguous and contradictory meanings expressed by the interviewee. The contradictions of interviewees may not merely be due to faulty communication in the interview situation, nor to their personality structures, but may in fact be adequate reflections of objective contradictions in the world in which they live.

9. *Change.* It may happen in the course of an interview that subjects change their descriptions of, and meanings about, a theme. The subjects may themselves have discovered new aspects of the themes they are describing, and suddenly see relations that they had not been conscious of earlier. Thus, in the therapeutic interview reported by Rogers (1965), the patient started, through her talking and the counselor's rephrasings of her statements, to obtain insight about her critique of the counselor as actually being directed at herself. On less dramatic levels the questioning in research interviews may instigate processes of reflection where the meanings of themes described by the subjects are no longer the same after the interview.

10. Sensitivity. Interviews obtained by different interviewers, using the same interview guide, may be different due to varying levels of sensitivity toward, and knowledge about, the topic of the interview. Thus an interviewer who has no ear for music may have difficulties obtaining nuanced descriptions of musical experiences from his or her interviewees, in particular with probing more intensively into the meaning of the music. If a common scientific requirement of obtaining intersubjectively reproducible data were to be followed here, the interview form might have to be standardized in a way that would restrict the understanding of musical experiences to more superficial aspects understandable to the average person. A qualitative research interview would instead seek to employ the varying abilities of the interviewers to obtain different nuances and depths of the themes of the interview.

The requirement of sensitivity to, and a foreknowledge about, the topic of the interview contrasts with the presuppositionless attitude advocated above. The tension between these two aspects may be expressed in the requirement for a deliberate conscious naïveté on the part of the interviewer, which is demonstrated in Socrates' interview of Agathon.

11. Interpersonal Situation. The research interview is an inter view, an interaction between two people. The interviewer and the subject act in relation to each other and reciprocally influence each other. A strong case of emotional interaction took place in the counseling session reported by Rogers (1965). Sullivan (1954) analyzed the psychiatric interview as an interpersonal situation where the relevant data are constituted by the interaction itself, in the specific situation created between interviewer and interviewee. He emphasized the subjective moment in obtaining knowledge in an interview situation—in participant observation it is the interviewer as a person who is the method, the instrument.

The interview situation may, for both parties, be characterized by positive feelings of a common intellectual curiosity and a reciprocal respect. The interview may also be anxiety provoking and evoke defense mechanisms in the interviewee as well as in the interviewer. The interviewer should be conscious of the interpersonal dynamics within the interaction and take them into account in the interview situation and in the later analysis of the finished interview. The reciprocal influence of interviewer and interviewee on a cognitive and an emotional level is, however, not necessarily a source of error, but can be a strong point of qualitative research interviewing. Rather than seeking to reduce the importance of this interaction, what matters in the research interview is to recognize and apply the knowledge gained from the interpersonal interaction.

12. Positive Experience. A qualitative research interview can be a favorable experience for the interviewee. An interview is a conversation in which two people talk about a theme of mutual interest. A well-conducted qualitative interview can be a rare and enriching experience for the interviewee. It is probably not a very common experience in everyday life that another person—for an hour or more—is interested only in, sensitive toward, and seeks to understand as well as possible another's experiences and views on a subject. In practice, it is often difficult to terminate a qualitative interview: Subjects may wish to continue the dialogue and explore further the themes and the insights of the interview interaction.

*   *   *   *   *

The 12 aspects outlined above illustrate the mode of understanding in the qualitative research interview treated in this book. In Chapter 3, philosophical positions congenial with this understanding of the research interview will be presented, and in Chapter 4 this mode of understanding is contrasted with established conceptions of social science research.

Interviews in Three Conversations

This chapter on the interview as a conversation concludes by showing the interviewer-traveler in three conversational contexts. First, the research interview is treated as a specific professional form of *conversational technique* in which knowledge is constructed through the interaction of interviewer and interviewee as outlined in the above description of the mode of understanding in the qualitative research interview. In contrast to the reciprocal interchanges of everyday life, as well as of philosophical conversations, it is the interviewer who, as a professional, asks and the interviewee who answers.

Second, the conversation may be conceived of as a *basic mode of knowing*. Rorty (1979), a neopragmatist philosopher close to postmodern thought, has emphasized the constitution of knowledge through the conversation. When we understand knowledge as the social justification of belief rather than as accuracy of representation, conversation replaces confrontation with nature. The notion of mind as re-presenting an objective world can be discarded, "If we see knowledge as a matter of conversation and social practice, rather than as an attempt to mirror nature" (Rorty, 1979, p. 171). The certainty of our knowledge is a matter of conversation between persons, rather than a matter of interaction with a nonhuman reality. If we regard knowing not as having an essence but as a right to believe, we may see "*conversation* as the ultimate context within which knowledge is understood" (p. 389).

Third, *human reality* may be understood as persons in conversation. To the hermeneutic philosopher Gadamer, we are conversational beings for whom language is a reality (see Bernstein, 1983). In a postmodern conversational version of social constructivism, Shotter (1993) attempts to describe the conversational worlds within which we have our being: "For conversation is not just *one* of our many activities in *the* world. On the contrary, we constitute both ourselves and our worlds in our conversational activity. For us they are foundational. They constitute the usually ignored background within which our lives are rooted" (p. vi).

The conversation in the present approach is not only a specific empirical method: It also involves a basic mode of constituting knowledge; and the human world is a conversational reality. These three understandings of conversation—methodological, epistemological, and ontological—will be applied throughout this book, but with a methodological emphasis on the interview as a specific form of conversational technique.

In Chapter 3, philosophical positions compatible with a conversational approach to interview research are outlined. The emphasis on conversation as a mode of knowing is particularly strong within postmodern and hermeneutical philosophy, and the social, power, and material aspects of the conversational interaction are prominent in postmodern and dialectical understandings of conversations.

3

Postmodern Thought, Hermeneutics, Phenomenology, and Dialectics

The techniques of interviewing have been extensively treated in literature, while the philosophical implications of the mode of under-standing in qualitative interviews have seldom been addressed. The terms used to describe the interview in the preceding chapter—such as *experience, consciousness, description, meaning, interpretation,* and *interaction*—were taken from the vernacular. In this chapter I present philosophical lines of thought that have analyzed the very themes central to qualitative research interviewing—postmodern thought, hermeneutics, phenomenology, and dialectics.

A *postmodern* approach focuses on interrelations in an interview, on the social construction of reality in an interview, on its linguistic and interactional aspects including the differences between oral dis-course and written text, and emphasizes the narratives constructed by the interview. From a *hermeneutical* understanding, the interpretation of meaning is the central theme, with a specification of the kinds of meanings sought and attention to the questions posed to a text. The concepts of *conversation* and of *text* are pivotal, and there is an emphasis on the interpreter's foreknowledge of a text's subject matter. A *phenomenological* perspective includes a focus on the life world, an openness to the experiences of the subjects, a primacy of precise descriptions, attempts to bracket foreknowledge, and a search for invariant essential meanings in the descriptions. A *dialectical* access focuses on the contradictions of a statement and their relations to the contradictions of the social and material world. There is an emphasis on the new, rather than on the status quo, and on the intrinsic relation of knowledge and action.

These four philosophies highlight different aspects of knowledge relevant to the qualitative interview. They differ in fundamental ways and some of their intricate relations and differences will be pointed out at the end of this chapter. The complex philosophical positions are presented here in a brief and dense form with an emphasis on their epistemological aspects as relevant to qualitative research interviewing. The presentations serve as contexts for reflection—in later chapters —on the theoretical and methodological issues raised by the use of interviewing as a research method.

Box 3.1 depicts some literature on the philosophical positions to be presented, pertaining in particular to their implications for research in the social sciences.

Box 3.1

Literature on Philosophies
Pertaining to Interview Research

Postmodern Thought

Andersen, W. T. (1995). (Ed.). *The truth about truth—De-confusing and re-constructing the postmodern world.* New York: Tarcher/Putnam.

Gergen, K. J. (1994). *Realities and relationships. Soundings in social constructionism.* Cambridge, MA: Harvard University Press.

Kvale, S. (1992). (Ed.). *Psychology and postmodernism.* London: Sage.

Lyotard, J. F. (1984). *The postmodern condition: A report on knowledge.* Manchester, UK: Manchester University Press.

Rosenau, M. P. (1992). *Postmodernism and the social sciences.* Princeton, NJ: Princeton University Press.

(continued)

Box 3.1 Continued

Hermeneutics

Gadamer, H. G. (1975). *Truth and method.* New York: Seabury.

Messer, S. B., Sass, L. A., & Woolfolk, R. L. (1988). (Eds.). *Hermeneutics and psychological theory.* New Brunswick, NJ: Rutgers University Press.

Packer, A. L., & Addison, R. B. (1989). *Entering the circle—Hermeneutic investigation in psychology.* Albany: SUNY Press.

Palmer, R. E. (1969). *Hermeneutics.* Evanston, IL: Northwestern University Press.

Radnitzky, G. (1970). *Contemporary schools of metascience.* Gothenburg, Sweden: Akademiforlaget.

Phenomenology

Giorgi, A. (1970). *Psychology as a human science.* New York: Harper & Row.

Giorgi, A. (1985). (Ed.). *Phenomenology and psychological research.* Pittsburgh: Duquesne University Press.

Moustakas, C. (1994). *Phenomenological research methods.* Thousand Oaks, CA: Sage.

Spiegelberg, H. (1960). *The phenomenological movement, Vol. II.* The Hague, The Netherlands: Martinus Nijhoff.

Dialectics

Cornforth, M. (1971). *Materialism and dialectical method.* New York: International Publishers.

Riegel, K. F. (1975). (Ed.). *The development of dialectical operations.* Basel, Switzerland: Karger.

Sartre, J.-P. (1963). *The problem of method.* London: Methuen.

Interrelations

Bernstein, R. J. (1983). *Beyond objectivism and relativism.* Philadelphia: University of Pennsylvania Press.

Madison, G. B. (1990). *The hermeneutics of postmodernity.* Bloomington: Indiana University Press.

Ryan, M. (1992). *Marxism and deconstruction.* Baltimore, MD: Johns Hopkins University Press.

Postmodern Construction

Postmodern thought represents a broad movement in current art and philosophy, particularly as expressed in different versions by such French thinkers as Baudrillard, Derrida, Foucault, and Lyotard (see Anderson, 1995). Though long influential in the humanities, postmodern thought has now reached the social sciences, too (Kvale, 1992; Rosenau, 1992). In his book *The Postmodern Condition: A Report on Knowledge,* Lyotard (1984) characterizes the postmodern age by a disbelief in universal systems of thought. There is a lack of credibility toward meta-narratives of legitimation—such as the Enlightenment belief of progress through knowledge and science, as well as the Marxist utopia to be reached through emancipation of the working class, and the modern belief in economic growth.

The philosophy of the Enlightenment was a reaction against the religious dogma of the medieval ages. The belief in one true and almighty God, for all people and from eternity to eternity, was replaced in the modern era by a belief in one true and objective reality, universal and stable. Today—with a delegitimation of global systems of thought—there is no longer a stable foundation to support a universal and objective reality. Rorty's (1979) critique of the objectivism implied by the conception of "knowledge as a mirror of nature" pertains in particular to the dominating mental representations of a cognitive psychology. "The illusion of the double world" entailed thereby has been criticized by marginal positions as diverse as the phenomenological philosophy of Sartre and Merleau-Ponty and the radical behaviorism of Skinner (Kvale & Grenness, 1967). The modern dichotomy of an objective world distinct from subjective images is today breaking down and being replaced by a hyperreality of signs referring to other signs, texts referring to other texts.

Philosophy in the past half century has been characterized by a series of "turns," such as the linguistic, the conversational, the narrative, and the pragmatic turn. The conception of knowledge as a mirror of reality is replaced by a conception of "the social construction of reality" (Berger & Luckmann, 1966), where the focus is on the interpretation and negotiation of the meaning of the social world.

With the breakdown of the universal meta-narratives of legitimation, there is an emphasis on the local context, on the social and linguistic construction of a perspectival reality where knowledge is validated through practice. There is an openness to qualitative diversity, to the multiplicity of meanings in local contexts; knowledge is perspectival, dependent on the viewpoint and values of the investigator. Human reality is understood as conversation and action, where knowledge becomes the ability to perform effective actions. Today, the legitimation question of whether a study is scientific tends to be replaced by the pragmatic question of whether it provides useful knowledge.

The *qualitative research interview* is a construction site of knowledge. The knowledge generated by interviews is related below to five features of a postmodern construction of knowledge: the conversational, the narrative, the linguistic, the contextual, and the interrelational nature of knowledge. These intertwined features are taken as a starting point for clarifying the nature of the knowledge yielded by the research interview and for developing its knowledge potentials.

Knowledge as Conversation. An interview is a conversation, a dialogue between two partners about a topic of mutual interest. With the loss of faith in an objective reality that could be mirrored and mapped in scientific models, there is a move toward discourse and negotiation about the meaning of the lived world. The Socratic concept of dialogue is coming to the fore. The primacy of conversation is broadly recognized within current philosophy as well as outside postmodern philosophy, such as in Gadamer's hermeneutic analyses of the conversation, and in the discourse philosophy of Habermas—where truth is to be sought through a rational discourse aiming at consensus. In Rorty's neopragmatic philosophy, conversation is a basic mode of knowing, and in Shotter's conversational constructionism we live in conversational realities (Chapter 2, Interviews in Three Conversations).

Both the research interview and the philosophical discourse rest on conversation as access to knowledge. The nature of the interview conversation can be clarified by drawing on a philosophical analysis of discourse. Thus in Potter and Wetherell's (1987) application of discourse analysis, interview texts do not merely refer to some reality beyond the texts, but the participants' discourse is of interest in its own right, and the authors pose questions, such as, How is the talk constructed? and What does it achieve? They emphasize discourse analysis as not so much a method as an approach, focusing on the constructive nature of questioning, transcribing, and analyzing in interview research.

Knowledge as Narrative. In open interviews people tell stories, narratives, about their lives. In current thought, there is a shift from modern formalized knowledge systems to the narrative knowledge embodied in storytelling (Lyotard, 1984). With a skepticism about global systems of thought, a renarrativization of culture takes place, with truth to be worked out locally in small narrative units and with the collective stories contributing to uphold the values of the community. The narrative character of the knowledge in the human sciences has been treated by Polkinghorne (1988) and the specific narrative nature of interview research by Mishler (1986), who analyzes the structures of the stories subjects tell.

Knowledge as Language. The medium of the interview is language, and the knowledge produced is linguistic. Current philosophy has undergone a linguistic turn, with an emphasis on language games, speech acts, linguistic and textual analyses, and hermeneutic interpretation. The linguistic turn has been radicalized in postmodern philosophy: Language constitutes reality, each language constructing reality in its own way. The focus on language shifts attention away from the notion of an objective reality, as well as away from the individual subject. There is no longer a unique self who uses language to describe an objective world or to express itself; it is the structures of language that speak through the person.

In interview research, language is both the tool of interviewing and, in the form of tapes and transcripts, also the object of textual interpretation. Nevertheless, it has been rare in the social sciences for interview researchers to analyze the language medium they use as tools for and objects of their research. As one exception, Jensen (1989) has argued for applying the techniques of linguistics as a "statistics" of qualitative research.

Knowledge as Context. The interview takes place in an interpersonal context, and the meaning of the interview statements depends on this context. With the collapse of the universal systems of knowledge, the local, manifold, and changing language contexts come into prominence. Knowledge obtained within one context is not automatically transferable to, nor commensurable with, the knowledge within other contexts. With the heterogeneity of contexts, the issues of translations between contexts—such as from the interviewers' conversations with their subjects to their conversations with other researchers —and of transitions from one modality to another—such as from oral to written knowledge—come into the foreground.

Interviews are sensitive to the qualitative differences and nuances of meaning, which may not be quantifiable and commensurable across contexts and modalities. The contextuality of the meaning obtained is central in the narrative approaches, as discussed by Mishler in his *Research Interviewing—Context and Narrative* (1986). The differences between the oral and the written language contexts become critical through the transcription from an oral to a written modality (Mishler, 1991).

Knowledge as Interrelational. An interview is literally an inter view, an inter change of views between two persons conversing about a common theme. In postmodern thought there is an emphasis on knowledge as interrelational and structural, interwoven in webs of networks. Knowledge is neither inside a person nor outside in the world, but exists in the relationship between person and world. In an introduction to phenomenological philosophy, Lyotard (1991) points out that the intentional relation of subject and situation does not unify two isolated poles; on the contrary, the subject and the situation cannot be defined except in and by this relationship. Merleau-Ponty, a phenomenological psychologist and philosopher whose work has also been regarded as a precursor to postmodern thought (Madison, 1990), emphasized the interrelational nature of knowledge in his development of a phenomenology of perspectivity. His *Phenomenology of Perception* (Merleau-Ponty, 1962), which is a critique of the prejudice of an objective world in psychology, thus concludes with a quote from Saint Exupery's *The Little Prince:* "Man is but a network of relations."

There is a shift today from the individual mind to relations between persons: "Constructionism replaces the individual with the relationship as the locus of knowledge" (Gergen, 1994, p. x). The knowledge created by the inter-view is inter-relational. The interrelational knowledge of the interview has been particularly recognized by therapists. To Sullivan (1954), the psychiatric interview is an inter-personal situation, the data obtained are neither objective nor subjective but inter-subjective. In an interview about the therapeutic interview, the Jungian therapist Hillman (1984) replied to the interviewer:

> The main thing is that we both get out of the way. What can block the interview is "us," your thinking about what you have to get done here, and my thinking about my own thoughts, opinions, biography, myself. The "you" and the "me" can prevent the "inter." It's not our views that matter, it's the "inter." (p. 8)

New Views on Inter Views. The current qualitative research wave in the social sciences may become comprehensible when situated in a postmodern frame of reference. The recent interest in interview research is, in the present analysis, not merely a result of internal developments in social science methodology, but reflects a broader historical and cultural questioning and construction of social reality. The implicit conceptions of the knowledge produced by interviews and the explicit analysis of knowledge construction by postmodern philosophers thus converge on the conversational, narratival, linguistic, contextual, and interrelational features of knowledge. None of these features of knowledge are specific, new postmodern insights of the past decades. The pervasiveness of these aspects of knowledge as expressions of a postmodern loss of belief in an objective reality *is* new, however, as is the recognition of their intertwinedness in the communal construction of knowledge of a social reality.

The affinities of knowledge construction in postmodern thought and in research interviews pointed out here do not imply that the interview is a postmodern method. Thematically, a common focus on experiences and intentions of individual subjects in interviews contrasts with a postmodern decentering of the individual. Historically, the conversation as a systematic tool for the creation of knowledge can be traced at least to Thucydides and Socrates. The psychoanalytic interview, developed by Freud, has since the turn of the century been a main production site of new psychological knowledge. Yet the extended use of qualitative interviews as a research method in the social sciences is a new phenomenon of the past decades, and has here been related to changes in the concept of knowledge in a postmodern era as introduced by the traveler metaphor in the first chapter.

Postmodern philosophy has been applied by Scheurich (1995) in an analysis of the power relationship between the interviewer and the interviewee, and by Lather (1995) in an extension of the concept of validity.

I now turn to the philosophical positions that to some extent provided the background from which postmodern thought developed —and reacted against—and that in their own right have provided analyses relevant to qualitative interviews.

Hermeneutical Interpretation

Hermeneutics is the study of the interpretation of texts. The purpose of hermeneutical interpretation is to obtain a valid and common understanding of the meaning of a text. Although the subject matter of classical hermeneutics was the texts of literature, religion, and law, there has been an extension of the concept of "text" to include discourse and even action. Thus, in *Truth and Method,* Gadamer (1975) starts with Plato's dialogues and regards both the conversation and the oral tradition as presuppositions for understanding the written texts, which historically are secondary phenomena. In his article "Human Action as a Text," Ricoeur (1971) extends the hermeneutic principles of interpretations of the texts of the humanities to the interpretation of the object of the social sciences—meaningful action.

The research interview is a conversation about the human life world, with the oral discourse transformed into texts to be interpreted. Hermeneutics is then doubly relevant to interview research, first by elucidating the dialogue producing the interview texts to be interpreted, and then by clarifying the subsequent process of interpreting the interview texts produced, which may again be conceived as a dialogue or a conversation with the text.

The hermeneutic discipline is an attempt to reflect upon the mode of understanding in the humanities, such as by interpretations in literature and historical research, as well as in theology and law. Radnitzky (1970, p. 22) offers a definition of hermeneutics, which I have abbreviated slightly: Hermeneutic human sciences study the objectivations of human cultural activity as texts with a view to interpreting them to find out the intended or expressed meaning, in order to establish a co-understanding, or possibly even a consent; and in general to mediate traditions so that the historical dialogue of mankind may be continued and deepened.

The topic of the so-called Betti-Gadamer controversy was whether hermeneutics involves specific techniques of literary interpretation, as maintained by Betti, or whether it entails a more fundamental questioning of the meaning of being, which was Gadamer's position (see Palmer, 1969). I emphasize below the methodological implications of hermeneutics and outline some aspects of hermeneutical interpretation.

The Hermeneutical Circle and Canons of Interpretation. The interpretation of meaning is characterized by a *hermeneutical circle*. The understanding of a text takes place through a process in which the meaning of the separate parts is determined by the global meaning of the text, as it is anticipated. The closer determination of the meaning of the separate parts may eventually change the originally anticipated meaning of the totality, which again influences the meaning of the separate parts, and so on. In principle, such a hermeneutical explication of the text is an infinite process, while it ends in practice when one has reached a sensible meaning, a valid unitary meaning, free of inner contradictions.

Box 3.2 describes seven canons of a hermeneutic meaning interpretation of literary texts. They are taken from Radnitzky's (1970) analysis of the hermeneutical circle, and their implications for the interpretation of interviews are pointed out.

Differences Between Literary and Interview Texts. Although the relevance of a hermeneutical approach to interview research has been suggested here, some reservations need to be made concerning differ-

Box 3.2

Hermeneutical Canons of Interpretation

A first canon involves the continuous *back and forth process between the parts and the whole* that follows from the hermeneutical circle. Starting with an often vague and intuitive understanding of the text as a whole, its different parts are interpreted, and out of these interpretations the parts are again related to the totality, and so on. In the hermeneutical tradition this circularity is not viewed as a "vicious circle," but rather as a *circulus fructuosis,* or spiral, which implies the possibility of a continuously deepened understanding of meaning. The problem is not to get away from the circularity in the explication of meanings, but to get into the circle in the right way. During the analysis of qualitative interviews, it is common to read an interview through first to get at the more or less general meaning. One then goes back to certain themes and special expressions, tries to develop their meaning, then again returns to the more global meaning of the interview in the light of the deepened meaning of the parts, and so on.

A second canon is that an interpretation of meaning ends when one has reached a *"good Gestalt,"* an inner unity of the text free of logical contradictions. Correspondingly the interpretations of an interview will stop when the meanings of the different themes make sensible patterns and enter into a coherent unity.

A third canon is the *testing* of part interpretations against the global meaning of the text and possibly also against other texts by the same author. In interview analysis this implies a comparison between interpretations of the single statements and the global meaning of the interview, and possibly with other information about the interviewee. In contrast to the interpretations of "dead" texts, there exists

---

Box 3.2 Continued

a possibility that the researcher may in a re-interview enter into a dialogue with the subjects about the meaning of their statements.

A fourth canon is the *autonomy of the text,* that the text should be understood on the basis of its own frame of reference, by explicating what the text itself states about a theme. For the analysis of interviews this means that the interpretation should stick to the content of the statements and try to understand what they express about the life world of the subject. The biography of the individual and psychological theories about the theme are of subordinate importance here; what matters is to deepen and extend the autonomous meaning of the interview statements.

A fifth canon of the hermeneutical explication of a text concerns *knowledge about the theme* of the text. Conducting a qualitative research interview requires an extensive knowledge of the theme so that the interviewer may be sensitive to the nuances of meanings expressed and the different contexts into which the meanings may enter.

A sixth principle is that an interpretation of a text is *not presuppositionless.* The interpreter cannot "jump outside" the tradition of understanding he or she lives in. The interpreter of a text may, however, attempt to make these presuppositions explicit, and try to become conscious of how certain formulations of a question to a text already determine which forms of answers are possible. Such a consciousness of presuppositions is necessary when using the interview as a research method, because the interviewer and the interpreter will unavoidably co-determine the results. What matters here is being as aware as possible about one's own presuppositions and modes of influence and to attempt to take them into account in the interpretation.

(continued)

Box 3.2 Continued

A seventh canon states that every interpretation involves innovation and *creativity*—*"Jedes Verstehen ist ein Besserverstehen"* (Every understanding is a better understanding). The interpretation goes beyond the immediately given and enriches the understanding by bringing forth new differentiations and interrelations in the text, extending its meaning. Correspondingly the immediately experienced meanings in the interview situations are expanded and refined through interpretation.

SOURCE: Adapted and extended from Radnitzky (1970).

---

ences between the literary texts of hermeneutics and the texts produced by interviews. First, hermeneutics has traditionally treated the interpretation of finished texts, whereas a research interview involves both the generation and the interpretation of a text. The interviewers are cocreators of the texts they interpret, and they may negotiate their interpretations with their subjects. The interview text is thus not a pre-given literary text, but emerges in the same process as its interpretation; it involves both the creation and the negotiated interpretation of the text.

Second, a literary text is an accomplished work intended as communication outside the situation in which it originated. The interview is tied to a specific interpersonal situation, it develops more or less spontaneously, the subjects addressing themselves to the interviewer not only by words but also through gestures and implicit references to their common situation. The transcribed interview text renders an incomplete account of the wealth of meanings expressed in the lived interview situation.

Third, literary texts contain well-articulated and highly condensed expressions of meanings; they are "eminent" texts. The transcribed interviews are often vague, repetitious, and have many digressions containing much "noise." An extended process of clarification and condensation may be necessary to arrive at the meanings intended by the interviewee. On the other hand, what appears to be "noise" from the standpoint of a "pure" meaning interpretation may yield important information through the deeper psychological interpretation of nonintended meanings as a form of "depth hermeneutics."

The nature of the qualitative research interview as a conversation has been treated from a hermeneutical perspective by Carson (1986) and by Weber (1986). The implications of hermeneutics for interpreting interview texts will be taken up in Chapter 12.

Knowledge and Interest. From a critical hermeneutical standpoint, Habermas (1971) has argued for an interlocking of knowledge and human interests. He has outlined three types of knowledge-constituting interests: a technical, an understanding, and an emancipatory interest.

The *natural sciences* are, according to Habermas, characterized by a technical knowledge interest directed toward technical control over objectified processes. This knowledge interest dominated a positivist philosophy of science in which the natural sciences were regarded as the methodological ideal for the social sciences. The explicit purpose of behaviorist psychology was thus the prediction and control of the behavior of other people.

Hermeneutical research in the *humanities* is guided by an interest in obtaining a possible consensus of understanding among actors within the frame of reference of self-understanding as mediated within the culture. The study of literature and history serves in this case to further the understanding of the human situation.

For the critical *social sciences,* Habermas has postulated an emancipatory knowledge interest. Information about social laws may instigate a process of reflection in the consciousness of the persons involved; and the unreflected consciousness, which belongs to the preconditions for such laws, may then change. Habermas relates psychoanalytical interpretations to the hermeneutics of text interpretations, and regards the psychoanalytic therapy as a model for an emancipatory self-reflection of the social sciences.

Several criticisms can be raised concerning Habermas's triad of knowledge-constituting interests. One is that the natural sciences are depicted in a narrow technical mode, in line with a positivist concep-

tion of natural science, neglecting other approaches such as an eco-
logical understanding of nature. Another is that psychoanalysis is
pictured in a rather idealized cognitive manner of hermeneutical
interpretations, with little weight on the emotional turmoils inherent
in the therapy situation, as these appear, for example, in the session
reported by Rogers (see Chapter 2, A Therapeutic Interview on Hate).
In spite of such limitations, Habermas's analysis is important because
it goes beyond the common dichotomy of facts or values to point out
how different human interests constitute different forms of scientific
knowledge.

In the present context we can include the emancipatory possibilities
that research interviews have for getting beyond the surface level of
the phenomena, for going deeper than common sense and instigating
a process of reflection on the phenomena studied. A social science
guided by an emancipatory knowledge interest would aim at communicating the insights obtained about the life world of the interviewees
back to the subjects concerned. Communicating a critical understanding of the life world, which still has an appearance of natural
necessity, may contribute to changes in the socially constructed world.

Phenomenological Description

A phenomenological approach in a general nonphilosophical sense
has been prevalent in qualitative research. In sociology, phenomenology was mediated by the Husserlian-based phenomenology of the
social world by Schuetz, and further by Berger and Luckmann in *The
Social Construction of Reality* (1966). Without explicitly drawing in
the phenomenological philosophy of Husserl, Taylor and Bogdan's
Introduction to Qualitative Research—The Search for Meanings (1984)
is based on phenomenology in the sense of understanding social
phenomena from the actors' own perspectives, describing the world
as experienced by the subjects, and with the assumption that the
important reality is what people perceive it to be.

Phenomenology was founded as a philosophy by Husserl at the turn
of the century and further developed as existential philosophy by
Heidegger, and then in an existential and dialectical direction by
Sartre and by Merleau-Ponty. The subject matter of phenomenology
began with consciousness and experience, was expanded to include

the human life world by Heidegger, and to include human action by Sartre. With the focus of the interview on the experienced meanings of the subjects' life world, phenomenology appears relevant for clarifying the mode of understanding in a qualitative research interview.

"Phenomenology is the study of the structure, and the variations of structure, of the consciousness to which any thing, event, or person appears" (Giorgi, 1975, p. 83). Phenomenology is interested in elucidating both that which appears and the manner in which it appears. It studies the subjects' perspectives on their world; attempts to describe in detail the content and structure of the subjects' consciousness, to grasp the qualitative diversity of their experiences and to explicate their essential meanings. Phenomenology attempts to get beyond immediately experienced meanings in order to articulate the prereflective level of lived meanings, to make the invisible visible. Two contributions of phenomenological philosophy to understanding qualitative interview research will be discussed here: the phenomenological method and the primacy of the life world.

The Phenomenological Method. Spiegelberg (1960; see also Giorgi, 1994) outlined a phenomenological method that includes description, investigation of essences, and phenomenological reduction. It is not possible to give precise instructions for an *open description,* and Spiegelberg illustrates the method by using metaphors; for example, "to the matters themselves," "seeing and listening," "keeping the eyes open," "not think, but see." According to Merleau-Ponty (1962), what matters is to describe the given as precisely and completely as possible; to describe rather than to explain or analyze. Phenomenology is the attempt at a direct description of experience, without any considerations about the origin or cause of an experience. In phenomenological philosophy, objectivity is reached through intentional acts of consciousness and is an expression of fidelity to the phenomena investigated.

In the *investigation of essences* one shifts from describing separate phenomena to searching for their common essence. Husserl termed one method of investigating essences as a "free variation in fantasy." This means varying a given phenomenon freely in its possible forms, and that which remains constant through the different variations is the essence of the phenomenon.

A *phenomenological reduction* calls for a suspension of judgment as to the existence or nonexistence of the content of an experience. The reduction can be pictured as a "bracketing," an attempt to place the common sense and scientific foreknowledge about the phenomena within parentheses in order to arrive at an unprejudiced description of the essence of the phenomena. Phenomenological reduction does not involve an absolute absence of presuppositions, but rather a critical analysis of one's own presuppositions.

The Primacy of the Life World. The qualitative research interview has a unique potential for obtaining access to and describing the lived everyday world. The attempt to obtain unprejudiced descriptions entails a rehabilitation of the *Lebenswelt*—the life world—in relation to the world of science. The life world is the world as it is encountered in everyday life and given in direct and immediate experience, independent of and prior to explanations. The qualitative interview may be seen as one realization of Merleau-Ponty's (1962) program for a phenomenological science starting from the primary experience of the world:

> All my knowledge of the world, even my scientific knowledge, is gained from my own particular point of view, or from some experience of the world without which the symbols of science would be meaningless. The whole universe of science is built upon the world as directly experienced, and if we want to subject science itself to rigorous scrutiny and arrive at a precise assessment of its meaning and scope, we must begin by re-awakening the basic experiences of the world of which science is the second order expression. (p. viii)

The geographer's map is thus an abstraction of the countryside where we first learned what a forest, a mountain, or a river was. In this phenomenological approach, the qualitative studies of subjects' experiences of their world are basic to the more abstract scientific studies of the social world; interviews are in this sense not merely a few entertaining curiosities in addition to some basic scientific quantitative facts obtained by experiments and questionnaires. The qualitative interview is a research method that gives a privileged access to our basic experience of the lived world. The descriptive focus on the lived interactions of the human world may counteract a technological colonization of the life world that reduces qualitative diversity to isolated facts and variables and that transforms intentional human interaction to a means-ends rationality.

The implications of phenomenological philosophy for qualitative research were developed in a series of studies at Duquesne University. Starting with van Kaam's (1959) study of "The experience of really being understood," the method was further applied, systematized, and reflected by Giorgi and co-workers (see Giorgi, 1970; Giorgi, Fischer, & Murray, 1975). The open phenomenological approach to the meanings of phenomena in the everyday world is illustrated in the interview reported by Giorgi (Chapter 2, A Research Interview on Learning) and will be taken up again in the analysis of the interview (Chapter 11, Meaning Condensation). In a review of recent literature on qualitative research, Giorgi (1994) outlines how a more comprehensive phenomenological approach would deepen the qualitative perspective. A general presentation of phenomenological method is given by Moustakas (1994). The phenomenographic research in education, which focuses on qualitative descriptions of our conceptions of the world, was inspired by phenomenology but does not share its philosophical assumptions (Marton, 1981). The mode of understanding in qualitative research interviews outlined earlier (Chapter 2, The Mode of Understanding in the Qualitative Research Interview) is in keeping with a phenomenological understanding, with the life world as the point of departure, the qualitative descriptions of meaning, and a deliberate naïveté as expression of phenomenological reduction.

Dialectical Situating

Dialectics is the study of internal contradictions—the contradiction between the general and the specific, between appearance and essence, between the quantitative and the qualitative. The development of contradictions is the driving force of change. Dialectical materialism involves the fundamental assumption that the contradictions of material and economic life are the basis of social relations and of consciousness. Men act upon the world, change it, and are again changed by the consequences of their actions. Human consciousness and behavior are studied within the concrete sociohistorical situation of a class society and its forces and relations of production. The objects of the human sciences are seen as multifaceted and contradictory, consisting of internally related opposites in continual change and development.

There are marked differences among the many different traditions of dialectics, such as the official dialectical materialism of the former socialist countries, the activity theory developed by Leontiev, the Frankfurt school of Adorno and Horkheimer, and the existential Marxism of Sartre, which will be described here. I will not discuss the differences, but will offer some general implications that dialectics has for understanding qualitative interview research.

Sartre attempted to mediate between Marxism, phenomenology and existentialism, and psychoanalysis in *The Problem of Method* (1963). His critique of the individualizing approach of psychoanalysis also pertains to much current interview research: "How many times has someone attempted the feat of psychoanalyzing Robespierre for us without even understanding that the contradictions in his behavior were conditioned by the objective contradictions of the situation" (p. 60). Sartre's critique of an objectifying Marxist reductionism might also be mentioned: "Valéry is a petit bourgeois intellectual, no doubt about it. But not every petit bourgeois intellectual is Valéry" (p. 56).

In dialectical thought there is an emphasis upon the new, what is under development. With a conception of the social world as being developed through contradictions, it is important to uncover the new developmental tendencies in order to obtain true knowledge of the social world. The statistical average or the representative case of the status quo is less important than the new tendencies developing as the *status nascendi*.

In a dialectical perspective, knowledge is intrinsically related to action. Marx, in his theses on Feuerbach, criticized the philosophers for merely interpreting the world differently; what matters is to change the world. Correspondingly, social scientists have tended to provide different interpretations of the social reality, rather than contribute to its change. For Sartre, knowledge and action are two abstracted aspects of an original concrete relation: Action is an uncovering of reality and at the same time a changing of this reality.

The implications of dialectical philosophy for qualitative interview research have been little addressed. I include it here in an attempt to counteract the prevalent individualistic and idealistic approach of much interview research. One example, an interview study based on

Marxist theory, treats the double work situation of women industrial workers who were also homemakers. Becker-Schmidt (1982) describes the economic and social aspects of the women's world and the conflicts that were generated by the contradictions in their life situation. The specific contradictions of the women's reactions and attitudes expressed in the interviews were then interpreted, not only in relation to the individual women's personalities, but were also systematically traced to the common economic and social contradictions of their everyday world, in particular the conflicting demands made by their work and their family situation.

Dialectics takes issue with the coherence criterion of truth involved in hermeneutics with a good interpretation as a coherent Gestalt free of contradictions. From a dialectical perspective, a truth criterion based on being free of contradictions in a contradictory world is false. Haug (1978) has criticized what she terms the need for consensus and harmony in qualitative research. If social reality is in itself contradictory, the task of social science is to investigate the real contradictions of the social situation and posit them against each other. In other words, if social processes are essentially contradictory, then empirical methods based on an exclusion of contradictions will be invalid for uncovering a contradictory social reality.

Philosophy and Interviews

Philosophy addresses the conditions for knowledge of the human situation; it does not provide specific methods for obtaining empirical knowledge of the human situation. The philosophies outlined above have analyzed major aspects of the mode of understanding in the interview, such as life world, meaning, description, ambiguity and contradictions, intersubjectivity, and change. By clarifying the nature of such phenomena these philosophies may contribute to conceptualizing and reflecting the mode of understanding in the qualitative research interview. In some instances they can also provide inspiration for a methodological development of interview research, such as the open phenomenological approach to conducting and analyzing interviews, or a hermeneutical approach to interpretation of interview texts.

There are important convergences as well as fundamental differences among the philosophies discussed above. Heidegger's existential philosophy, based on Husserl's phenomenology and on the hermeneutic tradition, is now regarded as anticipating postmodern thought, as is Merleau-Ponty's phenomenological philosophy. Sartre developed phenomenological and existential philosophy within a dialectical context, and Lyotard's early works focused on phenomenology and dialectics.

Though they converge on conceptual reflections of major aspects of the interview's mode of understanding, these philosophies were developed with different aims and for different areas. There are many conflicting assumptions among, as well as within, these philosophies. The idealistic focus on consciousness and texts in phenomenology and hermeneutics contrasts with a dialectical materialist emphasis on the social and economical contradictions of society. Both phenomenology and dialectics seek the essences beneath the manifest appearances, while in postmodern thought the appearance has become the essence. Phenomenology attempts to obtain presuppositionless descriptions, hermeneutics emphasizes foreknowledge by interpretations. Hermeneutics attempts to obtain interpretations free of contradictions, whereas dialectics focuses on these very contradictions of consciousness and action as reflections of social and material contradictions. And whereas hermeneutics aims at consensus of interpretation, postmodern thought emphasizes the plurality of diverging interpretations. Dialectical materialism presupposes a basic material reality, postmodern thought emphasizes the linguistic and social construction of a social reality.

These important differences will not be pursued in the present context; in the following chapters the philosophies will be used pragmatically to highlight different aspects of the qualitative research interview. The philosophies will be applied to conceptualize and reflect upon issues encountered throughout the method stages of an interview inquiry. These involve methodologic choices in questioning, interpreting, validating, and reporting interview studies, choices that are often at odds with traditional conceptions of method in the modern social sciences.

4

Qualitative Research
in Science and in Practice

Before turning from the philosophical understandings of interview research to the concrete procedures of designing an interview inquiry, I will address some current positions on qualitative research in academic and practical social research. I will first discuss conceptual controversies that are frequently brought up by mainstream social scientists, such as the scientific status of qualitative research and its relation to quantification and objectivity. Then I will discuss three areas in which qualitative interviewing has been prominent in practice: market research, feminist research, and psychoanalysis. Different as these areas may be, they have in common a use of qualitative interviews in attempts to develop knowledge that may change persons and conditions.

The Scientific Status of the Interview

The qualitative research interview has sometimes been dismissed as not being scientific—it may perhaps provide interesting results and serve as preparation to scientific investigations, but the interview as such is not a scientific method. Critical objections appear endemic to current qualitative research. In *Qualitative Research for Education*, Bogdan and Biklen (1982) list and discuss eight common questions about the value of qualitative research. The concluding chapter of *Designing Qualitative Research* (Marshall & Rossman, 1995) is titled

"Defending the Value and Logic of Qualitative Research." In this book's final chapter, Chapter 15, I will return to some of the standard objections to qualitative interview research.

Neither textbooks on social science methodology nor dictionaries of the English language provide any unequivocal and generally accepted definition of *science*. Some of the main definitions of science in Webster's dictionary (*Webster's,* 1967) are, in abbreviated form: Knowledge as distinguished from ignorance or misunderstanding, attained through study; systematized knowledge; one of the natural sciences; knowledge covering general truths or the operations of general sciences, especially as obtained and tested through scientific method; a system or method based on scientific principles. The characterization of qualitative interviews as scientific or unscientific will therefore depend on which definition of science is chosen; thus the interview does not belong to the methods of the natural sciences, though it can, as will be shown in this book, produce systematized knowledge.

An alternative, apparently simpler definition of science is as the activity of, and the knowledge produced by, scientists. Although circular, this operational definition points to the social and historical issues of who is a scientist and who has the power to define an activity as scientific or unscientific.

Some accepted core concepts of the meaning of science do exist in our culture. It is understood that science should produce knowledge, and that this knowledge should be new, systematic, and obtained methodologically. A broad definition of science that will be used here is therefore: *the methodological production of new, systematic knowledge.*

The concepts of this working definition—methodical, production, new, systematic, and knowledge—are again complex. Depending on how these five terms are defined, qualitative research may again be characterized as either scientific or as unscientific. For example, *systematic* may refer to intersubjectively reproducible data, to quantitative data, to objective results, to generalizable findings, and to knowledge obtained by a hypothetical, deductive method. Again, the scientific status of the interview depends on the definitions chosen. With the manifold meanings of the concept of science, any general characterization of qualitative interview research as scientific or unscientific is unwarranted. The automatic rejection of qualitative research as unscientific reflects a specific, limited conception of science, instead of seeing science as the topic of continual clarification and discussion. Throughout the following chapters I will argue that the qualitative research interview can produce scientific knowledge in the meaning of methodologically secured new and systematic knowledge.

Positivism

One philosophical position that has generally rejected qualitative research as a scientific method goes under the name of positivism (see, e.g., Kerlinger [1979] and Mandler & Kessen [1959] for positivism applied to the social sciences; Radnitzky [1970] for a critical discussion of the philosophical foundations of positivism, and Koch [1959] for a critique of its consequences for psychology). Truth was to be found through method, by following general rules of method that were largely independent of the content and context of the investigation. Any influence by the person of the researcher should be eliminated or minimized.

The founding of the social sciences was closely tied to positivism. Comte founded both positivist philosophy and sociology as a science in mid-19th-century France. Positivism began as a positive development; it reacted against religious dogma and metaphysical speculation and stressed a return to observable data. Positivist science was to provide determinate laws of society with possibilities of socially engineering society. The potential contributions of social science to social change were lost in the Vienna circle in the 1920s. Its strict focus on the logic and validity of scientific statements had a strong impact on the mid-century development of the social sciences, in particular in the United States.

Social scientists of different critical schools have often labeled positivism as uncritical. This may pertain to positivist scientists defining the political, historical, and social functions of social research as outside the scientific domain. When it comes to a critical approach to scientific evidence and the rigor of scientific arguments, the positivists have contributed to moving social research beyond myth and common sense.

According to positivist thought, the young social sciences should follow the experimental quantitative methods of the established natural sciences, in particular of the most advanced science at the turn of the century—physics. Social science should aim at the prediction and control of behavior. Scientific statements were to be based upon observable data; the observation of the data and interpretation of their meanings should be strictly separated. The scientific facts should be objective and quantifiable. Data should be unambiguous, intra- and intersubjectively reproducible. Scientific statements ought to be value neutral, facts were to be distinguished from values, and science from politics.

To a philosophy of science that takes as its point of departure the elimination of the human factor in research, the qualitative interview based on interpersonal interaction must appear unscientific. The mode of understanding in research interviews consistently violates the positivist demands of scientific knowledge. The main aspects of the interview, as outlined in Box 2.1 (see Chapter 2), either are irrelevant to or directly violate a positivist conception of science. The interview data consist of meaningful statements, themselves based on interpretations, and they are again subject to continual processes of interpretation; the data and their interpretations are thus not strictly separated. Quantified knowledge is not the goal of interview research; the main interview findings are expressed in language, frequently in everyday language. Interview statements can be ambiguous and contradictory and the findings may not be intersubjectively reproducible, for example, because of the interviewers' varying knowledge of and sensitivity to the interview topic. In conclusion, major features of the mode of understanding in the qualitative interview appear, from a positivist perspective, as methodological sources of error, and the interview therefore cannot be a scientific method.

Criticizing positivism and a quantitative hegemony in the social sciences is sometimes dismissed today as attacking a straw man. The quantitative man may indeed be made of straw in some disciplines, but as recently as the 1984 congress of the International Union of Scientific Psychology, the presidential address by Klix advocated the development of psychology as a natural science in accordance with the principle evolved by Galilei: Measure what is measurable, and make measurable what is not.

Though science was to build on objective, quantified data, the social and temporal practices of the researchers producing these data were neglected in the positivist social sciences. A closer look at the procedures for obtaining intersubjective agreement among observers about "objective" facts reveals the many theoretical presuppositions built into the observational procedures leading to the construction of social facts. This pertains to the transformation of meanings into data, for example in psychology by the categorization of group action, and the content analysis of texts into atomized meanings as facts (Kvale, 1976a). With a postmodern perspective, quantified data are not given, nor ideals for interview research to approximate; social facts are social constructions arising from a specific, chosen technological perspective on the social world.

Although positivist philosophy has had little influence on the natural sciences—one article even talks about "the physics of the physicist" and "the physics of the psychologist" as two entirely different realities (Brandt, 1973)—and is no longer current in the philosophy of science, a positivist understanding of science may still rule in some psychology departments. An extreme version of this attitude was the early behavioristic limitation of psychology to the objective observation of behavior, with a prohibition against entering into a dialogue with research subjects. Mishler (1986) documents how a behaviorist approach long dominated interview research, and that a mechanical behaviorist conception of interviews as responses (answers) emitted to stimuli (questions) led interviewers to neglect, and even suppress, the spontaneous tendency that people have to tell stories about their lives.

A closer look at the practices of formalizing and quantifying research in the social sciences may show that these are linked less to the actual practices of the natural sciences than to the administrative procedures of *bureaucratic* institutions and a general *technological* approach to human action (Kvale, 1976b), both of which attempt to eliminate or reduce the subjective dimensions of the subjects ruled. The strictly formalized procedures of categorization and quantification are ways of ordering and structuring the social world, with quantification as one means of legitimating administrative decisions. In the social sciences, positivism has entailed a philosophic bureaucracy that suppresses the subjective and social dimensions of social research.

Objectivity in Qualitative Research

It has often been claimed that the qualitative research interview lacks objectivity, due in particular to the human interaction inherent in the interview situation. Turning to social science texts on methodology and to ordinary language dictionaries, about a dozen meanings of *objectivity* may be found (see Polkinghorne, 1989; *Webster's*, 1967). *Objectivity* is often discussed as one side of a polarity: objective/ subjective; unbiased/biased; public/private; intersubjective/personal; reflects the nature of the object/personal impressions only; reality as it exists independent of the observer/reality as dependent on the observer; value free/value laden; impartial/partial; facts/values; physical/meaning; behavior/consciousness; quantitative/qualitative; stable/ changing; and universal/local.

According to a definition of objectivity as intersubjective agreement, the lack of intersubjective consensus testifies to objectivity being a rather subjective notion. With the variety of conceptions of objectivity, the qualitative interview cannot be objectively characterized as either an objective or a subjective method. The objectivity of the knowledge produced by the interview interaction must be discussed with specific respect to the different conceptions of objectivity and the topic of the concrete inquiry. Here three conceptions of objectivity will be discussed: as freedom from bias, as intersubjective knowledge, and as reflecting the nature of the object.

First, objectivity as *freedom from bias* refers to reliable knowledge, checked and controlled, undistorted by personal bias and prejudice. Such a commonsense conception of *objective* as being free of bias implies doing good, solid, craftsmanlike research, producing knowledge that has been systematically cross-checked and verified. In principle, the interview can be an objective research method in the sense of being unbiased. This will be argued later in relation to validity as craftsmanship (Chapter 13, Validity as Quality of Craftsmanship).

Second, a conception of objective as meaning *intersubjective* knowledge has been common in the social sciences. Scientific data must be intersubjectively testable and reproducible: Repeated observations of the same phenomenon by different observers should give the same data. Objectivity may here refer to what a number of subjects or judges observe, referred to as "coder reliability." Scriven (1972) criticized this quantitative conception of objectivity as the "fallacy of intersubjectivism"—the sheer number of observers reporting the same phenomenon is no guarantee of truth, the success of stage magicians being one of many possible counterexamples. I can add the extreme position of the main character in Ibsen's play, *An Enemy of the People*—"The most dangerous enemy of truth and freedom is the compact majority. . . . The minority is always right" (act IV).

Within a conception of objectivity as intersubjective agreement we may distinguish between an arithmetic and a dialogical conception of objectivity. *Arithmetic intersubjectivity* refers to reliability as measured mechanically by amount of agreement among independent observers. *Dialogical intersubjectivity* refers to agreement through a rational discourse and reciprocal critique among those identifying and interpreting a phenomenon. This may take the form of a communicative validation among researchers as well as between researchers and their subjects (Chapter 13, Communicative Validity).

In principle, qualitative interviews can approach objectivity in an arithmetic sense of intersubjectivity. Although a single interview can hardly be replicated, different interviewers may, when following similar procedures in a common interview guide, come up with closely similar interviews from their subjects. With a dialogical conception of intersubjectivity, the interview attains a privileged position—it involves a conversation and negotiation of meaning between the interviewer and his or her subjects.

Third, objective may also mean reflecting the nature of the object researched, letting the object speak, being *adequate to the object* investigated, expressing the real nature of the object studied. The objectivity of a method then depends on its relation to the nature of the object studied, and it involves a theoretical understanding of the content matter investigated. Again, the interview may in principle be objective. With the object of the interview understood as existing in a linguistically constituted and interpersonally negotiated social world, the qualitative research interview as a linguistic, interpersonal, and interpreting method becomes a more objective method in the social sciences than the methods of the natural sciences, which were developed for a nonhuman object domain. From this perspective the qualitative research interview obtains a privileged position concerning objective knowledge of the social world: The interview is sensitive to and reflects the nature of the object investigated, in the interview conversation the object speaks.

In conclusion, the interview as such is neither an objective nor a subjective method—its essence is intersubjective interaction. The issue of the objectivity of knowledge gained through an interview is linked to the pervasive dichotomy of objectivism and subjectivism in Western thought. Bernstein (1983), in *Beyond Objectivism and Relativism,* describes *objectivism* as the basic conviction that there exists some permanent, ahistorical matrix or framework to which we can ultimately appeal in determining the nature of knowledge, truth, reality, and goodness. A realist version of objectivism implies that an objective reality exists independently of the observer and that only one correct view can be taken of it. The counterposition of *relativism* involves a view that all concepts of knowledge, truth, reality, and goodness are relative to a specific theoretical framework, a form of life or culture. In an attempt to go beyond the polarity of an objectivist realism versus an "anything goes" relativism, Bernstein follows a hermeneutical tradition arguing for a dialogic conception of truth, where true knowledge is sought through rational argumentation by participants in a discourse. And the medium of a discourse is language, which is neither objective or universal, nor subjective or individual, but intersubjective.

Qualitative and Quantitative Research

One of the most persistent requirements in modern social science has been that scientific knowledge should be quantitative; for example,

> Quantitative research which does seek scientific explanation can be referred to simply as the scientific approach. (Calder, 1977, p. 355)

> Scientists are not and cannot be concerned with the individual case. They seek laws, systematic relations, explanations of phenomena. And their results are always statistical.

. . . the existential individual, the core of the individuality, forever escapes the scientist. He is chained to group data, statistical prediction, and probabilistic estimates. (Kerlinger, 1979, pp. 270, 272)

The degree to which the observations can be quantified (translated into numbers) is often a good index of the maturity of a science. (Mussen, Conger, & Kagan, 1977, p. 13)

According to the above views, the present introduction to qualitative interview research is without scientific relevance or is, at best, an indication of an immature science.

Some possible reasons for the strong demands for quantification in current social sciences will be mentioned. There may be an *ontological* assumption that the social world is basically a mathematically ordered universe in which everything that exists, exists in number form; and, accordingly, the objective data of a science of the social world must be quantitative. There may also be an *epistemological* demand that research data should be quantitative in order to be commensurable across theories. There may further be a *technical* interest in quantification, in that statistical techniques are powerful tools for handling large amounts of data. The demand for quantification may also stem from the anticipated audience of a research report, such as a dissertation committee, the scientific or the public community, or a government agency. The use of numbers may be *rhetorical* here; when it comes to convincing a modern audience, the hard quantified facts may appear more trustworthy than qualitative descriptions and interpretations.

I will go into some detail here about the dichotomization of quantitative versus qualitative research methods. *Quality* refers to what kind, to the essential character of something. *Quantity* refers to how much, how large, the amount of something. In *Webster's* (1967), *qualitative analysis* is described as a chemical analysis designed to identify the components of a substance, and *quantitative analysis* as a chemical analysis designed to determine the amounts of the components of a substance. In chemistry a qualitative analysis is then a presupposition for a quantitative analysis. In the practice of natural science, both forms of analysis are often required: For example, a recent job announcement for North Sea oil geologists listed the ability to do "qualitative and quantitative interpretations" of petrophysical sediments as a requirement. Although quantification is an important tool in the natural sciences, large areas of geology, biology, and zoology are based on qualitative descriptions and interpretations, such as studies by Darwin and by Lorenz of the interactions of animals with their habitats. In recent philosophical analyses of the practice of the natural sciences, such as those by Hesse, any sharp bifurcation of the human and the natural sciences breaks down (see Bernstein, 1983). Thus, apart from the more basic question of why the social sciences should try to imitate the natural sciences, a brief look at the actual practice of the natural sciences erodes any automatic outlawing of qualitative research as unscientific.

The issue of qualitative versus quantitative methods has been a heated topic in the social sciences for some time; attempts at bridging the gap (Lazarsfeld, 1944) and arguments that it is a pseudoissue (e.g., Reichardt & Cook, 1979; Tschudi, 1989) have had little impact. And the title of one article appears somewhat premature: "Closing Down the Conversation: The End of the Quantitative-Qualitative Debate Among Educational Researchers" (Smith & Heshusius, 1986). Some conceptual and practical problems with a strict qualitative-quantitative bifurcation will be pointed out here, and some reasons why a restricted quantitative conception of science still remains will be suggested.

In social science textbooks four basic types of measurement are distinguished: nominal, ordinal, interval, and ratio. Qualitative research leading to an either/or categorization of an interview statement as expressing, for example "competition" or "no competition" involves scaling on a nominal level. If the categories also include a ranking of more versus less, for example as "strong," "medium," "little," and "no" competition, scaling at an ordinal level is involved. Scaling at an equidistant interval level, as attempted by intelligence tests, and at a ratio level with an absolute zero, as by measurement of temperature, is, however, outside the realm of qualitative research. Qualitative research may thus lead to weaker forms of measurement—such as nominal and ordinal scaling—and no conceptual foundation to maintain a sharp dichotomy of quantitative versus qualitative methods appears here.

In the practice of social research, qualitative and quantitative approaches interact. In the "content analysis" tradition of media research, the content and form of communication, mainly in the form of texts, are quantified and made amenable for statistical treatment. In more open approaches to interview texts, qualitative and quantitative analyses intermingle. The relative emphasis will depend on the type of phenomena investigated and the purpose of the investigation. In media research of TV soap operas, for example, both linguistic and narrative analyses of the plot, and statistical analyses of viewer frequency and social distribution of the viewers may be required to understand and predict the impact of a TV series.

Not just the analysis phase, but the whole research process involves the interaction of qualitative and quantitative approaches (Mayring, 1983). An investigation starts with a qualitative analysis of the existing knowledge about a phenomenon and the development of qualitative concepts and hypotheses for the specific study. The phases of data collection and data analysis that follow can be mainly qualitative or quantitative, often with an interaction. The final phase, reporting the results, is predominantly qualitative; furthermore, tables and correlation coefficients require qualitative interpretations of their meanings. There may, however, be a tendency to downplay the qualitative aspects of the research process in published reports. Whether due to external editorial requirements, or to self-censorship by the researcher, the "soft" qualitative aspects of the research process and product tend to be washed away, leaving only the "hard" quantified facts as fit for public presentation.

In conclusion, qualitative and quantitative methods are tools, and their utility depends on their power to bear upon the research questions asked. As tools they require different competencies, with differences among researchers in their abilities to and interests in carrying out quantitative computations or conducting linguistic or empathic analysis of qualitative data. Despite the conceptual and practical interweaving of the qualitative and quantitative aspects of social science research, a dichotomized conception with a hegemony on the quantitative side may still prevail. Today's social science students acquire a professional competency in analyzing the social world as a mathematically constituted universe, but remain amateurs in the face of a linguistically constituted social world.

*   *   *   *   *

I now turn from academic debates on the position of qualitative research in social science to the role of qualitative research in some practice-oriented fields, such as market research, feminist research, and psychoanalysis. The legitimacy of using qualitative interviews in these rather different fields has rested less on their compatibility with the prevailing ideas of scientific method than on their contributions to effecting changes in persons and their conditions.

Qualitative Market Research

In some quarters, qualitative research has come to be regarded as progressive and quantitative research as repressive. It is maintained that qualitative research is sensitive to the human situation, it involves an empathic dialogue with the subjects studied, and it may contribute to their emancipation and empowerment.

The qualitative interview is a uniquely sensitive and powerful method for capturing the experiences and lived meanings of the subjects' everyday world. Interviews allow the subjects to convey to others their situation from their own perspective and in their own words. Several books by social researchers, journalists, and novelists have been based on interviews with groups who seldom participate in the public debate. Oscar Lewis's interviews with Mexican peasant families, *The Children of Sanchez* (1964), is one example. Such interview studies can have a politically emancipatory function by bringing to attention and documenting the living conditions of oppressed groups. It is, however, illusory to consider qualitative methods as such "progressive," which is evident from a look at the use of qualitative interviewing in market research.

In psychology, a technical interest in control over objectified processes has generally been associated with the natural science-oriented experiments of behaviorism, with the research interest in predicting and controlling the behavior of others. These behaviorist knowledge interests and methods were well in line with the human engineering approach Taylor instigated in industry at the turn of the century (Kvale, 1976b). This involved extensive time and motion studies controlling the worker's behavior, which was made more efficient by the assembly line introduced by Ford.

In the course of the 20th century, the emphasis in economy has changed from control of production to control of consumption and communication. In a consumer society, an extensive knowledge of the experiences, meanings, feelings, desires, and lifestyles of the consumers is essential for the design and marketing of consumer products. An empathic uncovering of experienced meanings and assuming the perspective of the potential consumers facilitates manipulation of their buying behavior.

Qualitative interviews are extensively used in today's market research to predict and control consumer behavior. What market researchers have called a "depth interview" or "motive interview" (Dichter, 1960) and "focused interviews" with groups (Morgan, 1988) come close to the qualitative research interview treated in this book. Dichter early developed market interviews inspired by the interpretational approach of psychoanalysis and in line with the sensitive nondirective interview techniques that Rogers used in therapy. Dichter's outline of central aspects of qualitative interview techniques was developed decades before the current qualitative wave in the social sciences.

In consumer research it is important to get beyond the surface meaning of a product and tap the more hidden, symbolic meanings it has for potential consumers. In *The Strategy of Desire* (1960), Dichter reports an automobile study he conducted for Plymouth. The original report from 1939 outlined "a new psychological research technique to get beyond the limits of current statistical research in an understanding of the factors which influence the sale of cars" (1960, p. 289). The study was based on case histories in the form of detailed conversational interviews that had been recorded in shorthand and transcribed for analysis. "Our interviews reveal that cars stand for something, they are not just a means of transportation. A car is really a symbol, an expression of human desires. Its appearance, its mechanical functions, and its social functions help to build up that symbolic value" (Dichter, 1960, p. 292). According to Dichter, the empathic psychological study from 1939 changed the style of automobile advertising by taking into account the many hidden meanings of products and introducing new marketing approaches, which have since become commonplace (Holbrook, 1995).

The issue of method is here simpler than in the social sciences: In consumer research, the legitimacy of a research method is based on its contribution to increased consumption which in turn increases the producer's sales and profits. It is paradoxical that qualitative interviews—which until recently had been dismissed as unscientific within a behaviorist psychology, whose explicitly stated purpose is to predict and control behavior—have found an extended application in market research, whose survival depends on its very ability to predict and control consumer behavior in practice.

Qualitative interviews are not in themselves progressive or oppressive; the value of the knowledge produced depends on the context and the use of the knowledge. Qualitative interviews can, for example, be used to investigate teenage attitudes toward smoking, and the knowledge obtained used to motivate teenagers to start smoking—or to refrain from smoking. Interviews are powerful tools for obtaining knowledge about human experience and behavior, and this knowledge is at the disposal of power and money.

In contrast to the more open technological prediction and control advocated in a natural science-oriented psychology, the softer humanistic forms of controlling feelings and experiences are more difficult to detect. In a Foucault-inspired deconstruction of psychotherapy and humanistic psychology, Richer (1992) points to these hidden forms of control as more efficient than the shaping techniques of behaviorism, concluding that, "Psychology—all of it—is a branch of the police; psychodynamic and humanistic psychologies are the secret police" (p. 118).

Feminism and Qualitative Research

Qualitative approaches to human interaction have gained a strong position within feminist research. In contrast to an often eclectic qualitative research, feminist approaches have in common a focus on the everyday world of women, work with methods appropriate for understanding the very lives and situations of women, and understanding is a means for changing the conditions studied. Feminist research centers on women's diverse situations and the frames that influence those situations, based on the assumption that interpretive human actions can be the focus of research (Olesen, 1994). Feminist research is "qualitative research by women 'on' women" with a desire to make sense of women's lives and experiences; it "must take women's oppression as one of its basic assumptions"; it is research informed at every stage by an acknowledged political commitment (Scottm 1989, pp. 69-70).

In a postmodern feminist approach, in contrast to the Enlightenment view, the moral and political have priority over scientific and epistemological theory. For feminist researchers, gender is a basic organizing principle that profoundly shapes the concrete conditions of our lives.

> Very simply, to do feminist research is to put the social construction of gender at the center of one's inquiry. . . . The overt ideological goal of feminist research in the human sciences is to correct both the *invisibility* and *distortion* of female experience in ways relevant to ending women's unequal social position. (Lather, 1991, p. 71)

The feminine side of science in general has been emphasized by Shepherd (1993), with a focus on feeling and research motivated by love, receptivity and listening, subjectivity, multiplicity and webs of interaction, long-term trusting relationships, cooperation and working in harmony, intuition, relatedness and a vision of wholeness, and the social responsibility of science. Specific affinities of a feminist approach and qualitative research are discussed by Olesen (1994) with regard to subjectivity and experiences, relationships and personal interaction, and the intersubjectivity between researcher and participants. Furthermore, some feminists believe that soft qualitative data are more appropriate for feminist research, because quantitative methods encourage an unhealthy separation between those who know and those who do not. Though the linear talk of men can be captured by questionnaires, the way women want to make connections among areas of their lives is better approached through qualitative in-depth interviews (see Scott, 1985).

A feminist conception of the relationship between researcher and researched is in line with the mode of understanding in qualitative research interviews outlined earlier (Chapter 2, The Mode of Understanding in the Qualitative Research Interview). There is also an openness to new ways of conceiving research in a postmodern context, with a conflict between feminist strands caught in a textual relativism and a change-oriented feminist political agenda.

Feminist research focuses on social movements, organizations, and the making of policy, which produces a tension in relation to post-modernist feminist researchers who regard "truth" as a destructive illusion. The endless play of signs and stories, the shifting sands of interpretation obscure the existing forms of oppression. The real lives of women get lost in texts leading to a relativist resignation that enforces the status quo in a world of inequality (see the critique by Olesen, 1994). O'Hara (1995), on the other hand, expresses the liberating and moral potentials of postmodern feminism like this:

> What I feel, and read in the work of feminist poststructuralists, is an enormous sense of relief, hope and responsibility. Far from despair, the idea that each of us recreates reality with each encounter fills me with wondrous hope, empowerment and community connection. If there is no absolute truth "out there" to create pristine "expert systems" that can somehow solve our problems mathematically; . . . if we accept that when we enter into dialogue we both change; if it is true that we co-create reality, which in turn creates us—then we are called to a new community. If I can make culture I must act responsibly. (p. 155)

Psychoanalytical Knowledge Production

I now turn to an innovative form of knowledge production that has largely remained outside the discussions of scientific method. Psycho-analysis is the one branch of psychology that, nearly a century after its inception, still has a strong professional impact in psychotherapy and that continues to be of interest to the general public, to other sciences, and to present a challenge to philosophers. Central areas of current psychology textbooks are based on knowledge originally obtained through the psychoanalytic interview regarding dreams and neurosis, sexuality, childhood development and personality, anxiety and motivation, and the unconscious forces (Rapaport, 1959).

PSYCHOANALYSIS AS A RESEARCH METHOD

The psychoanalytic interview, where knowledge production is not the primary purpose, has been *the* psychological method for providing

significant new knowledge about humankind. In textbooks of psychological methods, however, the major method by which psychoanalytical knowledge is obtained—the psychoanalytic interview—is absent.
Freud (1963) regarded the therapeutic interview as a research method:
"It is indeed one of the distinctions of psychoanalysis that research
and treatment proceed hand in hand" (p. 120).

Box 4.1 shows seven characteristics of the psychoanalytical interview based on Freud's (1963) writings on the therapeutic technique.
The counseling session based on Roger's client-centered approach
(Chapter 2, A Therapeutic Interview on Hate) gives an adequate
presentation of a dramatic episode in this form of therapeutic interview. Criticisms have been raised about the efficiency of psychoanalytical therapy, about the coherence of the theory, and about the
empirical validity of psychoanalytical observations (see Fisher &
Greenberg, 1977). I will not address those critiques here, but focus
instead on the fruitfulness of psychoanalytical therapy in bringing
forth new phenomena and new interconnections. The characteristics
of the psychoanalytic interview as outlined are in marked contrast to

---

Box 4.1

The Psychoanalytical Research Interview

The Individual Case Study. Psychoanalytical therapy is an
intensive case study of individual patients over several
years. The extensive knowledge of the patients' life world
and of their past thereby obtained provides the therapist
with a uniquely rich context for interpreting their dreams
and neurotic symptoms.

The Open Mode of Interviewing. The psychoanalytical interview takes place in the structured setting of the therapeutic hour, the content is free and nondirective; it is based
on psychoanalytical theory, yet proceeds in an open man-

(continued)

Box 4.1 Continued

ner. The patient's free associations correspond with the therapist's "evenly hovering attention." Freud (1963) warned against scientifically formulating a case during treatment, because that would interfere with the open therapeutic attitude with which one proceeds "aimlessly, and allows oneself to be overtaken by any surprises, always presenting to them an open mind, free from any expectations" (p. 120).

The Interpretation of Meaning. An essential aspect of psychoanalytical technique is the interpretation of the meaning of the patient's statements and actions. The psychoanalytical interpretations are open to ambiguity and contradictions, to the multiple layers of meaning in a dream or a symptom. They require an extensive context, with the possibility of continual reinterpretations: "The full interpretation of such a dream will coincide with the completion of the whole analysis: if a note is made of it at the beginning, it may be possible to understand it at the end, after many months" (Freud, 1963, p. 100).

The Temporal Dimension. Psychoanalytic therapy unfolds over several years, in a historical dimension, with a unique intertwinedness of past, present, and future. Freud's innovation was to see human phenomena in a meaningful historical perspective: The remembrance of the past is an active force of therapeutic change, and the therapy aims at overcoming the repressions of the past as well as the present resistance against making the unconscious conscious.

Human Interaction. Psychoanalytical therapy takes place through an emotional human interaction with a reciprocal personal involvement. Freud noticed that if the analyst allows the patient time, devotes serious interest to him, and behaves with tact, a deep attachment of the patient for the

(continued)

Box 4.1 Continued

therapist develops. Strong emotions, ranging from love to rage, were interpreted theoretically as a "transference" of childhood feelings for the parents to the therapist. This transference is deliberately employed by the therapist as a means to overcome the patient's emotional resistance to deeper self-knowledge and change. Different depths of layers of the patient's personality are disclosed, depending on the intensity of the emotional ties to the therapist. The influence of the therapist's own feelings for the patient, termed "counter-transference," is not sought eliminated, but employed in the therapeutic process as a reflected subjectivity.

Pathology as Topic of Investigation. The subject matter of psychoanalytical therapy is the abnormal and irrational behavior of patients in crisis, their apparently meaningless and bizarre symptoms and dreams. The pathological behavior serves as a magnifying glass for the less visible conflicts of average individuals; the neuroses and psychoses are extreme versions of normal behavior, they are the characteristic expressions of what has gone wrong in a given culture.

The Instigation of Change. The mutual interest of patient and therapist is to overcome the patient's suffering due to his neurotic symptoms. Despite patients having sought treatment voluntarily, they exhibit a deeply seated resistance to a change in self-understanding and action. "The whole theory of psychoanalysis is . . . in fact built up on the perception of the resistance offered to us by the patient when we attempt to make his unconscious conscious to him" (Freud, 1963, p. 68). Although understanding can lead to change, the implicit theory of knowledge in psychoanalysis is that a fundamental understanding of a phenomenon can first be obtained by attempting to change the phenomenon.

positivist criteria of scientific method as discussed above (Chapter 4, Positivism). This may be one reason why the psychoanalytical interview has not been regarded as a research method in psychology.

Although it was rejected by a positivist philosophy of science, the knowledge production in psychoanalysis has challenged thinkers in the philosophical traditions outlined in Chapter 3. Though generally critical of the speculative and reductionist trends of psychoanalytic theory, they have reflected on the unique nature of the personal interaction in the psychoanalytical interview and its potentials for personal change as well as its contributions to knowledge about the human situation. An early introduction to the area was given by May, Angel, and Ellenberger (1958) in *Existence: A New Dimension in Psychiatry and Psychology.* There are also Boss's (1963) *Psychoanalysis and Daseinsanalysis,* based on Heidegger's phenomenological existential and hermeneutical philosophy, and Laing's (1962) *The Self and Others,* inspired by Sartre's existentialism. Among the philosophers addressing psychoanalysis are Sartre's (1963) existential mediation of psychoanalysis and Marxism in *The Problem of Method;* Ricoeur's (1970) phenomenological and hermeneutical *Freud and Philosophy: An Essay on Interpretation;* and Habermas's (1971) critical hermeneutical analysis of psychoanalysis as a model for an emancipatory social science in *Knowledge and Human Interests.* The present discussion of the psychoanalytic interview and the mode of understanding in the research interview is inspired by these works.

The psychoanalytical interview is related to, and contrasts with, the research interview and its mode of understanding. The purpose of a therapeutic interview is the facilitation of changes in the patient, and the knowledge acquired from the individual patient is a means for instigating personality changes. The general knowledge of the human situation gained through the psychoanalytic process is a side effect of helping patients overcome their neurotic suffering. The qualitative research interview is a construction site of knowledge production; its purpose is to obtain knowledge of the phenomena investigated and any changes in the interviewed subject is a side effect. The intensive personal therapeutic relationship may open painful, hidden memories and deeper levels of personality, which are inaccessible through a brief research interview.

Despite such differences, it is possible for research interviewers to learn from the modes of questioning and interpreting developed in therapeutic interviews. There are many problems with psychoanalysis as a research method, and the scientific status of psychoanalytical knowledge is still debated. Some of the issues concerning the validity of interpretations will be discussed later, in Chapter 13. It is a continuing paradox that the therapeutic interview, which has not been accepted as a scientific method and for which general knowledge production is a side effect, has produced some of the most viable knowledge in the discipline of psychology.

THERAPEUTIC RESEARCH
BETWEEN SCYLLA AND CHARYBDIS

A therapeutic research project can be a dangerous voyage, a cruise between anecdotal case stories with little method on the one hand, and quantified physiological and behavioral measures with little psychological content on the other. Clinical research has produced a long history of rejected articles and shipwrecked dissertations. A therapeutic research voyage can be likened to Odysseus sailing the narrow strait between Charybdis and Scylla on his return from Troy, a passage that he declared was the most dangerous part of his long research voyage.

On one side of the perilous strait waits the monster Charybdis, swallowing whole ships and their crews. Here, the therapeutic researcher gets carried away by entertaining and exciting case histories, often with the therapist as the hero. There is seldom any methodical reflection on how the evidence for the story is obtained, nor analyses of the narrative structures involved, nor of the validity of the knowledge presented. After almost a century of psychoanalytical therapy and theory, the main evidence supporting the psychoanalytic theory still rests on knowledge accumulated through psychoanalytical interviews, a research method that has hardly been given any systematical thought in the social sciences.

Odysseus tried so hard to avoid Charybdis that he came too close to the other side of the narrow strait, where the six-headed monster Scylla devoured six members of his crew. Contemporary therapeutic researchers may try so hard to avoid therapeutic anecdotes that they get caught in the positivist straightjacket on the other side and lose the lived therapeutic relations in a multitude of statistical correlations and significances that may be insignificant to the therapeutic situation. In this form of imitative scientism, the clinical researcher may become "more Catholic than the Pope"—or, in psychoanalytical terminology —identify with the aggressor.

Vessels sailing the current qualitative research wave also appear to be caught in the narrow strait, blown back and forth between a "no-method" Charybdis and an "all-method" Scylla. Interview versions of this research can even fall prey to both monsters. On the one side there is hardly any methodological account of, or reflection on the productions of, the texts in the original conversations, or on the transformations from living conversations to written texts, or on the validity of the interpretations of meanings of the text. On the other, there is a qualitative hyperempiricism of quantified categorizations and endless quotes from interview transcripts. Such interview reports lose the lived reality of the conversation as well as the human situation portrayed in the subjects' stories.

I now will turn to the method stages of an interview investigation in Part III and suggest some guidelines for keeping clear of the no-method and all-method hazards in the dangerous passages of an interview inquiry on the way from an original vision to a final report. The goal for the interview researcher is to return from the stages of his or her qualitative inquiry with a tale that does justice to the subjects' stories of their lived world and that conveys new and valid knowledge and insights to the listeners to and the readers of the tale.

PART
III

The Seven Stages of an
Interview Investigation

I now turn from the meaning of the concepts in the book's subtitle—
qualitative research interviewing—to the methods of carrying out an
interview investigation. This methodological Part III follows the temporal course of a qualitative interview investigation through seven
stages: thematizing, designing, interviewing, transcribing, analyzing,
verifying, and reporting. In Chapter 5, the first two stages—thematizing and designing—are discussed with respect to the production of

knowledge. The moral aspects of an interview inquiry are brought up in Chapter 6, where ethical issues that may arise throughout the stages of an interview investigation are discussed.

The interview situation is treated in Chapter 7, with the aim of improving the quality of the knowledge produced. Preparing for and carrying out a research interview is discussed, and an interview about grades is reproduced to illustrate forms of questioning. Quality criteria for qualitative interviews are suggested in Chapter 8, where also ethical aspects of the interview situation and the issue of leading questions are also addressed.

The structuring of the interviews for subsequent analysis is addressed in Chapter 9. Technical questions of transcribing raise principal issues about the differences between oral and written language. The chapter concludes by outlining the use of computer programs for handling interview texts.

The next three chapters focus on the analysis of interviews. A discussion of "the 1,000-page question" in Chapter 10 highlights some key issues of interview analysis. Chapter 11 provides an overview of approaches to analysis, such as meaning condensation and categorization, narrative structuring and interpretation. In Chapter 12, the plurality of interpretations is related to the hermeneutic primacy of the question, and questions posed to interview statements about grading are discussed, drawing on different contexts of interpretation and validation. Finally, a modern quest for meaning is contrasted with a postmodern deconstruction of reified meanings.

Verification of the knowledge produced in interviews is treated in Chapter 13, where generalizability, reliability, and validity in qualitative research are discussed. Validation as a social construction is treated in some detail, and philosophical conceptions of knowledge as conversation and action are included and communicative and pragmatic forms of validation outlined.

With the emphasis on validation as communication and action, the reporting of interviews comes into the foreground. Purposes and forms of interview reports are discussed in Chapter 14. Writing is discussed as a social construction, and in order to get beyond the often boring interview-quoting reports, modes for enriching the reports are suggested.

5

Thematizing and Designing
an Interview Study

This chapter attempts to design an interview investigation that goes beyond the no-method or all-method dilemma by emphasizing the expertise and craftsmanship of the interview researcher. It starts by describing a contrast between the formal reports of social science studies and the openness of the semistructured interview. An emotional account of the hardships of an interview journey is given, showing how things can go wrong when the overall design of an interview investigation is not considered. Then a more structured, seven-stage route for investigating is discussed—thematizing, designing, interviewing, transcribing, interpreting, verifying, and reporting. The stages are illustrated by my study of the effects of grades on learning. The first two stages of an interview study, thematizing and designing, are then treated in some detail. Finally, going beyond method by conceiving of research as craftsmanship is suggested.

Openness and Emotions in Interview Studies

Articles in social science journals give rather formalized pictures of the research process. Editorial requirements promote a distorted technical picture of scientific research as a logical, linear process—which is far from the continually changing actual research process with its surprises, design changes, and reformulations of concepts and hypotheses. In a realistic presentation of designing qualitative research, Marshall and Rossman (1995) discuss how the formalistic outlining of an interview investigation might also be required on applications for research funding, where the emphasis is on clear and well-structured proposals.

One example of a more valid description of the vicissitudes of actual scientific research is "A Case History in Scientific Method," by the radical behaviorist Skinner (1961). He dismisses the formalistic way of presenting research and describes the many chance happenings and surprises from his own experimental research on behavior that led to significant discoveries of animal and human behavior. Thus, happenings such as the breakdown of feeding apparatuses and the experimental rats having babies led to discoveries of new contingencies of reinforcements for learning. Such realistic descriptions of scientific research behavior can be a solace to students mystified by the neat formal presentations of research publications and textbooks on methodology.

The very virtue of qualitative interviews is their openness. No standard techniques or rules exist for an interview investigation based on unstandardized qualitative interviews. There are, however, standard choices of methods at the different stages of an interview investigation. They include questions such as: How many interviews will be needed? Should the interviews be taped, and should they be transcribed? How should the interviews be analyzed? Should the interpretations be given to the interviewee?

Rather than prescribe standardized procedures and techniques, the present approach calls attention to standard methodological choices arising at the different stages of an interview investigation. The aim is to make decisions about method on a reflective level, based on knowledge of the topic of the study and of the methodological options available, and their likely consequences for the interview project as a whole. The very openness and flexibility of the interview, with its many on-the-spot decisions—for example, whether to follow up new leads in an interview situation or to stick to the interview guide—put strong demands on advance preparation and interviewer competence. The absence of prescribed sets of rules creates an open-ended field of opportunity for the interviewer's skills, knowledge, and intuition. Interviewing is a craft that is closer to art than to standardized social science methods.

The common term *unstandardized* may pertain to the interview situation, but an entire interview investigation tends to be a rather standardized affair, often going through five characteristic emotional phases.

Box 5.1 describes the emotional dynamics of an interview investigation. The empirical basis for the descriptions involves observations from colleagues and students undertaking interview studies as well as recollections from my own study of grading. The intensity of the emotional phases varies. Moments of enthusiasm, common at the beginning, can also occur in the later phases, such as when discovering new meanings through interpretation. The five phases can also be encountered through the use of other research methods. It seldom happens, however, that the contrast between an initial enthusiasm and the later hardships is as distinct as in interview studies.

Box 5.1

Emotional Dynamics of an Interview Study

Antipositivist Enthusiasm Phase. An interview project usually starts with enthusiasm and commitment. The researcher is strongly engaged in a problem and wants to carry out realistic natural life research. It is to be meaningful qualitative research of people's lives, and not a positivist, quantified data gathering based on abstract theories.

The Interview-Quoting Phase. By now the researcher will have recorded the initial interviews and is intensively engaged in what the interviewees have said. Forming a contrast to the ideological enthusiasm in the antipositivist phase, there is now personal engagement and a solitary identification with the subjects, who have revealed so much of their often oppressive life situation. At lunch the interviewer entertains his colleagues with a wealth of new quotations. Although exciting at first, it may after a while be difficult for the colleagues to remain fully involved in the interview stories.

(continued)

Box 5.1 Continued

The Working Phase of Silence.   After a time, silence falls upon the interview project. The researcher no longer brings up interview quotations at lunch. A colleague now asking about the project receives a laconic answer: "The interviews are being transcribed" or "The analysis has just started." This working phase is characterized by sobriety and patience.

The Aggressive Phase of Silence.   A long time has passed since the interviews were completed and still no results are presented. A colleague who now inquires about the project would run the risk of being met with distinct annoyance: the researcher bristles and more or less clearly signals "it's none of your business." As for the researcher, this midproject crisis is characterized by exceeded time limits, chaos, and stress.

The Final Phase of Exhaustion.   By now the interview project has become so overwhelming that there is hardly any time or energy left for reporting the originally interesting findings. One version of this phase is that "nothing is reported"—the many hundred pages of transcribed interviews remain in the files. In a "lecture version," the researcher conjures up some entertaining quotations in lectures, but the final report remains postponed. In a common "save what can possibly be saved" termination, the interviews appear as isolated quotations without methodological and conceptual analyses. In cases where a more systematic "final report" does appear, the researcher may feel resigned because he has not succeeded in passing on to the readers in a methodological justifiable way the original richness of the interview stories.

The depicted emotional phases of an interview project need not be an exclusively Danish phenomenon, nor are they unavoidable. The late Renata Tesch—who ran a consultation firm for qualitative research in the United States—read the description of these emotional hardships. She then wrote for permission to quote the descriptions in an advertising folder for her firm, and added after the five hardship phases: "There is one way to avoid this state of affairs, call Qualitative Research Management!"

Perhaps the description of the emotional hardships of interview research is becoming outdated; with many qualitative research milieus and courses and with an abundance of method literature, the novice researcher will have a good starting point for better getting through the stages of an interview investigation.

The Seven Stages of Interview Research

In this section I outline ways of designing an interview investigation that may assist the interviewer through the hardships of the research process and help to contribute to retaining the initial vision and engagement throughout the investigation. As a first step toward invalidating the description of the emotional hardships, seven stages of an interview investigation are outlined.

Box 5.2 shows the course of an interview investigation through seven stages, from the original ideas to the final report. In order to provide some structure to an open and flexible interview study, I will emphasize a linear progression through the seven method stages for an interview inquiry. In contrast, the interactive nature of qualitative research comes through quite well in Strauss and Corbin's (1990) presentation of the procedures and techniques of the grounded theory approach, which is less formal than the present focus on seven stages of an interview investigation. Strauss and Corbin depict a continual interplay among conceptualization, field studies, analyses, and new contacts with the field, which is downplayed in the present simplified linear presentation that attempts to structure the often chaotic field of interview studies.

The emotional dynamics of an interview study can now be related to the seven stages outlined here. The antipositivist enthusiasm dominates the usually quickly bypassed thematizing and designing stages. The engaged interview quoting covers the interviewing stage. The

Box 5.2

Seven Stages of an Interview Investigation

1. *Thematizing.* Formulate the purpose of an investigation and describe the concept of the topic to be investigated before the interviews start. The *why* and *what* of the investigation should be clarified before the question of *how*—method—is posed (Chapter 5).

2. *Designing.* Plan the design of the study, taking into consideration all seven stages of the investigation, before the interviewing starts. Designing the study is undertaken with regard to obtaining the intended *knowledge* (Chapter 5) and taking into account the *moral* implications of the study (Chapter 6).

3. *Interviewing.* Conduct the interviews based on an interview guide and with a reflective approach to the knowledge sought and the interpersonal relation of the interview situation (Chapters 7 & 8).

4. *Transcribing.* Prepare the interview material for analysis, which commonly includes a transcription from oral speech to written text (Chapter 9).

5. *Analyzing.* Decide, on the basis of the purpose and topic of the investigation, and on the nature of the interview material, which methods of analysis are appropriate for the interviews (Chapters 10, 11, & 12).

6. *Verifying.* Ascertain the generalizability, reliability, and validity of the interview findings. *Reliability* refers to how consistent the results are, and *validity* means whether an interview study investigates what is intended to be investigated (Chapter 13).

7. *Reporting.* Communicate the findings of the study and the methods applied in a form that lives up to scientific criteria, takes the ethical aspects of the investigation into consideration, and that results in a readable product (Chapter 14).

working and the aggressive quiet phases accompany the transcription and, in particular, the analyzing stage. The verifying stage is often skipped, and exhaustion comes to dominate the reporting stage. The root of these ordeals is in the quick bypassing of the stages of thematizing and designing, which are particularly important in a method as open as an interview inquiry.

The treatment of an interview investigation in a single book entails rather brief treatments of each of the seven method stages. My main purpose is to give an overview of an entire interview investigation, to outline the interactions among the stages, and to trace the interconnectedness of the practical issues of method and the philosophical conceptions of knowledge and truth.

Some books with more extensive treatments of the stages of qualitative investigation are depicted in Box 5.3. Thematizing is bound to specific subject areas and is not covered by any general book; several of the chapters in Denzin and Lincoln's (1994) handbook, however, do treat general conceptions of the subject matter of interviews. For designing qualitative research, interviewing, analyzing, and reporting there now is a rich method literature. Little literature is available on verification, however, and the ethics and transcription of interview research are barely treated.

Interviews About Grades

The slightly exaggerated emotional hardship phases are to some extent based on my own interview study of grading in Danish high schools; examples from this investigation are used throughout this book. The overview presented below illustrates the seven stages of an interview investigation. Thereafter I will return to more general outlines of the thematizing and designing stages.

1. Thematizing. Thematizing refers to a conceptual clarification and a theoretical analysis of the theme investigated, and the formulation of research questions. The grade study, which took place in 1978, was instigated by a public debate about the effects of grading in connection with a new policy of restricted admission to college based on grade point averages from high school (Kvale, 1980). A hypothesis

---

Box 5.3

Literature on Qualitative Research

1. Thematizing

Denzin, N. K., & Lincoln, Y. S. (Eds.). (1994). *Handbook of qualitative research*. Thousand Oaks, CA: Sage.

2. Designing

Research Design

Glesne, C., & Peshkin, A. (1992). *Becoming qualitative researchers*. White Plains, NY: Longman.
Marshall, C., & Rossman, G. B. (1995). *Designing qualitative research*. Thousand Oaks, CA: Sage.
Maykut, P., & Morehouse, R. (1994). *Beginning qualitative research*. London: Falmer.
Morse, J. M., & Field, P. A. (1995). *Qualitative research methods for professionals*. Thousand Oaks, CA: Sage.

Ethics

Eisner, E. W., & Peshkin, A. (Eds.). (1990). *Qualitative inquiry in education*. New York: Teachers College Press. (see the chapters by Lincoln, by Smith, & by Soltis)
Guidelines for the protection of human subjects. (1992). Berkeley: University of California Press.
Kimmel, A. J. (1988). *Ethics and values in applied social science research*. Newbury Park, CA: Sage.
Mathison, S., Ross, E. W., & Cornett, J. W. (1993). *A casebook for teaching about ethical issues in qualitative research*. Unpublished manuscript. (Available from: American Educational Research Association, Qualitative Research SIG, Washington, D.C.)

3. Interviewing

Rubin, H. J., & Rubin, I. S. (1995). *Qualitative interviewing*. Thousand Oaks, CA: Sage.
Seidman, I. E. (1991). *Interviewing as qualitative research*. New York: Teachers College Press.
Spradley, J. (1979). *The ethnographic interview*. New York: Holt, Rinehart & Winston.
Yow, V. R. (1994). *Recording oral history*. Thousand Oaks, CA: Sage.

---

of a grade perspective was formulated: Grading influences the process of learning and the social situation where learning occurs. A second

---

Box 5.3 Continued

4. Transcribing

Mishler, E. G. (1991). Representing discourse. The rhetoric of transcrip
tion. *Journal of Narrative and Life History, 1,* 255-280.

5. Analyzing

Miles, M. B., & Huberman, A. M. (1994). *Qualitative data analysis: An
expanded sourcebook.* Thousand Oaks, CA: Sage.

Silverman, D. (1993). *Interpreting qualitative data.* Thousand Oaks, CA:
Sage.

Tesch, R. (1990). *Qualitative research: Analysis types and software tools.*
London: Falmer.

Wolcott, H. F. (1994). *Transforming qualitative data.* Thousand Oaks, CA:
Sage.

6. Verifying

Eisner, E. W., & Peshkin, A. (Eds.). (1990). *Qualitative inquiry in education.* New York: Teachers College Press (see the chapters on generalization by Donmoyer and by Schofield).

Kirk, J., & Miller, M. L. (1986). *Reliability and validity in qualitative
research.* Newbury Park, CA: Sage.

Kvale, S. (Ed.). (1989). *Issues of validity in qualitative research.* Lund,
Sweden: Studentliteratur.

7. Reporting

American Psychological Association. (1989). *Publication manual* (3rd ed.).
Washington, DC: Author.

Richardson, L. (1990). *Writing strategies.* Newbury Park, CA: Sage.

Van Maanen, J. (1988). *Tales of the field.* Chicago: Chicago University
Press.

Wolcott, H. F. (1990). *Writing up qualitative research.* Newbury Park, CA:
Sage.

hypothesis stated that the prevalence of the grading perspective would
increase with a restricted admission to college based on grade point
averages.

Though hardly new, the hypotheses—which were based on common sense as well as on research literature on grading in other
countries—were contested in the public debate in Denmark. I had
been involved in a newspaper debate with the Danish minister of
education, who maintained that there would be hardly any educa-

tional or social impact from a restricted university admission based on grade point averages. The purpose of the interviews was to test the two hypotheses, which also included an exploration of the main dimensions of the effects of grading on the pupils. A third hypothesis postulated an instrumentalization of learning through grading: Learning for grades in school socializes pupils to work for wages in occupational life.

2. Design. Because the influence of grades was a controversial topic when the interview study was begun, special care was therefore taken to have a methodologically well-controlled design. As one way of investigating the influence of grades, 30 high school pupils were interviewed about their experiences with grades. This number was a compromise between obtaining a representative sample and the resources available for the study. In order to counteract possible special circumstances at a single high school, pupils from three schools were interviewed. They came from one class at each school and were selected by their alphabetical name order. Six teachers were also interviewed, to gain an alternative perspective on the effects of grading. To counteract special interviewer bias, the 30 pupils were distributed among four interviewers, three student assistants and myself.

The remaining five stages of the grade study are treated in more detail in the following chapters and only outlined briefly here.

- *Stage 3: Interviewing.* A detailed guide was used for the individual interviews, each of which lasted about 45 minutes and was taped.
- *Stage 4: Transcribing.* All 36 interviews—with pupils and teachers—were transcribed verbatim, resulting in about 1,000 pages of transcripts.
- *Stage 5: Analyzing.* The 30 pupil interviews were categorized with respect to different forms of grading behavior. The interviews with the pupils and the teachers were also subjected to more extensive qualitative interpretations.
- *Stage 6: Verifying.* Reliability and validity checks were attempted throughout the project, including interviewer and scorer reliability, and validity of interpretations.
- *Stage 7: Reporting.* The project resulted in a book, *Spillet om karakterer i gymnasiet* (*The Grading Game in High School*) (Kvale, 1980). The thematic and methodic aspects of the study were also treated in subsequent articles in professional journals.

The actual course of the investigation was less neat than that schematized here. The transcription and analysis of the 36 interviews, which were conducted in January, took far more time than planned. The preliminary results were not ready to be reported back to the pupils and teachers, as promised before the interviews, until June. By then most of the pupils were too busy with their final exams to be interested in discussing research about the effects of grades.

Interviews and Questionnaires. Two psychology students later used the interviews as a basis for constructing a questionnaire on grades (Hvolbøl & Kristensen, 1983). They included statements from the interviews in their questionnaire and asked new groups of pupils for their degree of agreement or disagreement with these statements. The questionnaire consisted of more than 150 questions and was administered to more than 200 pupils from six high schools across the country. The purpose was to obtain representative and generalizable findings. The results were analyzed by computer programs, which had been prepared in advance.

The two students were so confident of how quickly the analysis would be done that they had submitted a presentation to a Nordic educational conference to take place in Finland 2 weeks after the last questionnaire was scheduled to arrive. They actually managed to have the major findings from the questionnaires ready for presentation at the conference, with statistical computations of correlations and significances in neatly arranged tables and figures. A corresponding predictability and speed of analyzing and reporting for a qualitative interview study would have been out of the question. With the standardized structures and techniques for questionnaire construction and quantitative analysis, the likelihood of delays and of getting lost is less than with the little structured interview studies.

One of the statements included in the questionnaire was an assertion about a connection between talkativeness and grades from an interview passage quoted earlier (Chapter 1, Conversation as Research). The statement, depicted in Table 5.1, was split into two items in the questionnaire. The percentage of agreement among the 239 pupils on the two items is indicated in Table 5.1. It turned out that a majority of the pupils agreed with the first part of the statement—that grades are an expression of how much one talks, whereas a majority

TABLE 5.1 From Interview Statements to Questionnaire Items

Interview Statement

Pupil: Grades are often unjust, because very often—very often—they are only a
measure of how much you talk, and how much you agree with the teacher's opinion.

| | Percentage of 239 Pupils | | | |
Questionnaire Items	Strongly Agree	Agree	Disagree	Strongly Disagree
Grades are often an expression of how much one talks in class	20	62	15	3
Grades are often an expression of how much one follows the teacher's opinion	4	20	57	19

disagreed with the second part—that grades are often an expression
of how much one goes along with the teacher's opinion.

The example points out strengths and weaknesses in the two
methods. The interview brought out interesting beliefs about which
behaviors lead to good grades, whereas the questionnaire made it
possible to test how prevalent these beliefs were among a large number
of pupils. The questionnaire did not follow up on the pupils' statements, but an interviewer could closely question the strength of a
pupil's belief and might also obtain concrete examples supporting the
claims (see the context of this statement in Chapter 1, Conversation
as Research).

In retrospect, the interview study of grades would probably have
yielded more valuable knowledge with fewer but longer, more intensive interviews. The questionnaire developed on the basis of the
interviews could be used to test the generality of the interview findings
and the smaller number of qualitative interviews could have been
subjected to more penetrating interpretations.

Thematizing

The key questions for planning an interview investigation concern
the what, why, and how of the interview:

- *what:* obtaining a preknowledge of the subject matter to be investigated
- *why:* clarifying the purpose of the study
- *how:* acquiring a knowledge of different techniques of interviewing and analyzing, and deciding which to apply to obtain the intended knowledge

Method originally meant the way to the goal. In order to find or to show someone else the way to a goal, one needs to know what the goal is. When designing an interview project, it is necessary to know the content and the purpose of the study in order to make reflected decisions on which methods to use at the different stages of the study. Consultations on interview projects sometimes take the form of an explorative "counter"-interview. The counselor first needs to explore, by carefully questioning the investigator, what the research topic and basic questions of the interview study are before the specific questions asked about methods can be addressed. There is a standard reply to the questions of design of qualitative interviews—the answer depends on the thematic content and the purpose of the investigation. The thematic questions of "what" and "why" have to be answered before the "how" questions of design can be posed meaningfully.

CONTENT

Interview studies today often start without a theory of the themes investigated, and also without a review of the research literature in the area. One definition of science is the systematic production of new knowledge (Chapter 4, The Scientific Status of the Interview). Without any presentation of the existing knowledge about the topic of an investigation, it is difficult for both researcher and reader to ascertain whether the knowledge obtained by the interviews is new, and thus what the scientific contribution of the study is. The theoretical naïveté common in the many applied interview projects is not necessarily confined to qualitative research. The contributions of Freud and later psychotherapists testify to the potentials of theorizing on the basis of qualitative interviews.

A significant part of any interview project should take place before the tape recorder is turned on for the first actual interview. This involves developing a conceptual and theoretical understanding of the phenomena to be investigated, to establish the base to which new knowledge will be added and integrated. The thematic understanding of the topic of the study—the "what"—will further influence the "how" of the study: the many decisions on method that must be made. Knowledge of a phenomenon is required to be able to pose significant questions, whether they are on the essence of beauty, truth, and goodness in a Socratic dialogue, the tactics of a master chess player, or trends in rock music in a teenage interview.

Familiarity with the content of an investigation is not obtained only through literature and theoretical studies. Just hanging out in the environment where the interviews are to be conducted will give an introduction to the local language, the daily routines, and the power structures, and so provide a sense of what the interviewees will be talking about. Particularly for anthropological studies, a familiarity with the foreign culture is required for posing questions:

> One of the reasons for doing field trips is that you are presented with how abstract is the most concrete of your concepts and questions when you are at home in the library. When I first went to Brazil I made my way 2,000 miles into north central Brazil and I arrived in a small town. I heard that there were Indians who actually were in town. And I can remember an incredible sense of excitement. I rushed out and walked around town until I found this group of Indians and walked straight up to them—and then I didn't know what to say. I wanted to ask: "Have you got moiety systems?" (a special kind of kinship relations). And it didn't make sense to do that. In fact it took four months to find a way to ask a question with which I could discover from people whether they did have moiety systems. (Lave & Kvale, 1995, p. 221; slightly abbreviated)

The influence that theoretical conceptions of the content have upon method choices may be exemplified by an imagined interview with a pupil about the *meaning of teasing*. Different theories will lead to different emphasis on such phenomena as feelings, experiences, behavior —as well as on the temporal dimensions of past, present, and future. Say a school psychologist is interviewing a pupil who—the teacher complains—is continually teasing the other pupils and thereby disturbing the class. The interview might be conducted from a Rogerian client-centered approach, a Freudian psychoanalytic approach, and a Skinnerian behavior modification approach, respectively.

From a Rogerian perspective, the important questions would concern what the pupil experiences and feels when he is teasing the other pupils, and the questions would attempt to elaborate and differentiate the meaning of these experiences and help the pupil to express his feelings about them. From a Freudian perspective, the questions would be directed toward the pupil's interpersonal emotional dynamics and family situation. Relevant questions might address whether the teasing in school related to similar episodes in the family and to sibling rivalry. From a Skinnerian approach, the important information would concern the contingencies reinforcing the teasing behavior; that is, what happens after the teasing occurs. The reactions of others to a behavior are essential reinforcers of social learning, and the questioning would focus on what responses the teaser gets from the other pupils and the teacher; in short, What are the immediate consequences of the teasing behavior?

Different kinds of interview questions are required to obtain the kinds of information necessary to interpret the meaning of teasing with respect to the different theories. The three approaches, simplified here, would focus on present experiences and feelings, on family history and emotional dynamics, and on future behavioral consequences, respectively. These theoretical approaches highlight different aspects of the meaning of teasing. If they are not introduced until the analysis stage, after the interviews have been conducted, the relevant information for the theoretical interpretations may be lacking.

PURPOSE

Thematizing an interview study also involves clarifying the purpose of the study—the "why." Some common purposes of interview studies will be discussed here. Implications of different purposes will be addressed by the concrete decisions of design.

Interviews can be explorative and hypothesis testing: An *exploratory* interview is open and has little structure. The interviewer in this case introduces an issue, an area to be charted, or a problem complex to be uncovered, such as in the interview on the experience of learning reported by Giorgi. The interviewer follows up on the subject's answers and seeks new information about and new angles on the topic. Interviews that *test hypotheses* tend to be more structured. This can take the form of a comparison of interviews from different groups, for example, by testing a hypothesis that boys will express more competition about grades than will girls. When investigating group differences, it is best to standardize the wording and sequence of questions in order to compare the groups. The testing of hypotheses may also occur within a single interview, with the interview questions designed to test hypotheses about, for example, the structural similarities of learning for grades and of working for money.

The main purpose of an interview can be either empirical or theoretical. An investigation can be designed to gather *empirical* information about, say, the effects of grading. Or an investigation might also be designed to test the implications of a *theory* or, as in the grounded theory approach developed by Glaser and Strauss (1967), to develop an empirically grounded theory through observations and interviews.

There are more specific uses. Interviews are often applied in *case studies*. The purpose may be to develop knowledge about one specific person or institution or to use the case to illustrate more general phenomena. Interviews can also serve as an *auxiliary method* in conjunction with other methods. In studies of participant observation and in ethnographic studies, less or more informal interviews are important sources of information. Through the construction of questionnaires, pilot interviews can be used to chart the main aspects of a topic and to test questions for the questionnaire. In postexperimental interviews, subjects are questioned on how they understood the experimental design. Interviews may also be used as *background material* for other studies. In order to write a theoretical analysis of grading, one might interview pupils and teachers about grades, listen to the taped interviews, and then theorize. Here the interviews are not subjected to methodical analysis, but serve instead as background material for the theoretical work and to provide illustrations of the phenomena discussed.

Designing

After the first stage of thematizing an interview investigation—clarifying its content and purpose—the second stage, designing, consists of overall planning and preparing the methodical procedures for obtaining the intended knowledge. Procedures of design in the subsequent stages of interviewing—transcribing, analyzing, verifying, and reporting—are treated in detail in later chapters. In this section, I call attention to the temporal dimension of an entire interview inquiry from the first thematizing of the study topic to the final reporting. I also discuss some of the overall aspects of the design, such as interview types, number of interview subjects, and resources available for the study, as well as projects for which interviews are not particularly suitable.

THE TEMPORAL DIMENSION

The temporal dimension of an interview design should be kept in mind from the first thematizing to the final reporting, taking into account the interdependence of the seven stages. The final report should be envisaged from the start, and much of the analyzing and verifying tasks should be pushed forward to earlier stages. The implications of a researcher becoming wiser during the interviewing should also be considered.

Overview. A key factor is to develop a view over the entire investigation before the interviews start. When using the more standardized methods, such as experiments, questionnaires, and tests, the very structure of the instruments requires advance decisions about the way in which the study will be conducted. Methodological alternatives are in this case already built into the instruments, for instance by the response alternatives of questionnaires and by computer programs for statistical analysis and presentation of the numerical findings. In open and unstandardized interview studies, however, the choices of method can tend to make their first appearances throughout the investigation, often when it is too late to make decisions appropriate to the content and purpose of the study.

Interdependence. There are strong interconnections among the choices of method made at the different stages. A decision at one stage has consequences that both open and limit the alternatives available at the next stage. For example, generalizing the findings of an interview study to larger groups will require that certain criteria—regarding size and representativity of the sample of subjects—already be met at the design stage. If one were to make a linguistic analysis of interviews this would not be possible, or would require a time-consuming retranscription if the interviews had been edited into normal English by the transformation from oral to written language.

Keep the Endpoint in Sight. From the start of the investigation keep the endpoint in view. What is the study's purpose and how is the final product envisaged? Will a publication result from the study? A short article? A book? For a scientific forum or for a general audience? The answers to such questions can serve as guidelines throughout the stages of the research project, assisting the informed decisions made throughout the investigation and keeping it on track toward the goal. The nature of the final report is decisive for decisions at earlier stages on such issues as: Informing the interviewees about later use of what they say; obtaining written permission to quote extensively from their interviews; and handling any controversial and conflictual themes that might arise in the interviews. How personal and critical can the interpretations of the interviewees be in a public report?

Push Forward. Attempt to do much of the work of the later stages at earlier stages. Although the problems of an interview project tend to surface in the later stages, more often than not they originated in the earlier stages. The solution is to improve the quality of the original interviews. Thus, clarifying the meanings of expressions used during an interview will facilitate later analysis; asking control questions during the interview will facilitate the validation. Improving interview quality is not simply a question of better interview techniques or design; it also involves a reflective conception of the topic and purpose of the inquiry from the very beginning.

Getting Wiser. An interviewer may learn throughout an investigation: The conversations with the subjects may extend and alter the researcher's understanding of the phenomena investigated. The interviewees bring forth new and unexpected aspects of the phenomena studied; and during analysis of the transcribed interviews new distinctions may be discovered. One of the main purposes of an exploratory study is the discovery of new dimensions of the subject matter. In hypothesis-testing studies, however, realizing significant new insights during the study may well create problems for the interviewer. Novel dimensions of a phenomenon may be discovered in the middle of a series of interviews testing, for example, differences among pupils' learning motivations in a public versus an experimental school. The dilemma will then be whether to improve the interview guide to include in the new dimensions, and not have comparable groups, or to refrain from learning more about the new dimensions uncovered during the study. No easy solution to the dilemma of becoming wiser as a threat to standardized conditions is offered, except to be as clear as possible about the main purposes of a study from its inception.

INTERVIEW FORMS

There are many different forms of interviews and interview subjects, requiring different approaches, and a few will be mentioned briefly. Individual interviews vary according to content, such as seeking factual information, or opinions and attitudes, or narratives and life histories (see Flick et al., 1991). The interviewees can also be regarded as informants for recording oral history (Yow, 1994). Group interviews today are often referred to as focus groups and are frequently used in market research. The interaction among the interview subjects often leads to spontaneous and emotional statements about the topic being discussed. The group interaction, however, reduces the interviewer's control of the interview situation and the price may be a relatively chaotic data collection, with difficulties for systematic analysis of the intermingling voices (see Morgan, 1988). Different groups of subjects require different interview approaches. Interviews with elites thus involve problems of access to the interviewees, and generally require that the interviewer has a good grasp of the interview topic in order to entertain an informed conversation (see Hertz & Imber, 1995).

HOW MANY INTERVIEW SUBJECTS DO I NEED?

To the common question, "How many interview subjects do I need?" the answer is simply, "Interview as many subjects as necessary to find out what you need to know."

The number of subjects necessary depends on a study's purpose. In qualitative interview studies, the number of subjects tends to be either too small or too large. If the number of subjects is too small, it is not possible to make statistical generalizations or to test hypotheses of differences among groups. If the number of subjects is too large, then it is not possible to make penetrating interpretations of the interviews. If the goal is to predict the outcome of a national election, a representative sample of about 1,000 subjects is normally required, so qualitative interviews would be out of the question. If the purpose is to understand the world as experienced by one specific person, this one subject is sufficient.

If the purpose is to test hypotheses about the different attitudes of boys and girls toward competition for grades, the necessary sample may be as small as three boys and three girls for conducting a Fisher test of significance. Depending on the distribution of the findings, a test of statistically significant differences between the two groups can be made at a probability level of $p < .05$ (Siegel, 1956). If, however, the purpose of the study is to explore and describe in detail the attitudes of boys and girls toward grades, new interviews might be conducted until a point of saturation, where further interviews yield little new knowledge. In current interview studies, the number of interviews tend to be around 15 ± 10. This number may be due to a combination of the time and resources available for the investigation and of the law of diminishing returns.

A common critique of interview studies is that the findings are not generalizable because there are too few subjects. A paradoxical answer, from the history of psychology, is that if the aim of a study is to obtain general knowledge, then focus on a few intensive case studies. The contribution of Freud's case studies to the general knowledge of pathology and personality is one instance. Less attention has been given to the fact that a pioneer study of a natural science psychology, Ebbinghaus's experimental-statistical investigation of learning and remembering nonsense syllables, was a case study with a single subject—himself. Piaget's innovative studies of children's cognitive development originated with psychoanalytically inspired interviews with his own children. The radical behaviorist Skinner (1961) argued in "A Case History in Scientific Method" against the frequent use of large groups and statistics in psychology: Statistical averages are excuses for researchers who do not work hard enough to find the specific reinforcement schedules controlling the behavior investigated.

Taking into account the differences among the pioneering studies mentioned above, two reasons for obtaining significant knowledge from a few subjects, which has later been found generalizable to larger groups, may be suggested. Quantitatively, each case contained an immense number of observations of single individuals. Qualitatively, the focus on single cases made it possible to investigate in detail the relationship of a specific behavior to its context, to work out the logic of the relationship between the individual and the situation. The specific kind of relationship varied from transference of a psychoanalytic therapy to the reinforcement schedules of learning. What they have in common is the working out of consistent and recurrent patterns through intensive case studies.

RESOURCES AVAILABLE

Time and Money. The amount of resources necessary for an interview study can be easily overlooked at the design stage; that is when one should ask such questions as: How much time does the researcher have available for the study? How much money is available for assistance—for example, for typing the interview transcripts? Conducting the interviews themselves is generally not time-consuming; transcribing them requires much more time and is therefore expensive. The subsequent analysis of the transcripts is usually the most time-consuming part of the interview study.

Quality Versus Quantity. A general impression from current interview studies is that many of them would have profited from having fewer interviews in the study, and from taking more time to prepare the interviews and to analyze them. Perhaps as a defensive overreaction, some qualitative interview studies appear to be designed on a quantitative presupposition—the more interviews, the more scientific. In contrast, the present approach emphasizes the quality rather than the quantity of the interviews.

Expertise. Good interviews require expertise—in both subject matter and human interaction. If assistants are to be hired to conduct some of the interviews, intensive training of these "new" interviewers may be required to obtain interviews of good quality. Specific forms of analysis, say, of the linguistic aspects of the interviews, also require a special competence.

WHEN NOT TO INTERVIEW

In recent social research there has been an inflationary use of interviews; also in areas better covered by other methods. In some instances, the primary motive for using qualitative interviews appears to be a flight from statistics. When planning an interview study, it may be useful to consider whether other methods might be more appropriate for the topic and the purpose of the investigation. Marshall and Rossman (1995) offer a clear discussion of different methods of doing qualitative research for different purposes and topics.

Here, it may be pertinent to mention some topics and purposes to which qualitative interviews are little suited. If a study seeks to predict the behavior of larger groups, such as voting behavior, larger samples of respondents are necessary than would be possible to cover with time-consuming qualitative interviews; in such cases, survey questionnaires with precoded answers are the relevant method. Also, when there is little time available for a project, questionnaires will usually be faster to administer, analyze, and report than interview studies.

If you want to study people's behavior and their interaction with their environment, the observations of field studies will usually give more valid knowledge than merely asking subjects about their behavior. If the research topic concerns more implicit meanings and tacit understandings, like the taken-for-granted assumptions of a group or a culture, then participant observation and field studies of actual behavior supplemented by informal interviews may give more valid information.

If the purpose of a study is to obtain deeper knowledge about a person, focusing on personal emotional conflicts, then this may best be obtained through the trust developed in the close, personal interaction developed through a long and emotional therapy process. The challenges to a person's established self-image and the strong feelings provoked are necessary parts of therapy, as in the session reported by Rogers (Chapter 2, A Therapeutic Interview on Hate). Creating these kinds of strong emotional dynamics merely to serve research purposes would be unethical.

One purpose of the present book is to lead some readers *away* from using research interviews, by pointing out that other methods may be more appropriate for the subject matter and purpose of their research. This being said, it should not be forgotten that interviews are particularly suited for studying people's understanding of the meanings in their lived world, describing their experiences and self-understanding, and clarifying and elaborating their own perspective on their lived world.

From Method to Craftsmanship

Chapter 4, on qualitative research, concluded with an outline of the dilemma of therapeutic research as caught in a narrow strait between the monsters of a no-method Charybdis and an all-method Scylla. The present guidelines for designing an interview investigation may appear to steer an interview inquiry into the dangerous vicinity of an all-method monster. The systematic planning may, invoking the introductory metaphors, remind one more of an interviewer as a mining engineer than as a conversing traveler.

In order to develop the qualitative interview as a form of research it is necessary to go beyond the dichotomy of all method versus no method. I will discuss a craftsmanlike approach that bypasses this opposition of rigid formalism or naive spontaneity. Craftsmanship here includes a shift from method to the person of the researcher, relating science to art, a skill model of transition from novice to expert, and the learning of research through apprenticeship.

Interviewing is a craft: It does not follow content- and context-free rules of method, but rests on the judgments of a qualified researcher. For the therapeutic as well as the research interview, the interviewer is the instrument. The outcome of an interview depends on the knowledge, sensitivity, and empathy of the interviewer. Its relation to the survey questionnaire and therapy can again be mentioned: Because there are explicit and standard rules for administering questionnaires, new interviewers can be fully trained in a matter of hours or days. In contrast, the qualifications for conducting an open psychoanalytic interview require years of academic training and one's own psycho-analytic therapy over several years.

When the person of the qualitative researcher takes on a methodo-logical dimension, a broad spectrum of qualifications is desirable. In a discussion of validity in qualitative research, Salner (1989) proposes requirements for the human science researcher—such as an acquain-tance with philosophical analysis, an understanding of the develop-ment of rational thought in Western culture, a critical perspective on society, training in the formal analysis of everyday language, expertise in a variety of research methods, an awareness of the ethical dimension of human science, and an aesthetic sensibility.

An emphasis on the crucial role of the person of the researcher does not imply a neglect of techniques and knowledge. For an artist, a mastery of the different techniques of oil painting, watercolors, and pencil drawing, as well as knowledge of the laws of perspective and of color contrast, are preconditions for a mastery of the art of painting. A work of art cannot, however, be produced by merely following methodical rules; the primary instrument remains the artist, with his or her sensitivity and creativity. Art is a genre that can serve as an inspiration for interview inquiries. Eisner (1991, 1993) has looked at educational practice and research from the viewpoint of an artist. He pointed out that the connoisseur's sensitivity to qualitative distinctions and the critic's ability to communicate new perspectives and to evalu-ate the quality of a work of art are qualifications equally desirable for the educational researcher.

Dreyfus and Dreyfus (1986) have presented a model of skill learning with a temporal solution to a dichotomy of learning either by explicit rules or by intuition. The road to the mastery of a skill leads from a rule-guided "knowing that" to an experience-based "knowing how." Drawing on examples from driving, playing chess, making medical diagnoses, and nursing, they outline five qualitatively different stages of adults' skill acquisition through instruction and experience: novice, advanced beginner, competence, proficiency, and expertise. What stands out is a progression from the analytic behavior of a detached subject, of a novice learning through instruction of "context-free" elements and combining the facts by "context-free rules," to emotion-ally involved intuitive skillful behavior. The expert "sees" or "feels" solutions by relying on an intuitive knowledge generalized from extensive case experience.

The novice-expert model of the learning of skills as developing from explicit rule following to intuitive mastery is not the only mode of acquiring skillful behavior. Learning by means of an apprenticeship is usually more informal and has little verbal rule-governed behavior at either the novice or the expert level. The novice participates in communities of practice; learns through hands-on practice, with observation and imitation of expert performances; and gradually acquires a mastery of the craft (Lave & Wenger, 1991).

Relational, tacit, and pragmatic aspects of professional knowledge, including research, can hardly be presented verbally in the form of explicit rules. Altheide and Johnson (1994) have addressed the implications of tacit knowledge when assessing interpretative validity in qualitative research. They point to a bias of communication when the tacit knowledge is transformed into the logic of a more shareable textual communication form. Important aspects of the therapeutic knowledge is best communicated by exemplars, anecdotes, case stories, narratives, and metaphors and is tested by its implication for practice (Polkinghorne, 1992). Such forms of transmission of knowledge come closer to craftsmanship and art than to formal bureaucratic models of research design, and are best transmitted by participation in local forms of practice. Today there is an increasing recognition of indirect and context-bound forms of communicating knowledge through such practices as apprenticeship and mentoring, not only in the crafts, but also for the higher professions, including scientific research (Kvale, 1993a; Mishler, 1990).

Formal apprenticeship in a trade, where students learn interviewing through the interaction of research communities with masters of the craft, are not commonly available. When the option is to be self-taught, a manual may be better than nothing. The present book spells out guidelines for the practice of interview research, provides cases and examples of the methods discussed, and gives examples of breaking the rules—which tend to be as numerous as the exceptions in German grammar. Knowledge of interviewing is less embedded in determinate rules of methods than in examples of the method in use. The aim is to arrive at a transparency of the technical equipment, where the proficient craftsman does not focus on the methods but on the task—in Heidegger's analysis of craftwork it is not the hammer the carpenter focuses on, but the nail and the table.

The present outlines of methodical stages and specific guidelines are substitutes for learning in practice, they are preliminary tools for the gradual mastering of the craft of interviewing. In order to navigate safely through difficult waters it is, however, not sufficient simply to steer one's vessel; an extensive knowledge of the waters and the coastline, through drafts or personal experience, is also necessary. In an interview inquiry, a substantial familiarity with the theme and context of the inquiry is a precondition for the expert use of the interview method. In conclusion, method as rule following is replaced in qualitative interview research by the researcher's expert knowledge of the theme to be investigated and by mastery of the techniques required throughout an interview inquiry.

The issue of research as resting on rule following versus on qualified personal judgment pertains not only to the knowledge dimension of the interview inquiry, but to its moral dimension as well. This will be addressed in Chapter 6 on ethics in interview research.

6

Ethical Issues in
Interview Inquiries

An interview inquiry is a moral enterprise: The personal interaction in the interview affects the interviewee, and the knowledge produced by the interview affects our understanding of the human situation. In Chapter 5, an interview design was treated with regard to acquiring knowledge of the human situation. In this chapter, the moral implications of an interview inquiry will be addressed.

Explicit rules or clear solutions to ethical problems that may arise during an interview study can hardly be provided, but contexts will be suggested for the researcher's reflection on the normative and value themes involved. First, some ethical issues that may arise at the different stages of an interview project are outlined and discussed in relation to the ethical guidelines of informed consent, confidentiality, and consequences. Thereafter, the three ethical theories of duty, utility, and virtue are presented as broader contexts for reflection on moral dilemmas encountered in interview inquiries.

A central aim of social science is to contribute knowledge to ameliorate the human condition and enhance human dignity. The preamble to the American Psychological Association's ethical principles states,

> Psychologists respect the dignity and worth of the individual and strive for the preservation and protection of fundamental human rights. They are committed to increasing knowledge of human behavior and of people's understanding of themselves and others and to the utilization of such knowledge for the promotion of human welfare. (American Psychological Association [APA], 1981, p. 633)

Research with human participants must serve scientific *and* human interests: "The decision to undertake research rests upon a considered judgment by the individual psychologist about how best to contribute to psychological science and human welfare" (p. 637).

Ethical Issues at Seven Research Stages

Ethical decisions do not belong to a separate stage of interview investigations, but arise throughout the entire research process. When ethics is discussed here as a part of the designing stage, it is in order to emphasize the importance of taking ethical questions into consideration from the very start of an investigation through to the final report.

Box 6.1 gives an overview of some of the ethical issues that can arise during the seven stages of an interview investigation. Issues related to the thematizing and designing stages are discussed in this chapter; those pertaining to the later stages will be taken up in following chapters.

Ethical Guidelines

ETHICAL CODES

With a foreknowledge of the moral issues that typically arise at the various stages of an interview investigation, the researcher can make reflected choices while designing a study and watch for critical or sensitive issues that may turn up during the inquiry. Professional ethical codes for human research and philosophical ethical theories serve as contexts for reflection on the specific ethical decisions to be considered.

Ethical codes and theories seldom provide definite answers to the normative choices to be made during a research project. They are more like texts to be interpreted than rules to be followed: They provide guidelines that must be judged according to their relevance to specific situations. Examples and case studies may serve as aids for the transition from general principles to specific practices.

Box 6.1

Ethical Issues of the Seven Research Stages

Thematizing.   The purpose of an interview study should, beyond the scientific value of the knowledge sought, also be considered with regard to improvement of the human situation investigated.

Designing.   Ethical issues of design involve obtaining the subjects' informed consent to participate in the study, securing confidentiality, and considering the possible consequences of the study for the subjects.

Interview Situation.   Here the confidentiality of the subjects' reports needs to be clarified and the consequences of the interview interaction for the subjects to be taken into account, such as stress during the interview and changes in self-image. Also the potential closeness of the research interview to the therapeutic interview should be considered.

Transcription.   Here again is the issue of confidentiality, as well as the question of what is a loyal written transcription of an interviewee's oral statements.

Analysis.   Ethical issues in analysis involve the question of how deeply and critically the interviews can be analyzed and of whether the subjects should have a say in how their statements are interpreted.

Verification.   It is the ethical responsibility of the researcher to report knowledge that is as secured and verified as possible.

Reporting.   Here again is the issue of confidentiality when reporting the interviews, as well as the question of consequences of the published report for the interviewees as well as for the group or institution they represent.

When preparing an outline of the research design, it can be useful also to draft a parallel *ethical protocol* treating ethical issues that can be anticipated in an investigation. In some settings this may be an institutional requirement; thus, in addition to the research protocol submitted to a mentor or sponsor, a "human subjects protocol" for an ethics committee may be required before the project can be accepted (see *Guidelines for the Protection of Human Subjects* [*Guidelines*], 1992). Even when not a formal requirement, the advance preparation of an ethical protocol will allow the investigator to consider ethical and moral issues, and to have them in mind during the designing of the study and when making normative decisions later in the project. Some of the questions to be considered in an ethical protocol for an interview study were depicted in Box 6.1.

Besides having a project accepted by an ethics committee, there is a possibility of conducting an ongoing discussion of its value issues with more experienced members in the research community. The ethical skills embodied in local professional communities represent an important extension of the written ethical principles, rules, and examples.

Three ethical guidelines for human research are now discussed in some detail: informed consent, confidentiality, and consequences (see, e.g., Eisner & Peshkin, 1990; Kimmel, 1988).

INFORMED CONSENT

Informed consent entails informing the research subjects about the overall purpose of the investigation and the main features of the design, as well as of any possible risks and benefits from participation in the research project. Informed consent further involves obtaining the voluntary participation of the subject, with his or her right to withdraw from the study at any time, thus counteracting potential undue influence and coercion (see Moustakas [1994] and Yow [1994] for examples of letters of agreement with subjects).

On a principal level the requirements of information for and consent from the research subjects are sound and reasonable. The principle of informed consent is, however, not without problems in practice—such as the question of *who should give the consent.* Issues about consent may arise with interviews in institutions, where a superior's consent to a study may imply a more or less subtle pressure on employees to participate. With school children, the question arises about *who* should give the consent—the children themselves, the school superintendent, the school board, the teacher, or the parents?

Informed consent also involves the question of *how much information should be given and when.* Full information about design and purpose rules out any deception of the subjects. Providing information about a study involves a careful balance between detailed over-information and leaving out aspects of the design that may be significant to the subjects. In some interview investigations, the specific purposes of a study are initially withheld in order to obtain the interviewees' natural views on a topic and to avoid leading them to specific answers. In such cases any misleading information should be corrected in a debriefing after the study.

In the *grading study,* the high school pupils were interviewed at school. The principal was fully informed about the design and the purpose of investigating the effects of grades. The pupils were told in advance only that the interviews concerned the school situation and that participation was voluntary. Consent was easily obtained because the pupils would be free from a school hour during the interview. The decision to withhold the information about grading as the main interview topic was made in order to investigate how prominent a place grades had in the pupils' everyday school life. Thus the first 5 minutes of the interview consisted of questions about the general school situation, and the earlier the pupils spontaneously mentioned grades, the stronger the indication was that grades were central in their school life. After an interview, each pupil was debriefed about the interview topic and purpose, which had already become evident during the interview itself. Withholding of information was here considered as not going against the pupil's interests and was done with the intention of obtaining knowledge as uncontaminated by the researcher's hypotheses as possible.

Meeting the requirement of full disclosure may be difficult to fulfil when changes in purpose and design occur due to new knowledge and insight gained during a research project. Some ethics review boards may want to approve every interview question in advance, whereas the semistructured interview treated here relies on the possibility of following up unanticipated leads from the subjects and of posing questions not prepared in advance. In "Can Qualitative Studies Be

Informed?" Eisner (1991) has pointed out that the concept of informed consent implies that the researcher knows *before* the event to
be observed what the event will be and its possible effects. This may
be possible in carefully planned experimental studies, but is hardly
feasible in field research and explorative studies, where an important
tactic is to follow up unanticipated leads: "Thus we all like the idea
of informed consent, but we are less sure just who is to provide that
consent, just how much consent is needed, and how we can inform
others so as to obtain consent when we have such a hard time predicting what we need to get consent about" (Eisner, 1991, p. 215).

Lincoln (1990) has proposed replacing the concept of informed
consent with a dialogue that runs throughout an investigation, with
"the negotiation of research processes and products with one's respondents, so that there is a mutual shaping of the final research results"
(p. 286). Such a continual dialogue approach to informed consent
presupposes ideals of egalitarianism and a mutuality of interests of
researcher and researched that may be hard to find in many actual
social settings. Thus in some institutions there may be radically
opposing conceptions of the phenomena investigated, and with some
interests vested in upholding specific conceptions of the institutional
reality. The dialogue approach also involves a rationalism that hardly
pertains to therapeutic situations, where the patient's resistance to the
therapist's interpretations is a main aspect of the therapeutic process,
and may require years to overcome.

CONFIDENTIALITY

Confidentiality in research implies that private data identifying the
subjects will not be reported. If a study involves publishing information potentially recognizable to others, the subjects need to agree to
the release of identifiable information. In such cases this should be
stated explicitly in a written agreement. The protection of subjects'
privacy by changing their names and identifying features is an important issue in the reporting of interviews.

In the *grading study,* the pupils and teachers interviewed were
guaranteed that their interviews would be treated confidentially. In
the book about the study, many quotes from the interviews were given,

but with any information that could jeopardize the anonymity of the pupils removed. There was one exception. The decision to publish a book about the interviews for the general market was first made during the analysis half a year after the interviewing. I then wanted to reproduce a specific interview in full, because it gave a particularly vivid description of the influence of grades on the pupils' life situation. In this instance, the interviewee would be recognized by others, and I wrote for his permission to reproduce his interview. By then, however, he had left school to travel around the world; many months after my request I received a telegram from Jerusalem with his permission to publish the interview.

The principle of the research subjects' right to privacy is not without ethical and scientific dilemmas. Thus there is concern about what information should be available, and to whom. Should, for example, interviews with children be available to their parents and teachers? In studies where several parties are involved, such as interviews with married or divorced couples and in organizations, it should be made clear before the interviewing who will later have access to the material.

Protecting confidentiality can involve serious legal problems, such as in cases when a researcher—through the promise of confidentiality and the trust of the relationship—has obtained knowledge of mistreatment, malpractice, child abuse, the use of drugs, or other criminal behavior either by the interviewee or others. There are instances where research studies have come to contain information that was subpoenaed in legal proceedings, and there exists cases where researchers have gone to jail rather than reveal information disclosed by their subjects. If there is any preknowledge that a research topic might become involved in a legal conflict, it is possible in the United States to obtain a certificate of confidentiality from the federal government, which protects researchers against being compelled to disclose the identity of their subjects in any legal proceeding (see *Guidelines,* 1992, p. 6).

A conflict exists between the ethical demand for confidentiality and the basic principles of scientific research, such as intersubjective control and the possibility of reproducing the findings by other scientists. As expressed by Smith (1990): How can research results be checked by other researchers if no one knows who participated in a study, and where and when it took place?

CONSEQUENCES

The ethical principle of *beneficence* means that the risk of harm to a subject should be the least possible. The sum of potential benefits to a subject and the importance of the knowledge gained should outweigh the risk of harm to the subject and thus warrant a decision to carry out the study (*Guidelines,* 1992, p. 15).

The consequences of an interview study need to be addressed with respect to possible harm to the subjects as well as the expected benefits of participating in the study. This involves a researcher's responsibility to reflect on the possible consequences not only for the persons taking part in the study, but for the larger group they represent, as well.

Ideally there should be a reciprocity in what the subjects give and what they receive from participation in a study. In interview reports there are sometimes accounts by astonished researchers that their subjects have experienced the interviews as positive experiences. Just listening to what people have to say for an extended period of time, as well as the quality of the listening, can make an interview a unique experience. The interview researcher thus can offer benefits to the subjects through their participation in the investigation. The interviewer should also be aware that the openness and intimacy of the interview may be seductive and lead subjects to disclose information they may later regret. The personal closeness of the interview situation puts strong demands on the sensitivity of the interviewer regarding how far to go in his or her questioning.

At the thematizing stage of the *grade study,* the general purpose was formulated as the documentation of the effects of grading on learning and social relations in school. These effects were assumed to be in contrast to the central values of the official Danish high school curriculum, such as promoting independence, cooperation, and creativity and an intrinsic interest in lifelong learning. It was hypothesized that a newly introduced grade-based restriction on entering a university would promote dependence, competition, conformity, and negative attitudes toward learning. At the time, I believed that the investigation would serve the interests of the pupils by documenting the effects of grading in contrast with the official curriculum, and that this could result in instigating institutional changes that would improve their learning and social conditions at school.

The broader consequences of interview research involve political judgments about the desirable uses of the acquired knowledge. As mentioned at the beginning of this chapter, the American Psychological Association's ethical guidelines state that one aim of psychological research is contribution to human welfare, which leads to political issues of what are human welfare and a just society. Market studies of consumer experience are undertaken with the purpose of predicting and manipulating consumer behavior in the interest of increased profits for producers (Chapter 4, Qualitative Market Research). One aim of feminist research is to overcome the oppression of women through giving priority to the moral and politic over the scientific (Chapter 4, Feminism and Qualitative Research). The immediate aim of psychotherapy is to overcome the patients' suffering, and Habermas, in his discussion of the interlocking of knowledge and human interests, posited psychoanalytical therapy as a paradigm of a critical emancipatory social science (Chapter 3, Hermeneutical Interpretation).

THE ROLE OF THE RESEARCHER

Moral research behavior is more than ethical knowledge and cognitive choices; it involves the person of the researcher, his or her sensitivity and commitment to moral issues and action: "Clearly, researchers need both cases and principles from which to learn more about ethical behavior. More than this, they need two attributes: the sensitivity to identify an ethical issue and the responsibility to feel committed to acting appropriately in regard to such issues" (Eisner & Peshkin, 1990, p. 244).

The person of the researcher is critical for the quality of the scientific knowledge and for the soundness of ethical decisions in any research project. By interviewing, the importance of the researcher as a person is magnified because the interviewer him-or herself is the main instrument for obtaining knowledge. Being familiar with value issues, ethical guidelines, and ethical theories may help in choices that weigh ethical versus scientific concerns in a study. In the end, however, the integrity of the researcher—his or her honesty and fairness, knowledge, and experience—are the decisive factors.

Three ethical aspects of the researcher's role concern scientific responsibility, relation to the subjects, and researcher independence. The researcher has a *scientific responsibility* to his profession and his subjects that a research project yield knowledge worth knowing and that it is as controlled and verified as possible. Researchers take on different roles in *relation to their subjects.* Glesne and Peshkin (1992) have depicted some roles that qualitative researchers easily assume: exploiter, reformer, advocate, and friend. They go on to discuss ethical issues in the different roles, such as whether a researcher in an advocative role should publish information that may put his or her subjects in a negative light.

The *independence of research* can be co-opted from "above" as well as "below," by the funders of a project as well as by its participants. Ties to either group may lead the researcher to ignore some findings and emphasize others to the detriment of as full and unbiased an investigation of the phenomena as possible. Interviewing is interactive research; through close interpersonal interactions with their subjects, interviewers may be particularly prone to co-optation by them. Interviewers may so closely identify with their subjects that they do not maintain a professional distance, but instead report and interpret everything from their subjects' perspectives. There is a risk that interviewers can—in psychoanalytic terminology—become victims of unrecognized "countertransference," or—to use an anthropological expression—"go native."

ETHICAL ISSUES AT THE START OF A STUDY

Box 6.2 depicts some of the ethical questions to consider when beginning an interview study. These questions summarize the above discussion of the thematizing and designing stages, and outline some of the issues to be raised in the following chapters about the later stages. There are no easy answers to these questions; the ethical guidelines give some principal directions, and participating in research communities will provide additional concrete background knowledge for making ethical decisions. Theories of ethics provide broader contexts for reflecting on the moral issues of research, and some key theories are now discussed.

Box 6.2

Ethical Questions at the
Start of an Interview Study

- What are the *beneficial* consequences of the study?

  How can the study contribute to enhancing the human condition?

  Will potential contributions be primarily for the participating subjects? Or for their group? Or will the contribution be in the form of general knowledge of the human situation?

- How can the *informed consent* of the participating subjects be obtained?

  Should informed consent be agreed on orally or should there be a written contract?

  Who should give the consent—the subjects or their superiors?

  How much information about the study needs to be given in advance, and what information can wait until a debriefing after the interviews?

  How can informed consent be handled in exploratory studies where the investigators themselves will have little advance knowledge of how the interviews will proceed?

- How can the *confidentiality* of the interview subjects be protected?

  How important is it that the subjects remain anonymous?

  Who will have access to the interviews?

  How can the identity of the subjects be disguised?

  Can legal problems concerning protection of the subjects' anonymity be expected?

  (continued)

Box 6.2 Continued

- What are the *consequences* of the study for the participating subjects?

Will any potential harm to the subjects be outweighed by
potential benefits?

Will the interviews touch on therapeutic issues, and if so,
what precautions can be taken?

When publishing the study, what consequences can be
anticipated for the subjects and for the groups they
represent?

- How will the *researcher's role* affect the study?

How can the researcher ensure the scientific quality of
the study and protect the independence of the research?

How can the researcher avoid or counteract being co-
opted from above by his sponsors?

How can the researcher avoid or counteract overidenti-
fication with his subjects, thereby losing critical perspective on the knowledge obtained?

Ethical Theories

From a historical perspective, scientific knowledge has been intrinsically related to human values and interests. The sciences that are
today termed "social sciences," in earlier centuries went under the
name "moral sciences." With the rise of modern social science, a split
developed between facts and values, between the descriptive and the
normative, between what is and what should be. This dichotomy was
prominent in positivist philosophy, with its sharp distinction between
an objective scientific and a subjective human side of research. The
moral aspects of research, belonging to the value side of the dichotomy, became secondary and were left to the ethical codes of the
profession and the integrity of the researcher.

The split between factual knowledge and ethical values is being questioned today; for example, by Habermas's outline of the interlocking of human interests and scientific knowledge (Chapter 3, Hermeneutical Interpretation) as well as within feminist research (Chapter 4, Feminism and Qualitative Research). With a loss of faith in the Enlightenment belief in emancipation through knowledge, and human progress through the advance of scientific knowledge, the ends and means of scientific research are being closely questioned in the postmodern era, where the moral side of research becomes as important as the scientific side.

Theories of ethics provide frames of reference for thinking about specific moral issues in research. They contain more comprehensive contexts for considering ethical choices than the specific guidelines outlined above. There are three major philosophical ethical positions: a duty ethics of principles, a utilitarian ethics of consequences, and a virtue ethics of skills (see, e.g., Eisner & Peshkin, 1990; Kimmel, 1988).

The *duty* ethics of principles, also termed a deontological and an intentional position, judges an action independently of its consequences. Moral actions are those that live up to principles, such as honesty, justice, and respect for the person. An ethics of duty is expressed by Kant's maxims: "Treat every man as an end in himself, and never as a means only" and "Act as if the maxim of thy act were to become by thy will a universal law of nature." These general ethical principles may be specified as ethical rules for different types of research. Carried to its extreme, the intentional position can become a moral absolutism, with intentions of living up to absolute principles of right action, regardless of the human consequences of an act.

The *utilitarian* position, also termed a teleological position, emphasizes the consequences of an action—an action is judged pragmatically by its effects. In the final analysis it is the results of an action that determine its rightness. The end purpose might be the greatest good for the greatest number; what is good might be determined to be an increase in happiness, wealth, or knowledge. In an extreme version of a utilitarian consequence position, the ends come to justify the means.

The contrasting practical implications of a duty and a utilitarian theory may be highlighted by an extreme example:

Patient over telephone to therapist: I am going out now to jump into Lake Sortedamssøen and drown myself.

Therapist replies: Go and jump in the lake then!

Patient, a few days later: Forwards a complaint against the therapist to the Ethical Committee of the Danish Psychological Association for encouraging him to commit suicide and thus not respecting his dignity as a human being.

The therapist appears here to have acted spontaneously from a utilitarian position of survival, and used a paradoxical therapeutic technique when answering the patient on the phone. The patient, who apparently has profited from the therapist's pragmatic intervention, adopts a duty position of the principle of absolute respect for his person, which he complains that his therapist has violated.

Both a consequential ethics of utility and an intentional ethics of duty raise questions of whether there are universal ethical principles, or whether they would depend on the values of specific communities. A third position, departing from Aristotle's concepts of *virtue* and practical reasoning, involves a contextual ethical position. Ethical behavior is seen less as the application of general principles and rules, than as the researcher internalizing moral values. The personal integrity of the researcher, the interaction with the community studied, and the relation to their ethical values is essential. The emphasis is on the researcher's ethical intuitions, feelings, and skills as well as on negotiations between actors in a specific community. The learning of ethical research behavior is a matter of being initiated into the mores of the local professional culture. Through practice and interaction with more experienced members of the profession, which may be in the form of master-apprentice relationships, the newcomer gradually acquires the context sensibility and the wisdom of mature ethical behavior.

The duty, the utilitarian, and the virtue philosophies emphasize different aspects of ethical choices. On some specific issues they may lead to different decisions, such as deception of research subjects. An intentional duty ethic would emphasize honesty as an absolute principle, and thus reject any deception of research subjects in the interest of a greater good. A utilitarian-consequence position could justify deception in view of the positive consequences of knowledge and the betterment of the human situation that the research could entail. A contextual-virtue position would be based on the researcher's practical ethical skills and reasoning and, in cases of doubt, on a dialogue with others in the relevant communities.

A contextual-ethical position has been argued by Dreyfus and Dreyfus (1990) in a phenomenological account of the development of ethical expertise. The authors describe their five-step ladder of learning, from novice to expert (Chapter 5, From Method to Craftsmanship), and postulate that with increasing expertise, explicit rules and reasoning disappear into the background of skill or habit. Moral consciousness expresses itself in everyday life through unreflective responses to interpersonal situations, and Dreyfus and Dreyfus suggest that we begin our investigation of ethical experience on the level of this spontaneous coping. The highest form of ethical comportment consists of being able to stay involved and to refine one's intuitions. Ethical choices need not remain on the level of individual spontaneous choices; in cases of disagreement, the wise decision maker will enter into a dialogue with those who have reached different conclusions.

Within a virtue conception of ethics, Løvlie (1993) has attempted to overcome an opposition of explicit rules versus tacit skills by the introduction of examples. These may be in the form of parables, allegories, myths, sagas, morality plays, case stories, and personal examples. As riddles subject to contextual interpretation, the examples are pieces of texts to be interpreted: "The application of moral knowledge and wisdom then turns out to be governed as much by reflective judgement as by rule-following and the practising of skills" (p. 76).

In the next two chapters I turn to knowledge production in the interview situation, and will return (Chapter 8, The Ethics of Interviewing) to some of the ethical issues raised here; in particular, consequences of the interview interaction for the interviewees and the proximity of research interviews to therapeutic interviews.

7

The Interview Situation

In the interview, knowledge is created inter the points of view of the interviewer and the interviewee. The interviews with the subjects are the most engaging stage of an interview inquiry. The personal contact and the continually new insights into the subjects' lived world make interviewing an exciting and enriching experience. Different forms of interview conversations were discussed in Chapter 2 and the mode of understanding in the qualitative research interview described. In this chapter I outline in more detail some guidelines and techniques for carrying out interviews and give an illustration with an interview on grading.

The Interview Conversation

The purpose of a qualitative research interview was described earlier as obtaining qualitative descriptions of the life world of the subject with respect to interpretation of their meaning. The interview form treated here is a semistructured interview: It has a sequence of themes to be covered, as well as suggested questions. Yet at the same time there is an openness to changes of sequence and forms of questions in order to follow up the answers given and the stories told by the subjects. I will discuss the interview interaction in line with the mode of understanding depicted earlier with respect to 12 aspects of the interview: life world, meaning, qualitative, descriptive, specificity, deliberate naïveté, focus, ambiguity, change, sensitivity, interpersonal situation, and a positive experience (see Box 2.1 in Chapter 2).

An open phenomenological approach to learning from the interviewee is well expressed in this introduction from Spradley (1979):

> I want to understand the world from your point of view. I want to know what you know in the way you know it. I want to understand the meaning of your experience, to walk in your shoes, to feel things as you feel them, to explain things as you explain them. Will you become my teacher and help me understand? (p. 34)

The research interview is an interpersonal situation, a conversation between two partners about a theme of mutual interest. It is a specific form of human interaction in which knowledge evolves through a dialogue. The interaction is neither as anonymous and neutral as when a subject responds to a survey questionnaire, nor as personal and emotional as a therapeutic interview. Patients seek therapists for help: They are motivated to be as open as possible with the therapist, with whom a trusting relationship is established over time. In a research setting it is up to the interviewer to create in a short time a contact that allows the interaction to get beyond merely a polite conversation or exchange of ideas. The interviewer must establish an atmosphere in which the subject feels safe enough to talk freely about his or her experiences and feelings. This involves a delicate balance between cognitive knowledge seeking and the ethical aspects of emotional human interaction. Thus, at the same time that personal expressions and emotions are encouraged, the interviewer must avoid allowing the interview to turn into a therapeutic situation, which he or she may not be able to handle.

The interviewer has an empathic access to the world of the interviewee; the interviewee's lived meanings may be immediately accessible in the situation, communicated not only by words, but by tone of voice, expressions, and gestures in the natural flow of a conversation. The research interviewer uses him- or herself as a research instrument, drawing upon an implicit bodily and emotional mode of knowing that allows a privileged access to the subject's lived world.

A research interview follows an unwritten script, with different roles specified for the two actors. The implicit rules of their interaction become visible when they are broken, such as in this interview exchange with an unemployed man about traveling, in which the interviewer is caught off guard when the subject reverses the roles:

Subject: When you are on vacation there is some silly time factor, the only thing you have time for is to go down and throw yourself on the beach. Do you sunbathe?

Interviewer: What?

S: Do you sunbathe?

I: Well, no I do not.

S: You have a nice color.

I: I don't spend one single summer day on that, but as a whole I look tanned. F   urthermore I get very easily tanned, I only need to put one finger out of the window to catch the sun.

S: A lot of people would envy you that.

I: Well, where do we begin. What are you doing with your friends? (Berg Sørensen, 1988, p. 124).

The conversation in a research interview is not the reciprocal interaction of two equal partners. There is a definite asymmetry of power: The interviewer defines the situation, introduces the topics of the conversation, and through further questions steers the course of the interview. This was the case in the rather open interview reported by Giorgi (Chapter 2). Socrates' interview, despite the conversational partners being formally equal and the polite introduction, took the form of harsh interrogation, relentlessly driving Agathon around in his contradictory conceptions of love and beauty, until Agathon throws in the towel and concedes that he knows nothing of what he was talking about (Chapter 2).

Advance preparation is essential to the interaction and outcome of an interview. A substantial part of the investigation should take place before the tape recorder is turned on in the actual interview situation. The key issues of the interview concern what, why, and how: *what*— acquiring a preknowledge of the subject matter to be investigated; *why*—formulating a clear purpose for the interview; and *how*—being familiar with different interview techniques and deciding which to apply in the investigation. Also, before the first interviews in a study are undertaken, thought should have been given to how the interviews will be analyzed and how the findings will be verified and reported.

Research interviews vary on a series of dimensions. They differ in degree of *structure*, from well-organized interviews that follow a sequence of standard question formulations, to open interviews where specific themes are in focus but without a predetermined sequence and formulation of questions. Sometimes only a first, topic-introducing question is asked and the remainder of the interview proceeds as a follow-up and expansion on the interviewee's answer to the first questions, such as in the interview on learning reported by Giorgi. The interviews also differ in their *openness of purpose;* the interviewer can explain the purpose and pose direct questions from the start or can adopt a roundabout approach, with indirect questions, and reveal the purpose only when the interview is over.

The interviews can differ further in their emphasis on *exploration versus hypothesis testing,* as mentioned in the discussion of design. Interviews also vary concerning *description versus interpretation.* The interviewer might seek mainly to obtain nuanced descriptions of the phenomena investigated or can, during the interview, also attempt to clarify and interpret the descriptions together with the subject. Interviews also vary on an *intellectual-emotional dimension,* from a rational logical discourse between interviewer and subject analytically clarifying conceptions of the phenomena investigated, to the interviewer attempting to get spontaneous and emotional descriptions of, and reactions about, a topic. Two extreme interviews on the intellectual-emotional dimension were presented earlier—the discursive argumentation of Socrates and the emotional therapeutic interchange reported by Rogers.

Framing the Interview

The interview is a stage upon which knowledge is constructed through the interaction of interviewer and interviewee roles. Some directions are suggested here for setting the interview stage so the interviewees will be encouraged to put words to their points of view on their lives and worlds. The directions pertain to interviews with middle-class persons in Northern Europe and North America. In other cultures, different norms may hold for interactions with strangers concerning initiative, directness, openness, and the like.

The interviewees should be provided with a context for the interview by a briefing before and a debriefing afterward. The context is introduced with a *briefing* in which the interviewer defines the situation for the subject; briefly tells about the purpose of the interview, the use of a tape recorder, and so on; and asks if the subject has any questions before starting the interview. Further explanations about the interview investigation should preferably wait until the interview is over.

The first minutes of an interview are decisive. The subjects will want to have a grasp of the interviewer before they allow themselves to talk freely, exposing their experiences and feelings to a stranger. A good contact is established by attentive listening, with the interviewer showing interest, understanding, and respect for what the subject says; at the same time, the interviewer is at ease and clear about what he or she wants to know.

The initial briefing should be followed up by a *debriefing* after the interview. At the end of the interview there may be some tension or anxiety, because the subject has been open about often personal and emotional experiences and may be wondering about the interview's purpose and how it will be used. There may perhaps also be feelings of emptiness; the subject has given much information about his or her life and may not have received anything in return. This being said, a common experience after research interviews is that the subjects have experienced the interview as genuinely enriching, have enjoyed talking freely with an attentive listener, and have sometimes obtained new insights into important themes of their life world.

The interaction can be rounded off by the interviewer mentioning some of the main points learned from the interview. The subject may then want to comment on this feedback. The interaction can thereafter be concluded by the interviewer saying, for example, "I have no further questions. Do you have anything more you want to bring up, or ask about, before we finish the interview?" This gives the subject an additional opportunity to deal with issues he or she has been thinking or worrying about during the interview.

The debriefing is likely to continue after the tape recorder has been turned off. After a first gasp of relief, the interviewee may bring up topics he or she did not feel safe raising with the tape recorder on. And the interviewer can now, insofar as the subject is interested, tell more fully about the purpose and design of the interview study.

The lived interview situation, with the interviewee's voice and facial and bodily expressions accompanying the statements, provides a richer access to the subjects' meanings than the transcribed texts will later. It may be worthwhile for the interviewer to set aside 10 minutes of quiet time after each interview to recall and reflect on what has been learned from the particular interview, including the interpersonal interaction. These immediate impressions, based on the interviewer's empathic access to the meanings communicated, may—in the form of notes or simply recorded onto the interview tape—provide a valuable context for the later analysis of transcripts.

The Interview Guide

An interview guide indicates the topics and their sequence in the interview. The guide can contain just some rough topics to be covered or it can be a detailed sequence of carefully worded questions. For the semistructured type of interview discussed here, the guide will contain an outline of topics to be covered, with suggested questions. It will depend on the particular design chosen whether the questions and their sequence are strictly predetermined and binding on the interviewers, or whether it is up to an interviewer's judgment and tact how closely to follow the guide and how strongly to pursue an individual subject's answers.

Each interview question can be evaluated with respect to both a thematic and a dynamic dimension: thematically with regard to its relevance for the research theme, and dynamically with regard to the interpersonal relationship in the interview. A good interview question should contribute thematically to knowledge production and dynamically to promoting a good interview interaction.

Thematically the questions relate to the topic of the interview, to the theoretical conceptions at the root of an investigation, and to the subsequent analysis. The questions will be different when interviewing for spontaneous descriptions of the lived world, or interviewing for a conceptual analysis of the person's concepts of a topic. Simply expressed, the more spontaneous the interview procedure, the more likely one is to obtain spontaneous, lively, and unexpected answers from the interviewees. And vice versa: The more structured the interview situation is, the easier the later structuring of the interview by analysis will be.

In line with the principle of "pushing forward" in an interview project, the later stages should be taken into account when preparing the interview questions. If the method of analysis will involve categorizing the answers, then clarify continually during the interview the meanings of the answers with respect to the categories to be used later. If a narrative analysis is to be employed, then give the subjects ample freedom and time to unfold their own stories, and follow up with questions to clarify the main episodes and characters in their narratives.

Dynamically, the questions should promote a positive interaction; keep the flow of the conversation going and motivate the subjects to talk about their experiences and feelings. The questions should be easy to understand, short, and devoid of academic language.

A good conceptual thematic research question need not be a good dynamic interview question. When preparing an interview it may be useful to develop two guides, one with the project's main thematic research questions and the other with the questions to be posed during the interview, which takes both the thematic and the dynamic dimensions into account.

Table 7.1 depicts the translation of thematic research questions in the grading study into interview questions to provide thematic knowledge and contribute dynamically to a natural conversational flow. The abstract wording of the research questions would hardly lead to off-the-cuff answers from high school pupils. The academic research questions need to be translated into an easy-going, colloquial form to generate spontaneous and rich descriptions. One research question can be investigated through several interview questions, thus obtaining rich and varied information by approaching a topic from several angles. And one interview question might provide answers to several research questions.

The roles of the "why," "what," and "how" questions are different in research versus interview questions. It has been repeatedly emphasized that when designing an interview project, the "why" and "what" questions should be asked and answered before the question of "how" is posed. In the interview situation, the priority of the question types change. In the interview itself, the main questions should be in a descriptive form: "What happened and how did it happen?" "How

TABLE 7.1 Research Questions and Interview Questions

Research Questions	Interview Questions
	Do you find the subjects you learn important?
Which form of learning motivation dominates in high school?	Do you find learning interesting in itself?
	What is your main purpose in going to high school?
Do the grades promote an external, instrumental motivation at the expense of an intrinsic interest motivation for learning? →	Have you experienced a conflict between what you wanted to read (study) and what you had to read to obtain a good grade?
Does learning for grades socialize to working for wages?	Have you been rewarded with money for good grades?
	Do you see any connection between money and grades?

did you feel then?" "What did you experience?" and the like. The aim is to elicit spontaneous descriptions from the subjects rather than to get their own, more or less speculative explanations of why something took place. "Why" questions about the subjects' own reasons for their actions may be important in their own right. Many "why" questions in an interview may, however, lead to an intellectualized interview, perhaps evoking memories of oral examinations. Figuring out the reasons and explanations for why something happened is primarily the task of the investigator.

Interview Questions

The research interview proceeds rather like a normal conversation but has a specific purpose and structure: It is characterized by a systematic form of questioning. The interviewer's questions should be brief and simple. In the life world interviews described here, an opening question may ask about a concrete situation. The different dimensions introduced in the answer can then be pursued. The decisive issue is the interviewer's ability to sense the immediate meaning of an answer and the horizon of possible meanings that it opens up. This, again, requires a knowledge of, and interest in, both the theme and the human interaction of the interview. Decisions about which of the many dimensions to pursue that are introduced by a subject's answer will depend on the purpose and content of the interview, as well as on the social interaction in the interview situation.

Box 7.1 depicts some main types of questions that may be useful in the semistructured interview form treated here. A more extended discussion of interview questions is given by Seidman (1991). In addition to paying attention to the thematic and dynamic aspects of the questions, the interviewer should also try to keep in mind the later analysis, verification, and reporting of the interviews. Interviewers who know what they are asking about, and why they are asking, will attempt to clarify the meanings relevant to the project during the interview, obtaining a disambiguation of the statements made, and thereby provide a more trustworthy point of departure for the later analysis. Such a process of meaning clarification during the interview may also communicate to the subjects that the interviewer actually is listening to and interested in what they are saying. Ideally, the testing of hypotheses and interpretations is finished by the end of the interview, with the interviewer's hypotheses having been verified or falsified during the interview.

If an interview is to be reported, perhaps quoted at length, then attempt when feasible to make the social context explicit during the interview, and when possible the emotional tone of the interaction, so that what is said is understandable for the readers, who have not witnessed the live interview situation. Much is to be learned from journalists and novelists about conveying the setting and mood of a conversation.

The focus here has been on the interviewer's questions. Active listening—the interviewer's ability to listen actively to what the interviewee says—can be more important than the specific mastery of questioning techniques. Therapists' education emphasizes their skills

Box 7.1

Types of Interview Questions

A. *Introducing Questions*: "Can you tell me about . . . ?"; "Do you remember an occasion when . . . ?"; "What happened in the episode you mentioned?"; and "Could you describe in as much detail as possible a situation in which learning occurred for you?" Such opening questions may yield spontaneous, rich, descriptions where the subjects themselves provide what they experience as the main dimensions of the phenomena investigated. The remainder of the interview can then proceed as following up of dimensions introduced in the story told in response to the initial question.

B. *Follow-Up Questions*: The subjects' answers may be extended through a curious, persistent, and critical attitude of the interviewer. This can be done through direct questioning of what has just been said. Also a mere nod, or "mm," or just a pause can indicate to the subject to go on with the description. Repeating significant words of an answer can lead to further elaborations. Interviewers can train themselves to notice "red lights" in the answers—such as unusual terms, strong intonations, and the like—which may signal a whole complex of topics important to the subject. The key issue here is the interviewer's ability to listen to what is important to the subjects, and at the same time to keep in mind the research questions of an investigation.

C. *Probing Questions*: "Could you say something more about that?"; "Can you give a more detailed description of what happened?"; "Do you have further examples of this?" The interviewer here pursues the answers, probing their content but without stating what dimensions are to be taken into account.

(continued)

Box 7.1 Continued

D. *Specifying Questions*: The interviewer may also follow up with more operationalizing questions, for instance: "What did you think then?"; "What did you actually do when you felt a mounting anxiety?"; "How did your body react?" In an interview with many general statements, the interviewer can attempt to get more precise descriptions by asking "Have you also experienced this yourself?"

E. *Direct Questions*: The interviewer here directly introduces topics and dimensions, for example: "Have you ever received money for good grades?"; "When you mention competition, do you then think of a sportsmanlike or a destructive competition?" Such direct questions may preferably be postponed until the later parts of the interview, after the subjects have given their own spontaneous descriptions and thereby indicated what aspects of the phenomena are central to them.

F. *Indirect Questions*: Here the interviewer may apply projective questions such as "How do you believe other pupils regard the competition for grades?" The answer may refer directly to the attitudes of others; it may also be an indirect statement of the pupil's own attitude, which he or she does not state directly. Careful further questioning will be necessary here to interpret the answer.

G. *Structuring Questions*: The interviewer is responsible for the course of the interview and should indicate when a theme has been exhausted. The interviewer may directly and politely break off long answers that are irrelevant to the topic of the investigation, for example by saying, "I would now like to introduce another topic: . . . "

H. *Silence*: Rather than making the interview a cross examination by continually firing off questions, the research interviewer can take a lead from therapists in employing silence to further the interview. By allowing pauses in the

---

Box 7.1 Continued

conversation the subjects have ample time to associate and reflect and then break the silence themselves with significant information.

I. *Interpreting Questions*: The degree of interpretation may involve merely rephrasing an answer, for instance: "You then mean that . . . ?" or attempts at clarification: "Is it correct that you feel that . . . ?"; "Does the expression . . . cover what you have just expressed?" There may also be more direct interpretations of what the pupil has said: "Is it correct that your main anxiety about the grades concerns the reaction from your parents?" More speculative questions can take the form of: "Do you see any connections between the two situations of competing with the other pupils for grades and the relation to your siblings at home?"

---

as listeners, furthering an empathic active listening to the many nuances and layers of meanings of what their patients tell them. Freud (1963) recommended that therapists listen to their patients with an "evenly hovering attention" to attend to the meaning of their accounts (Chapter 4, Psychoanalytical Knowledge Production).

The importance of listening also appears in phenomenological and hermeneutical approaches to interviewing (Chapter 3, sections titled Hermeneutical Interpretation; and Phenomenological Description). There is the phenomenological ideal of listening without prejudice, allowing the interviewees' descriptions of their experiences unfold without interruptions from interviewer questions and the presuppositions these involve. A hermeneutical approach involves an interpretative listening to the multiple horizons of meaning involved in the interviewees' statements, with an attention to the possibilities of continual reinterpretations within the hermeneutical circle of the interview. Attention will also be paid to the influence of the presuppositions of the subjects' answers as well as the presuppositions of the interviewer's questions.

An Interview About Grades

An interview will be reproduced here to illustrate the mode of questioning in a qualitative research interview. An interview guide that combined explorative and hypothesis-testing approaches was prepared in advance. The interview was conducted before a class at a research workshop at Saybrook Institute, San Francisco, in 1987. Although the interview situation is artificial, it gives in a condensed form a fair picture of the semistructured interview form under discussion. The interview is reproduced virtually verbatim, with only a few minor changes in linguistic style.

SK: I will now attempt to demonstrate the mode of understanding in a qualitative research interview, and I need a volunteer. It will be a rather neutral topic, it's not a psychoanalytic depth interview. The interview will take about ten minutes and afterwards we will discuss it here.

A woman in her thirties volunteers.

SK 1: Thank you for your willingness to participate and be interviewed here. I have been studying the effects of grades in Europe for some years, and now I'm interested in the meaning of grades for American students and pupils.

I want to first ask you a maybe difficult question. If you'll try to remember back when you went to primary school, are you able to remember the first time you ever had any grades?

Student 1: I remember a time; but it might not have been the first time.

SK 2: Let's take that time. Can you tell me what happened?

Student 2: I did very well. I remember getting a red star on the top of my paper with 100; and that stands out in my memory as exciting and interesting.

SK 3: Yes. Is it only the red star that stands out, or what happened around it?

Student 3: [laughter] I remember the color very very well. It was shining. I remember getting rewarded all the way around. I remember being honored by my classmates and the teacher and my parents—them making a fuss. And some of the other kids not responding so well who didn't do so well. It was mixed emotions, but generally I remember the celebration aspect.

SK 4: You said mixed emotions. Are you able to describe them?

Student 4: Well, at that time I was the teacher's pet and some people would say, "Aha, maybe she didn't earn it, maybe it's just because the teacher likes her so well." And some kind of stratification occurring because I was not only the teacher's pet but I was maybe getting better grades and it created some kind of dissonance within my classmates' experience of me socially.

SK 5: Could you describe that dissonance?

Student 5: Well, I think there's always some kind of demarcation between students who do well and students who don't do as well, and that's determined, especially in the primary grades, by the number that you get on top of your paper.

SK 6: Was this early in school? Was it first grade?

Student 6: Third grade.

SK 7: Third grade. Well, that's a long time ago. Are you able to remember what they said? Or—

Student 7: No; it was more feeling—

SK 8: The feeling—

Student 8: Yeah, it was the feeling of, I'd put some space between me and the peer group—

SK 9: Because of your good grades.

Student 9: Yeah.

SK 10: Did you try to do anything about that?

Student 10: I didn't do so well after that. It really affected me in a large way. I wanted to be with them more than I wanted to be with the teacher, or on the teacher's good list. So it was significant.

SK 11: It was a significant experience— (Yes) —to you, and you got in a conflict between teacher and your peers, or you experienced it as a conflict. (Yes) Did your parents enter into the situation?

Student 11: Not that I recall, because it was—to me it was a significant alteration in how I experienced grades. To them it was maybe just a little bit less. But it was still satisfactory, still acceptable, and I was still rewarded in general terms for doing well and not failing. So that dichotomy was respected.

SK 12: That kind of dissonance between say loyalty to your teacher and the affection of the classmates, is that a situation you have been into other times? Does it remind you of—other—?

Student 12: It keeps repeating itself in my life, yes. Whenever I start taking my friends or my peer group for granted, I get some kind of message saying, Huh-uh, what's more important to me? And what's more important to me is my friendships.

SK 13: Um-hmm. That is the basic issue.
    You mentioned several times before "rewarded"—what do you mean by "rewarded"?

Student 13: Oh, getting to stay up to watch TV when I was in third grade, maybe; or getting to go some place or stay out later or maybe just getting ice cream, some food—

SK 14: So you got tangible rewards (Yes) for the grades? Did that make you learn more or was it more incidental?

Student 14: It made me want to do well, so it was—do better.

SK 15: I've heard some place about the term "grade money"—

Student 15: Grade?

SK 16: Money. That some people get "grade money."

Student 16: Oh, if they do well?

SK 17: Yes, did you ever get that?

Student 17: No. Only food! [laughter] Ice cream.

SK 18: There's a term called "wheedling" or "apple polishing." Or playing up to the teacher. Were you ever accused of that?

Student 18: Yes.

SK 19: You were. How did you take that?

Student 19: —No; it was upsetting, yes.

SK 20: The Danish pupils I've interviewed, they've also mentioned that conflict. They get good relations with the teacher and almost automatically other pupils may start saying it's wheedling — —
    — — —
    Let's see. If we jump ahead to—If you try to remember the last time you ever got a grade.

Student 20: Other than a Pass/Fail?

SK 21: Yes.

Student 21: I remember failing English in college! That was pretty traumatic. It meant I couldn't graduate with my class. Completely unexpected. It made me feel bad. But I wound up by taking the test over the phone with the teacher and finally graduating with my class, in undergraduate school. That was very sweet of them.

SK 22: There you were at the other end of the continuum.

Student 22: I had a lot of friends say so! [laughter]

SK 23: So there seems to be an almost ongoing conflict in both relation to the teacher and the relation to the classmates. And where is your own self? Is that pulling apart?

Student 23: I'm glad I don't have to deal with that any more.

SK 24: Yes. I can see that—

And asking more specifically about the learning process, did the fact that you were getting graded, did that have any influence on the way you learned?

Student 24: Yes; I was very worried about picking the right theme subject to write about and getting the right research, and right meaning not necessarily the best. So now [at Saybrook, a nonresidential Ph.D. program with only pass/fail evaluation] I'm taking more chances with writing essays, personal opinion essays. I think "Gee, let me try this, it might not be accepted, but I won't fail." This is a much more creative experience for me, and the risk-taking factor has expanded. There wasn't a lot of risk-taking when I knew I was going to get graded, 'cause I needed to get the confirmation of my peer group, talk about it, and make sure that it was in line with everybody else's. This experience is so individual and so nonthreatening that I'm more willing to take creative risks.

SK 25: Do I understand you correctly when I'm saying that your experience with the grading you had to play it safe, not to be too creative or take any risks? (Yes) Whereas with Pass/Fail, you are allowed to think creatively and take risks?

Student 25: Yeah. And in this situation [at Saybrook] in particular it's very difficult to compare and contrast with classmates who aren't very close, so it's a better situation.

SK 26: Okay.—Are there any more things you would want to say before we end the interview?

Student 26: No; I don't think so.

SK 27: Okay; thank you very much for your cooperation.

The interview was then discussed in class, including the following exchange:

SK 28: How did you experience being interviewed about it [the grades] up in front here?

Student 27: I thought it was a really good opportunity for me to explore that. I haven't even thought about it in a long time, but I knew from therapy that I've had recently that that was a big time in my life when I was closer to my teacher than I was to my friends and I've had to face that a lot. It was fun for me to talk about it 'cause I'm pretty clear about what happened.

The modes of questioning and the topics covered in this artificial demonstration interview about grades are representative of the 30 interviews on grades in Danish high schools discussed throughout this book. Few of the pupils, however, gave such rich and eloquent descriptions of their experiences with grades.

Knowledge Produced in the Interview. Several important aspects of the social effects of grading are evident in this short interview—primarily a pervasive loyalty conflict between teacher and peers; being a teacher's pet getting high grades created a dissonance in her classmates' experiences of her, it put a space between her and the peer group. This dissonance kept repeating itself in her life, with her friendships being the most important (Student 3 & 5). In the third grade this even led the student deliberately to seek lower grades in order not to be separated from her peers (Student 10). In a pass/fail evaluation system in the present Ph.D. program, she was relieved that this made it difficult to compare and contrast evaluations with classmates. Learning thereby became a more creative experience for the student, with more risk taking (Student 24).

In the interview guide, the meanings of grading were to be addressed from the three theoretical perspectives mentioned earlier—a

Rogerian, a Freudian, and a Skinnerian approach (Chapter 5, Design-ing). These were used as general approaches in this interview to investigate different aspects of the meanings of grades. Thus when the student described "mixed emotions" (3) and "it was more the feeling" (7), I sought, in line with a Rogerian approach, to encourage further elaboration of the feeling and the mixed emotions by repeating these very words (SK4 & 8). A Freudian approach in a broad sense was tried by asking, "Did your parents enter into the situation?" (SK 11) and, later, whether the loyalty conflict between teacher and pupils re-minded her of other situations (SK 12). The student's answer confirms that this keeps repeating itself in her life, but she does not bring up family relations. I here had in mind her grade-loyalty conflict as possibly reactivating childhood conflicts of jealousy and sibling rivalry for the affection of parents.

A Skinnerian reinforcement approach was pursued (SK 13) by probing the meaning of the student's term "rewarded" (3 & 11). The student then tells about being rewarded for good grades as a child by getting to stay up late to watch TV or by being given ice cream. Earlier in the interview the student (3) had mentioned reinforcements for good grades, such as being honored by her classmates, teacher, and parents. If this had not been a demonstration interview in front of a class, and had lasted longer, one or more of the three theoretical approaches would have been more extensively followed up.

The Interview Situation. In spite of the interview taking place in front of a class, the atmosphere was rather relaxed. One reason is the student's openness: She had volunteered, indicating thereby that she was not afraid of being interviewed in front of an audience; she had also been in therapy and was thus comfortable with talking about her personal experiences. And, as it turned out, the topic of the inter-view—grades—had had quite some personal impact on her school life.

My experience from previous interviews about grades made it relatively easy to listen to and follow up on significant themes about grades from the perspective of the student. I did, however, appear more influenced by the audience than the subject was, sometimes not following up important leads in the answers and not tolerating pauses (SK 20 & 24). I felt the topics here might be too sensitive to explore in front of the other students.

The interview was introduced by a briefing about the purpose and context of the interview before, and also at the start, of the interview (SK 1). It was rounded off by a debriefing—before ending the interview by asking if the student had anything more to say (SK 26), and after the interview by asking her about her experience of the interview (SK 28).

Question Types. The application of some of the question types outlined in Table 7.1 from (A) through (I) will now be pointed out. The introductory question, asking about a specific episode of grading (SK 1/A), hit home, and the first two thirds of the interview were mainly a following up (B) of the student's answer (2) about the "red star." The term was a "red light" signaling that I stop and probe; the very word, and probably also her tone of the voice and facial expression, had indicated that this was a symbol of some significant experience. The follow-up question, repeating the term "red star" (SK 3/B), led to an emotional response rich in information (Student 3).

Continued probing, repeating another significant expression— "mixed emotions"—and probing for further description (SK 4/B & C) opened up a basic conflict for the subject between loyalty to the teacher or to her peers. This topic was pursued in the following sequence until the concluding student (12) remark, "And what's more important to me is my friendships." In some of the answers in this sequence I overheard potentially significant expressions like "demarcation" and "space" (Student 5 & 8), and instead of following them up posed specifying (SK 6/D) and interpreting (SK 9/I) questions.

I then "went back" in the interview and repeated a term introduced by the student that was of theoretical interest to me—"rewarded"— and asked for its meaning (SK 13/B & C). This led to a concrete answer about ice cream and TV as rewards, whereas a direct follow-up question about receiving money for grades (SK 15/E) gave no confirmation.

Then for the first time since the opening question I turned to the interview guide and posed a direct question about whether the student had been accused of wheedling (SK 18/E). This was confirmed by the student (18 & 19) but in such a tense way that I chose not to follow up and attempted a consoling remark (SK 20). The subject did not expand on the situation, and there was a pause whereupon I changed the topic by asking about a recent grading episode. I sought to follow up on the answers (Student 20-22) with an interpretation in the direction of the loyalty conflict (SK 23/I), but this time was politely put off by a "double entendre" remark by the student (23): "I am glad I don't have to deal with that anymore." A second topic from the interview guide about learning and grading (SK 24/E) was then introduced, and this opened to a long student (24) answer about grades as suppressing creativity and risk taking, which again led into the loyalty conflict described extensively earlier in the interview.

The majority of questions in this interview were probing (C)—often by repeating significant words from the student's answers to a few direct questions about episodes and effects of grading. There were a few interpreting questions, such as the meaning-clarifying question, "Do I understand you correctly when I'm saying that you experience with the grading you had to play it safe, . . ." (SK 25/I), which is followed by a confirmation and further elaboration (Student 25). Earlier in the interview, a direct interpretation of the student's statement (8) as "Because of your good grades" (SK 9/I) was immediately confirmed, "Yeah" (Student 9).

Extensive interpretations and follow-ups checking the reliability of the answers and testing of hypotheses were not undertaken in this interview. This was due to the short time, to the social situation in front of the class, and to the sensitivity of the subject to some of the topics raised. This interview therefore does not live up to the ideal requirements posed earlier of being interpreted, validated, and communicated by the time the tape recorder is shut off. In Chapter 8 I will address some of the factors contributing to the quality of an interview.

8

The Quality of the Interview

In the first parts of this chapter I will address issues of quality in interview research. Criteria for evaluating the quality of a research interview are suggested and related to characteristics of the interviewees and the interviewers. An interview by Hamlet is then presented as an illustration of problems that may arise when using fixed criteria for appraising the quality of an interview. Thereafter, the moral quality of an interview is discussed in relation to ethical research guidelines, and finally, a common objection to the scientific quality of an interview is addressed—the question of leading questions.

Interview Quality

The interview is the raw material for the later process of meaning analysis. The quality of the original interview is decisive for the quality of the later analysis, verification, and reporting of the interviews.

Of the six quality criteria for an interview depicted in Box 8.1, the last three in particular refer to an ideal interview—requiring that the meaning of what is said is interpreted, verified, and communicated by the time the tape recorder is turned off. This demands craftsmanship and expertise and presupposes that the interviewer knows what he or she is interviewing about, as well as why and how. Although such quality criteria might seem to be unreachable ideals, they can serve as guidelines.

Box 8.1

Quality Criteria for an Interview

- The extent of spontaneous, rich, specific, and relevant answers from the interviewee.

- The shorter the interviewer's questions and the longer the subjects' answers, the better.

- The degree to which the interviewer follows up and clarifies the meanings of the relevant aspects of the answers.

- The ideal interview is to a large extent interpreted throughout the interview.

- The interviewer attempts to verify his or her interpretations of the subject's answers in the course of the interview.

- The interview is "self-communicating"—it is a story contained in itself that hardly requires much extra descriptions and explanations.

The three interviews in Chapter 2 live up to the quality criteria suggested here in different ways. Thus the interview reported by Giorgi has brief questions and long answers; it provides rich and spontaneous relevant answers about learning in everyday life, and the answers are followed up and clarified. In the session reported by Rogers the counselor follows up and clarifies the meanings of the client's answers, and at the end the client herself spontaneously interprets the meaning of the interaction. In the third example, Socrates critically interprets the meanings and contradictions of Agathon's statements about love and beauty, and concludes by constructing a logical chain of arguments, the validity of which Agathon ends up accepting. All three interviews are in one respect self-communicating— they convey important knowledge as they stand, and they also open to further interpretations.

These quality criteria are not without exceptions. At a workshop, one participant told about an unsuccessful interview she had conducted with a young author at a "writing school." The topic was the author's own writing process; the contact during the interview had, however, been poor, and the author's statements were fragmented and superficial. There were no coherent stories and descriptions, the interviewer could not find any unity or deeper meaning in the answers. The resulting interview appeared worthless to her. Then she ventured the information that the author had told her that he was trying to be a postmodern author. From this perspective, the fragmentation, the incoherence, and the surface statements that abstain from deeper interpretations of meaning need not be due to a poor interview technique, but stem from the very topic—writing literature—with the interviewee playing the role of a postmodern author.

The Interview Subject

Some interview subjects appear to be better than others. Good interviewees are cooperative and well motivated, they are eloquent and knowledgeable. They are truthful and consistent, they give concise and precise answers to the interviewer's questions, they provide coherent accounts and do not continually contradict themselves, they stick to the interview topic and do not repeatedly wander off. Good subjects can give long and lively descriptions of their life situation, they tell capturing stories well suited for reporting. The subjects of the learning interview reported by Giorgi and of the interview on grades were both good interview subjects according to these criteria.

As pleasant as such interview subjects may appear to the interviewer, it is by no means a given that they provide the most valuable knowledge about the research topics in question. The above idealized subject appears rather similar to an upper-middle-class intellectual whose views are not necessarily representative of the general population. Well-polished eloquence and coherency may in some instances gloss over more contradictory relations to the research themes.

The ideal interview subject does not exist—different persons are suitable for different types of interviews, such as providing accurate witness observations, versus giving sensitive accounts of personal experiences and emotional states, versus telling capturing stories. The subjects of the three interviews in Chapter 2 were thus all good subjects with respect to different purposes—Agathon providing logical contradictions for Socrates to clarify; the therapeutic client living out, and learning from, the emotional nature of the therapeutic relationship; and the woman learning interior decorating giving rich, spontaneous descriptions of learning in everyday life.

Recognizing that some people may be harder to interview than others, it remains the task of the interviewer to motivate and facilitate the subjects' accounts and to obtain interviews rich in knowledge from virtually every subject.

Interviewer Qualifications

The interviewer is him- or herself the research instrument. A good interviewer is an expert in the topic of the interview as well as in human interaction. The interviewer must continually make quick choices about what to ask and how; which aspects of a subject's answer to follow up—and which not; which answers to interpret—and which not. Interviewers should be knowledgeable in the topics investigated, master conversational skills, and be proficient in language with an ear for their subjects' linguistic style. The interviewer should have a sense for good stories and be able to assist the subjects in the unfolding of their narratives.

Learning to become an interviewer takes place through interviewing. Reading books may give some guidelines, but practice remains the main road to mastering the craft of interviewing. This involves reading interviews, listening to interview tapes, and watching more experienced interviewers, but learning is primarily through one's own experience with interviewing. An interviewer's self-confidence is acquired through practice; conducting several pilot interviews before the actual project interviews will increase his or her ability to create safe and stimulating interactions.

Role playing can be included in pilot interviews for the purpose of training, with subjects playing such roles as the Tacit Oyster, the Nonstop Talker, the Intellectualizing Academician, and the Power Player who tries to take control of the interview.

Box 8.2 outlines some criteria for interviewer qualifications that may lead to good interviews in the sense of producing rich knowledge and doing justice to the ethical demand of creating a beneficial situation for the subjects.

Recall once more the three interviews in Chapter 2. The interviewer inquiring about interior decorating poses clear questions, is gentle and open to what is said, follows up sensitively, and steers the interview

---

Box 8.2

Qualification Criteria for the Interviewer

1. *Knowledgeable:* Has an extensive knowledge of the interview theme, can conduct an informed conversation about the topic; being familiar with its main aspects the interviewer will know what issues are important to pursue, without attempting to shine with his or her extensive knowledge.

2. *Structuring:* Introduces a purpose for the interview, outlines the procedure in passing, and rounds off the interview by, for example, briefly telling what was learned in the course of the conversation and asking whether the interviewee has any questions concerning the situation.

3. *Clear:* Poses clear, simple, easy, and short questions; speaks distinctly and understandably, does not use academic language or professional jargon. The exception is in a stress interview: Then the questions can be complex and ambiguous, with the subjects' answers revealing their reactions to stress.

4. *Gentle:* Allows subjects to finish what they are saying, lets them proceed at their own rate of thinking and speaking. Is easy-going, tolerates pauses, indicates that it is acceptable to put forward unconventional and provocative opinions and to treat emotional issues.

in the direction of what she wants to know about the learning experience. The therapeutic interviewer is gentle and safe, allows the

---

Box 8.2 Continued

5. *Sensitive:* Listens actively to the content of what is said, hears the many nuances of meaning in an answer, and seeks to get the nuances of meaning described more fully. The interviewer is empathic, listens to the emotional message in what is said, not only hearing what is said but also how it is said, and notices as well what is not said. The interviewer feels when a topic is too emotional to pursue in the interview.

6. *Open:* Hears which aspects of the interview topic are important for the interviewee. Listens with an evenly hovering attention, is open to new aspects that can be introduced by the interviewee, and follows them up.

7. *Steering:* Knows what he or she wants to find out: is familiar with the purpose of the interview, what it is important to acquire knowledge about. The interviewer controls the course of the interview and is not afraid of interrupting digressions from the interviewee.

8. *Critical:* Does not take everything that is said at face value, but questions critically to test the reliability and validity of what the interviewees tell. This critical checking can pertain to the observational evidence of the interviewee's statements as well as to their logical consistency.

9. *Remembering:* Retains what a subject has said during the interview, can recall earlier statements and ask to have them elaborated, and can relate what has been said during different parts of the interview to each other.

10. *Interpreting:* Manages throughout the interview to clarify and extend the meanings of the interviewee's statements; provides interpretations of what is said, which may then be disconfirmed or confirmed by the interviewee.

client to state her emotional critique of himself, is sensitive to what the client says, and reflects it back to her with a mild degree of interpretation. Socrates structures his interview by starting with Agathon's speech and stating the purpose of his questioning about the nature of love; he then steers his opponent through relentless questioning, remembers well Agathon's earlier answers, interprets contradictions in and among the answers, and critically questions their logic on the basis of his own thorough conceptual knowledge of love and beauty.

The brief interview passage on talkativity and grades (Chapter 1, Conversation as Research) can also be mentioned. By bringing up an answer from earlier in the interview and asking in an open way, the interviewer obtains two interesting pupil hypotheses about a connection between how much a pupil talks and his grades as well as between agreement with a teacher's opinions and grades. The interviewer does not take the statements at face value, but follows up first by questioning the postulated connection in an open, rather naive way, and then in a second question openly disputes the connection, with the pupil who still holds to his own offering to provide examples of his postulate.

In spite of such criteria as those given in Box 8.2, there are no absolute standards for interviewer qualifications. In interviews in which the topic really matters, the above technical rules and criteria may lose relevance in face of the existential importance of the interview topic. With extensive practice in different interview forms and with different subjects, an experienced interviewer might go beyond technical recommendations and criteria, and—sometimes—deliberately disregard or break the rules.

One example of breaking rules in the interest of good interviewing took place at an interview workshop. The participants were divided into groups in which one of the group members interviewed another. The instruction to the interviewers was to explore the meaning of authority for the subjects. All but one group returned to the plenary session with lively positive reports. The negative experience came from a group where the interviewer had been demanding, hostile, and aloof and had continually interrupted the interviewee's answers, breaking most of the above criteria for good interviewing, with the result that his group returned disintegrated and angry. The interviewer's explanation of his bad behavior was simple—instead of asking about the meaning of authority, he had played the role of an authoritarian interviewer, thereby obtaining a rich spectrum of spontaneous interviewee reactions to the phenomenon of authority.

Hamlet's Interview

There are no definite criteria for evaluating the quality of an interview. An example from literature may show how the appraisal of an interview technique depends on the purpose and the content of the interview.

Hamlet: Do you see yonder cloud that's almost in shape of a camel?

Polonius: By th' mass, and 'tis like a camel indeed.

Hamlet: Methinks it is like a weasel.

Polonius: It is back'd like a weasel.

Hamlet: Or like a whale?

Polonius: Very like a whale.

Hamlet: . . . (Aside) They fool me to the top of my bent.
  (*Hamlet,* act III, scene 2)

A first comment on the quality of this interview concerns its length. Hamlet's interview is brief. The seven lines are, however, dense and rich enough to be the subject of more lengthy comments. In contrast, current research interviews are often too long and filled with idle chatter. If one knows what to ask for, why one is asking, and how to ask, one can conduct short interviews rich in meaning.

The quality of Hamlet's interview technique depends on how the interview is interpreted. This short passage gives rise to several interpretations. At first glance the interview is an example of an unreliable technique—by using three leading questions Hamlet leads Polonius to give three entirely different answers. The interview thus does not yield any reproducible, reliable knowledge about the *shape of the cloud* in question.

At a second glance, the topic of the interview might change: The figure in question is no longer the cloud, but the *personality of Polonius,* his trustworthiness. The interview then provides reliable, thrice-checked knowledge about Polonius as an unreliable person—to all three questions his answers are led by Hamlet's questions. With the change in the purpose and the topic of the interview the leading questions do not produce unreliable knowledge, but become a sophisticated, indirect, interview technique.

Hamlet's interview then approximates the threefold ideal of being interpreted, validated, and communicated by the end of the interview. By repeating the question in different versions and each time getting the "same" indirect answer about Polonius's personality, the interview is "self-interpreted" before Hamlet closes off with his aside interpretation: "They fool me to the top of my bent." As to the second requirement—verification—few interview researchers today repeat so consistently as Hamlet a question in different versions to test the reliability of the answers. Regarding the third requirement—communication—the short interview has been carried out so well that it speaks for itself. I would think that, when watching the play, the audience would generally experience a Gestalt switch from cloud shape to personal credibility as the interview topic even before Hamlet gives his aside conclusion.

So far, I have discussed Hamlet's interview isolated from its context, its position in the broader drama. At a third glance the interview appears as a display of the *power relations* at a royal court. The prince demonstrates his power to make a courtier say anything he wants. Or, the courtier demonstrates his mode of managing the power relations at the court. In an earlier scene in the play, Polonius himself gave a lesson in what in current textbooks of method is called an indirect, funnel-shaped, interview technique. Polonius requests a messenger going to Paris to inquire into the behavior of his son studying music in the city. The messenger is instructed to start with a broad approach: "Enquire me first what Danskers are in Paris" and then gradually to advance the subject, to end up with suggesting such vices as drinking, quarreling, and visiting brothels, where "Your bait of falsehood take this carp of truth," concluding the lesson, "By indirections find directions out" (*Hamlet,* act II, scene 1). When Polonius is that well versed in indirect questioning techniques, is he actually caught by Hamlet's questioning technique? Or does he see through the scheme and play up to Hamlet as a courtier?

A central theme of the play, which was written at the transition from the medieval to the modern age, is a questioning of reality; not just a suspicion of the motives of others, but also a preoccupation with the frail nature of reality. Hamlet's interview may in that case be seen as an illustration of a *pervasive doubt about the appearance of the world,* including the shape of a cloud and the personalities of fellow players.

From an ethical perspective, the evaluation of Hamlet's interview again depends on the interpretation of its purpose and content. In the first reading, the leading questions merely lead to unreliable knowledge of the shape of the cloud. In the second reading, the interview entails the deliberate deception of Polonius; there is no question of informed consent, and the consequences may be a matter of life and death for the protagonists. An ethics of principles is here overruled by a utilitarian interest in survival.

In conclusion, the quality of the knowledge obtained by Hamlet's interview, as well as the ethical evaluation of the interview, depends on the interpretation of the purpose and the topic of the interview. Some further issues of ethics and of leading questions will now be addressed more specifically. Neither are mere technical problems: They raise basic questions as to the nature of the human interaction in the interview and the reality the interview is about.

The Ethics of Interviewing

The moral qualities of an interview are here first addressed with regard to the ethical guidelines of informed consent, confidentiality, and consequences. Thereafter, comparisons with therapeutic interviews will serve to emphasize some of the ethical issues involved in research interviews.

Informed Consent. Through briefing and debriefing, the subjects should be informed about the purpose and the procedure of the interview. When it comes to later use of the interview it may be preferable to have a written agreement, signed by both interviewer and subject, thereby obtaining the informed consent of the interviewee to participate in the study and allow future use of the interviews. This may include information about confidentiality and who will have access to the interview; the researcher's right to publish the whole interview or parts of it; and the interviewee's possible right to see the transcription and the interpretations. In most cases such issues may not matter much to the subjects interviewed, but if the investigation should treat or instigate issues of conflict, particularly within institutional settings, a written agreement may serve as a protection for both the interviewees and the researcher.

Confidentiality. The qualitative research interview involves different ethical issues than those of a standardized questionnaire or a therapeutic conversation. Confidentiality in these cases is assured by the computed averages in survey responses and by the closed doors of the therapist's office. It is more problematic in a research interview. Confidentiality issues involved in transcribing and reporting interviews will be addressed in later chapters (Chapter 9, Transcribing Interviews; Chapter 14, Ethics of Reporting).

Consequences. The consequences for the interviewees concern the situation itself as well as later effects of participating in the interviews. In the *grading study* the general benefits of the investigation appeared unproblematic, no harms were foreseen for the pupils interviewed, and more knowledge about the effects of grades was considered to be in their own interests. There were, however, some problematic consequences for the subjects. The Danish pupils appeared rather embarrassed when describing their own relation to certain forms of grading behavior, such as competition about, and wheedling for, good grades (see also the interview on grades, Chapter 7, An Interview About Grades). At such points their accounts often became general and vague; for research purposes it would have been desirable to probe more intensively and critically in order to obtain reliable knowledge about such grade-affected behaviors. This was not done out of concern for the pupils' well-being; when consenting to be interviewed, they had not been told that they might be questioned about topics that could be penible to themselves or might involve changes in their self-concept.

Research and Therapeutic Interviews. Some consequences of a research interview can be highlighted by a comparison with therapeutic interviews. Although the research interviewer can learn much from therapeutic interviews, it is important to distinguish between the two types. The main goal in therapy is change in the patient; in research it is the acquisition of knowledge. A research interviewer's ability to listen attentively may, however, in some cases lead to quasi-therapeutic relationships, for which most research interviewers have neither the training nor the time. A research interview can come to approximate a therapeutic interview, depending on the extent, the topic, and the subjects of the interview. A quasi-therapeutic relationship may be promoted through long and repeated interviews with the same subject, where a close personal rapport may develop. If the interview topics involve strongly personal and emotional issues, they may in some cases bring forth deeper personal problems requiring therapeutic assistance. Emotionally unstable subjects, more or less consciously seeking the advice of a professional, may attempt to turn a research interview into personal therapy.

Any possibility that an interview situation might come close to a therapeutic relationship should be taken into account when designing the study. This can be done by seeing to it that the interviews do not promote a therapeutic relation. If sensitive issues and subjects are involved in an interview study, arrangements might be made with a therapist to serve as a "backup" for dealing with personal problems that might be brought up by the interviews.

In some cases it may be possible to give interview subjects a fair return for their services. One such study concerned the transition of mental patients from living in a state hospital to living under normal circumstances in the city of Aarhus. For their combined master's thesis, three psychology students conducted intensive personal interviews with the patients during the transition period, and in return organized a consultation group to facilitate the patients' transition to normal living situations. In some cases, such as in therapeutic research, it may thus be possible to exchange therapy for information, to offer benefits that may alleviate troubles the interviewees may have had.

A suspicious attitude toward the subjects' statements, as in Hamlet's interview, has also been common in some forms of psychological interview research and may be based in a therapeutic frame of reference. In therapy it is ethical to be skeptical of what patients say: They are at a loss about the meaning and purpose of their life and go to a therapist for help in learning what they really mean and want. In contrast to the therapeutic interview, where a suspicious attitude toward the patients' statements may be part of an implicit therapeutic contract, using concealed techniques and interpreting meanings implying a distrust of the subjects' motives in a research interview would raise ethical problems.

When a researcher makes interpretations going beyond the self-understanding of the interviewees, a series of issues are raised: Should subjects be confronted with interpretations of themselves, which they may not have asked for? During the interview? In the course of the analysis of the interviews? When reporting the interviews? And what should be done about disagreements between the subject's and the researcher's interpretations of a theme? In therapy the answer to such questions is relatively simple: Patients have sought therapy and they are paying the therapist to help them change, involving often painful changes in self-understanding and that may take place in a dialogue that continues over many years. In psychoanalysis, the working through of the patient's resistance to the therapist's interpretations is an essential part of the therapeutic process. In research, however, it is the interviewer who has sought out the interviewees; they have not asked for interpretations leading to fundamental changes in the way they understand themselves and their world. To emphasize the point: In therapy it may be unethical if the therapeutic conversations the patient has asked for, and often paid highly for, do not lead to new insights or emotional changes. But in a research interview, which the interviewee has not asked for, it may be unethical to instigate new self-interpretations or emotional changes.

An inherent contradiction between pursuing scientific knowledge and ethically respecting the integrity of the interviewee is illustrated in the following example (see Fog, 1992). As a therapist conducting research interviews, Fog addresses the dilemma of the researcher wanting the interview to be as deep and probing as possible, with the risk of trespassing on the person, but on the other hand to be as respectful of the interviewed person as possible and thereby risk getting empirical material that only scratches the surface. She mentions a woman who repeatedly and energetically tells the interviewer how happy she is in her marriage. The woman also gives many verbal and nonverbal signals denying the happiness and reports situations where she is angry about the marriage. The information obtained in the interview is thus ambiguous and puts the interviewer in a difficult situation between scientific and ethical considerations. Should she leave the woman's version uncommented, or should she follow her own hunch that the woman is denying the realities of the marriage and probe further and point out to the woman the many inconsistencies and contradictions in what she tells about her marriage? A consequence of the latter could be a radical challenge of the woman's understanding of herself and her marriage. This would have been part of an implicit contract in a therapeutic interview, but it is definitely beyond the contract of a normal research interview and was not attempted in this case.

Leading Questions

The most frequently asked question about interview studies today probably concerns the effects of leading questions. The issue is sometimes raised in the form of a question such as: "Can the interview results not be due to leading questions?" The very form of the question involves a liar's paradox—an answer of "Yes, this is a serious danger" may be due to the suggestive formulation of the question leading to this answer. And a "No, this is not the case" may demonstrate that leading questions are not that powerful.

It is a well-documented finding that even a slight rewording of a question in a questionnaire or in the interrogation of eye witnesses may influence the answer. When the results of public opinion polls are published, the proponents of a political party receiving low support are usually quick to find biases in the wording of the poll's questions. In a psychological experiment on witness reliability, different subjects were shown the same film of two cars colliding and were then asked about the cars' speed. The average speed estimate in reply to the question "About how fast were the cars going when they smashed into each other?" was 41 mph. Other subjects—seeing the same film, but with *smashed* replaced by *contacted* in the question above—gave an average speed estimate of 32 mph (Loftus & Palmer, 1974). Politicians are well experienced in warding off leading questions from reporters; but if leading questions are posed to subjects who are easily suggestible, such as small children, research findings may be invalidated, a key issue in the current focus on child abuse.

Although the wording of a question can inadvertently shape the content of an answer, it is often overlooked that leading questions are also necessary parts of many questioning procedures; their use depends on the topic and purpose of the investigation. Leading questions may be deliberately posed by interrogators to obtain information they suspect is being withheld. The burden of denial is then put on the subject, as with the question, "When did you stop beating your wife?" Police officers and lawyers also systematically apply leading questions to test the consistency and reliability of a person's statements. In the Rorschach personality test, leading questions are employed by the psychologist to "test the limits" for specific forms of perceiving the ambiguous ink blots. In Piaget's interviews with children about their understanding of physical concepts, questions leading in wrong directions were used to test the strength of the child's concept of, for example, weight. In Socrates' dialogue on love, he repeatedly employed such leading questions as "Surely you would say . . . would you not?" with the intention of exposing the contradictions of Agathon's understanding of love and beauty.

The qualitative research interview is particularly well suited for employing leading questions to check repeatedly the reliability of the interviewees' answers, as well as to verify the interviewer's interpretations. Thus, contrary to popular opinion, leading questions do not always reduce the reliability of interviews, but may enhance it; rather than being used too much, deliberately leading questions are today probably applied too little in qualitative research interviews.

It should be noted that not only may the questions preceding an answer be leading, but the interviewer's own verbal and bodily responses following an answer can act as positive or negative reinforcers for the answer given and thereby influence the subject's answers to further questions. The technical issue of using leading questions in an interview has been rather overemphasized, but the leading effects of project-based research questions have received less attention. Recall the different kinds of answers obtained by a Rogerian, Freudian, and

Skinnerian approach in the imaginary interview on teasing (Chapter 5, Thematizing). A project's orienting research questions determine what kind of answers may be obtained. The task is, again, not to avoid leading research questions, but to recognize the primacy of the question and attempt to make the orienting questions explicit, thereby providing the reader with the possibility of evaluating their influence on the research findings and of assessing the validity of the findings.

The fact that the issue of leading questions has received so much attention in interview research may be due to a naive empiricism. There may be a belief in a neutral observational access to an objective social reality independent of the investigator, implying that an interviewer collects verbal responses like a botanist collects plants in nature or a miner unearths precious buried metals. In an alternative view, which follows from a postmodern perspective on knowledge construction, the interview is a conversation in which the data arise in an interpersonal relationship, coauthored and coproduced by interviewer and interviewee. The decisive issue is then not whether to lead or not to lead, but where the interview questions should lead, and whether they will lead in important directions, producing new, trustworthy, and interesting knowledge.

9

From Speech to Text

Before turning to the analysis of the knowledge constructed in the interview interaction, I will address the transcription of interviews. Rather than being a simple clerical task, transcription is itself an interpretative process. Whereas the interaction of the interview situation has been extensively treated in the literature on method, the translation from oral conversations to written texts has received less attention. This chapter addresses the procedures for making interview conversations accessible to analysis—taping the oral interview interaction, transcribing the tapes into written texts, and the use of computer programs to assist the analysis of the interviews. The practical problems of transcription raise theoretical issues about the differences between oral and written language, which leads to the rather neglected position of language in interview research.

Recording Interviews

Methods of recording interviews for documentation and later analysis include audiotape recording, videotape recording, note taking, and remembering. The usual way of recording interviews today is with a *tape recorder*. The interviewer can then concentrate on the topic and the dynamics of the interview. The words and their tone, pauses, and the like, are recorded in a permanent form that can be returned to again and again for relistening. The audiotape gives a decontextualized version of the interview, however: It does not include the visual aspects of the situation, neither the setting nor the facial and bodily expressions of the participants.

A *videotape recorder* will encompass the visual aspects of the interview. With the inclusion of facial expressions and bodily posture, a videotape provides richer contexts for interpretations than does audiotape. Video recordings offer a unique opportunity for analyzing the interpersonal interaction in an interview, an aspect that has led to extensive use of videos in research on, and training for, therapy.

The wealth of information makes videotape analysis a time-consuming process. For most interview projects, particularly those with many interviews and where the main interest is the content of what is said, video recordings may be too cumbersome for analysis. A video is useful for the training of interviewers, making them aware of their facial and bodily expressions during an interview that could either inhibit or promote communication. The same is true of subtle ways of reinforcing specific types of answers by nods, smiles, and bodily postures that the interviewer may not be aware of and that are not recorded on the audiotape.

It should be noted that the inclusion of the visual setting does not solve the issue of an objective representation of the interview situation. Researchers who use videotape recordings are today rather sensitive to the constructive natures of their documentation, which are products of the researcher's many choices of angles and framing, as well as the sequence of shots (see, e.g., Harel & Papert, 1991).

An interview may also be recorded through a reflected use of the researcher's subjectivity and *remembering,* relying on his or her empathy and memory and then writing down the main aspects of the interview after the session, sometimes assisted by notes taken during the interview. There are obvious limitations to a reliance on memory for interview analysis, such as the rapid forgetting of details and the influence of a selective memory. The interviewer's immediate memory will, however, include the visual information of the situation as well as the social atmosphere and personal interaction, which to a large extent is lost in the audiotape recording. The interviewer's active listening and remembering may ideally also work as a selective filter, retaining those very meanings that are essential for the topic and purpose of the study.

While remembering is today often decried as a subjective method replete with biases, it should not be overlooked that the main empirical basis of psychoanalytic theory came from the therapist's empathic listening to and remembering of therapeutic interviews. Freud developed his psychoanalytical theory at a time when tape recorders did not exist. He refrained from taking notes during the therapeutic hours and listened with an even-hovering attention, attended to the meaning of what was said, and first made notes after the therapeutic session (Freud, 1963). This form of recollection is based on active listening during the situation; it requires sensitivity and training, which interview researchers today may forgo, treating the tapes and transcripts as their real data. One might speculate that if tape recorders had existed in Freud's time, psychoanalytical theory might not have developed beyond infinite series of verbatim quotes from the patients, and psychoanalysis might today have remained confined to a small Viennese sect of psychoanalysts lost in a chaos of tapes and transcriptions from their therapies.

Taping. In the present context, the most common method of recording interviews today—audiotape recording and subsequent transcription—will be treated more extensively. The first requirement for transcribing a recorded interview is that it was in fact recorded. Some interviewers have painful memories of an exceptional interview where nothing got on the tape due to technical faults or, most often, human error. The interviewer may have been so caught by the newness and complexities of the interview situation that he or she simply forgot to turn the recorder on, or a special interview may have been so engaging that any thought of technicalities was lost.

A second requirement for transcription is that the conversation on the tape is audible. A good tape recorder and microphone are basic requirements. So is finding a room without background noise such as voices in neighboring rooms and heavy outside traffic. To secure good recording quality it is necessary that the microphone is close enough to both participants; that the interviewer is not afraid to ask a mumbling interviewee to speak up; and that the transcriber's coming work is kept in mind, for example by avoiding coffee cups and the like hitting the table, sending bolts of thunder into the transcriber's ears (see Yow [1994] and Poland [1995] for more extensive treatments of the recording quality of interviews).

Transcription Reliability and Validity

Interviews are today seldom analyzed directly from tape recordings. The usual procedure for analyzing is to have the taped interviews transcribed into written texts. Although this seems like an apparently simple and reasonable procedure, transcriptions involve a series of methodical and theoretical problems. For example, once the interview transcriptions are made, they tend to be regarded as *the* solid empirical data in the interview project. The transcripts are, however, not the rock-bottom data of interview research, they are artificial constructions from an oral to a written mode of communication. Every transcription from one context to another involves a series of judgments and decisions. I will introduce the constructive nature of transcripts by taking a closer look at their reliability and validity.

Reliability. Questions of interviewer reliability in interview research are frequently raised. Yet in contrast to sociolinguistic research, transcriber reliability is rarely mentioned for social science interviews. Technically regarded, it is an easy check to have two persons independently type the same passage of a taped interview, and then have a computer program list and count the number of words that differ between the two transcriptions, thus providing a quantified reliability check.

The interpretational character of transcription is evident from the two transcripts of the same tape recording in Table 9.1. The words that are different in the two transcriptions are italicized. The transcriptions were made by two psychologists who were instructed to transcribe as accurately as possible. Still, the transcribers adopted different styles: Transcriber A appears to write more verbatim, includes more words, and seems to guess more than transcriber B, who records only what is clear and distinct, and who also produces a more coherent written style. The most marked discrepancy between the two is rendering the interviewer's question as "because you don't get grades?" versus "of course you don't like grades?" It thereby becomes ambiguous what the subject's answer—"Yes, I think that's true . . ."—refers to.

The quality of transcriptions can be improved by clear instructions about the procedures and purposes of the transcriptions, preferably accompanied by a reliability check. Yet even with detailed typing

TABLE 9.1 Two Transcriptions of the Same Interview Passage

Transcription A:

I: And are you also saying *because* you don't *get* grades? *Is that true?*

S: Yes, I think that's true because if I got grades I would work toward the grade as opposed to working toward . . . *umm,* expanding what I know, or, pushing *a limit* back *in myself or, something* . . . contributing new ideas . . .

Transcription B:

I: And are you also saying *that of course* you don't *like* grades?

S: Yes, I think that's true, because if I got grades I would work toward the grade as opposed to working toward expanding what I know or pushing *those limits* back . . . (tape unclear) contributing new ideas.

---

instructions it may be difficult for two transcribers to reach full agreement on what was said. Listening again to the tape might show that some of the differences are due to poor recording quality and mishearing. Other differences, which are of interest from an inter-relational perspective, may not be unequivocally solved, as for example: Where does a sentence end? Where is there a pause? How long is a silence before it becomes a pause in a conversation? Does a specific pause belong to the subject or to the interviewer? And if the emotional aspects of the conversation are included, for instance "tense voice," "giggling," "nervous laughter," and so on, the intersubjective reliability of the transcription could develop into a research project of its own.

Validity. Ascertaining the validity of the interview transcripts is more complex than assuring their reliability. The issue of what a valid transcription is may be exemplified by two different transcriptions of a story told by a 7-year-old Afro-American pupil (see Table 9.2). The two transcriptions are from a segment of a longer story from a classroom exercise, transcribed by two different researchers and discussed by Mishler (1991). Transcript A is a verbatim rendering of the oral form of the story; the school teacher found the whole story disconnected and rambling, not living up to acceptable criteria of coherence and language use. Transcript B is an idealized realization of the same story passage, retranscribed into a poetic form by a researcher familiar with the linguistic practices of black oral style.

TABLE 9.2 Two Transcriptions of Leona's Story of Her Puppy

Transcription A:

. . . and then my puppy came / he was asleep / and he was—he was /
he tried to get up / and he ripped my pants / and he dropped the oatmeal—
all over him / and / my father came / and he said

. . .

Transcription B:

an' then my puppy came
    he was asleep
    he tried to get up
    an' he ripped my pants
    an' he dropped the oatmeal all over him
an' my father came
    an' he said

. . .

SOURCE: From Mishler (1991).

Here the story appears as a literary tour de force, yielding a remarkable narrative. Neither transcription is more objective than the other; they are, rather, different written constructions from the same oral passage: "Different transcripts are constructions of different worlds, each designed to fit our particular theoretical assumptions and to allow us to explore their implications" (Mishler, 1991, p. 271).

Transcribing involves translating from an oral language, with its own set of rules, to a written language with another set of rules. Transcripts are not copies or representations of some original reality, they are interpretative constructions that are useful tools for given purposes. Transcripts are decontextualized conversations, they are abstractions, as topographical maps are abstractions from the original landscape from which they are derived. Maps emphasize some aspects of the countryside and omit others, the selection of features depending on the intended use. Maps of the same topographical area for purposes of driving, aviation, agriculture, and mining will tend to be rather different. An objective map representing, for example, the island of Greenland does not exist: The shape depends on the selected mode of projection from a curved to a flat plane, which again depends on the intended use of the map.

Correspondingly, the question "What is the correct transcription?" cannot be answered—there is no true, objective transformation from the oral to the written mode. A more constructive question is: "What is a useful transcription for my research purposes?" Thus verbatim descriptions are necessary for linguistic analyses; the inclusion of pauses, repetitions, and tone of voice are relevant for psychological interpretations of, for example, level of anxiety or the meaning of denials. Transforming the conversation into a literary style facilitates communication of the meaning of the subject's stories to readers.

Oral and Written Language

By neglecting issues of transcription, the interview researcher's road to hell becomes paved with transcripts. The interview is an evolving conversation between two people. The transcriptions are frozen in time and abstracted from their base in a social interaction. The lived face-to-face conversation becomes fixated into transcripts. A transcript is a transgression, a transformation of one narrative mode—oral discourse—into another narrative mode—written discourse. To *trans*scribe means to *trans*form, to change from one form to another. Attempts at verbatim interview transcriptions produce hybrids, artificial constructs that are adequate to neither the lived oral conversation nor the formal style of written texts. Transcriptions are translations from one language to another; what is said in the hermeneutical tradition of translators also pertains to transcribers: *traduire traittori*—translators are traitors.

The different rhetorical forms of oral and written language are frequently overlooked during the transcription of social science interviews; one exception is Poland (1995). Recognizing the socially constructed nature of the transcript, he discusses in detail procedures for increasing the trustworthiness of transcripts and thus enhancing rigor in qualitative research. Sociolinguistics and ethnomethodology have brought the differences between oral and written language into focus (Ong, 1982; Tannen, 1990; Tedlock, 1983). In a historical linguistic study, in particular of Homer's work, Ong outlines the thought and expression of a primarily oral culture as being close to the human life world, situational, empathic and participatory, additive, aggregative, agonistic, and redundant. In contrast, a written culture is characterized by analytic, abstract, and objectively distanced forms of thought and expression.

Interview transcriptions are often boring to read, ennui ensues in face of the repetitions, the incomplete sentences, and the many digressions. The apparently incoherent statements may be coherent within the context of a living conversation, with vocal intonation, facial expressions, and body language supporting, giving nuances to, or even contradicting what is said. Such discrepancies between what is said and the accompanying bodily expressions are deliberately used in some forms of comical and ironical statements.

The problems with interview transcripts are due less to the technicalities of transcription than to the inherent differences between an oral and a written mode of discourse. Transcripts are decontextualized conversations. If one accepts as a main premise of interpretation that meaning depends on context, then transcripts in isolation make an impoverished basis for interpretation. An interview takes place in a context, of which the spatial, temporal, and social dimensions are immediately given to the participants in the face-to-face conversation, but not to the out-of-context reader of the transcript. In contrast to a taped interview, a novel will report the immediate context of a conversation, including nonverbal communication to the extent the author finds it relevant for the story he or she wants to tell. Similar considerations hold for journalistic interviews.

The transcriptions are detemporalized; a living, ongoing conversation is frozen into a written text. The words of the conversation, fleeting as the steps of an improvised dance, are fixated into static written words, open to repeated public inspections. The words of the transcripts take on a solidity that was not intended in the immediate conversational context. The flow of conversation, with its open horizon of directions and meanings to be followed up, is replaced by the fixated, stable written text.

In a conversation we normally have immediate access to the meaning of what the other says. When analyzing the interviews, the tape recording, and in particular the ensuing transcript, tends to become an opaque screen between the researcher and the original situation. Attention is drawn to the formal recorded language and the empathically experienced, lived meanings of the original conversation fade away; the dried pale flowers in the herbarium replace the fresh

colorful flowers of the field. The transcripts become a kind of fundamental verbal data for interview research, rather than a means to evoke
and revive the personal interaction of the interview situation.

The rather interpretative basis of the transcripts is often forgotten
in the analysis, where the transcripts tend to become a rock-bottom
basis for the ensuing interpretations. Ignorance of the many technical
and theoretical issues of transforming conversations into texts may be
due to a neglect in social science of the linguistic medium of interview
research. Social scientists are today naive users of the language that
their professional practice and research rests on. Although most social
science programs today require courses in statistical analysis of quantitative data, even a rudimentary introduction to linguistic analysis of
linguistic, qualitative data is a rarity.

"Not being able to rely on a conception of a stable, universal,
noncontextual, and transparent relation between representation and
reality, and between language and meaning, confronts researchers
with serious and difficult theoretical and methodological problems"
(Mishler, 1991, p. 278). Neglecting linguistic complexities during
transcription from an oral to a written language may be related to a
philosophy of naive realism, with an implicit constancy hypothesis of
some real meaning nuggets remaining constant by their transfer from
one context to another. In contrast, postmodern conceptions of
knowledge emphasize the contextuality of meaning with an intrinsic
relation of meaning and form, and focus on the very ruptures of
communication, the breaks of meaning. The nuances and the differences, the transformations and discontinuities of meaning become the
very pores of knowledge. Postmodern approaches to knowledge do
not solve the many technical and theoretical issues of transcription.
The emphasis on the linguistic constitution of reality, on the contextuality of meaning, and on knowledge as arising from the transitions
and breaks, however, involves a sensitivity to and a focus on the often
overlooked transcription stage of interview research.

Transcribing Interviews

Transcribing the interviews from an oral to a written mode structures the interview conversations in a form amenable for closer
analysis. Structuring the material into texts facilitates an overview and

is in itself a beginning analysis. The amount and form of transcribing depends on such factors as the nature of the material and the purpose of the investigation, the time and money available, and—not to be forgotten—the availability of a reliable and patient typist. Transcription from tape to text involves a series of technical and interpretational issues for which, again, there are few standard rules, but rather a series of choices to be made.

It is a useful exercise for interviewers to type one or more pilot interviews themselves. This will sensitize them to the importance of the acoustic quality of the recording, to paying attention to asking clear audible questions and getting equally clear answers in the interview situation. The transcribing experience will also make interviewers aware of some of the many decisions involved in transforming oral speech to written texts, and it will give an impression of the time and effort the transcription of an interview requires.

Typing. The time needed to transcribe an interview will depend on the quality of the recording, the typing experience of the transcriber, and the demands for detail and exactitude. Transcribing large amounts of interview material is often a tiresome and stressing job; the stress can be reduced by securing recordings of high acoustic quality.

For the interviews in the grading study, an experienced secretary took about 5 hours to type verbatim an interview of 1 hour. A 1-hour interview results in 20 to 25 single-spaced pages, depending on the amount of speech and how it is set up in typing.

Who Should Transcribe? In most studies the tapes are transcribed by a secretary, who is likely to be more efficient at typing than the researcher. Investigators who emphasize the modes of communication and linguistic style may choose to do their own transcribing in order to secure the many details relevant to their specific analysis. Some have a typist do a first transcription of all the interviews in a study; then after reading them through, the researcher goes back and retypes those interviews, or those parts of the interviews, that will be subjected to intensive analysis.

Style. There is one basic rule in transcription—state explicitly in the report how the transcriptions were made. This should preferably be based on written instructions to the transcribers. If there are several transcribers for the interviews of a single study, care should be taken that they use the same procedures for typing. If this is not done, cross-comparisons among the interviews will be difficult to make.

Although there is no standard form or code for transcription of research interviews, there are some standard choices to be made. They involve such issues as: Should the statements be transcribed verbatim and word by word, including the often frequent repetitions, or should the interview be transformed into a more formal, written style? Should the entire interview be reproduced verbatim, or should the transcriber condense and summarize some of the parts that have little relevant information? Should pauses, emphases in intonation, and emotional expressions like laughter and sighing be included? And if pauses are to be included, how much detail should be indicated?

There are no correct, standard answers to such questions; the answers will depend on the intended use of the transcript. One possible guideline for editing, doing justice to the interviewees, is to imagine how they themselves would have wanted to formulate their statements in writing. The transcriber then on behalf of the subjects translates their oral style into a written form in harmony with the specific subjects' general modes of expression. The extent of detail in a transcription will depend on its use; regarding pauses, for example, it may be sufficient for some purposes simply to note "a short pause" or "a long pause," whereas for detailed sociolinguistic analyses the length of a pause will be indicated in milliseconds.

Decisions concerning style of transcription depend on the audience for which a text is intended. For the investigator, as an aid in remembering the interviews? For the interview subjects, to confirm that their views are adequately rendered in the interview and possibly also as an invitation to expand upon what they have said? For a research group that will make extensive analyses of the interviews, or for critical colleagues who want to check the basis on which the researcher draws his or her conclusions? Or for general readers who want some concrete illustrations from the interviews?

The decisions about style of transcribing depend on the use of the transcriptions. If they are to give some general impressions of the subjects' views, rephrasing and condensing of statements may be in order. Also, if the analysis is to be in a form that categorizes or condenses the general meaning of what is said, a certain amount of

editing of the transcription may be desirable. If, however, the transcriptions are to serve as material for sociolinguistic or psychological
analysis, they need to be in a detailed, verbatim form. Even the many
"hm"s of an ordinary conversation, disturbing when reading a transcript, can be relevant for later analysis: for example, whether the
"hm"s of the interviewer selectively follow, and thus reinforce, special
types of answers by the subject. And, if psychological interpretations
are to be made, the emotional tone of the conversation should also be
included. Here the very pauses, repetitions, and so forth may yield
important material for interpretation.

In Jacobsen's (1981) study of the university socialization of students
of Danish and of medicine to their respective professional cultures,
the interviews were transcribed verbatim, including the many "hm"s,
"ain't it true," and the like. Jacobsen counted the use of such fillers
by the students of Danish and of medicine, respectively, and found a
markedly more frequent use of "ain't it true" by the students of
Danish. He interpreted this, together with other indications, as being
in line with the culture of the humanities, in which there is an emphasis
on dialogue with attempts to obtain consensual validation of interpretations, involving appeals to the others, such as "ain't it true." In
contrast, the medical profession is more characterized by lectures as
monologues authoritatively stating nondebatable truths.

The issue of how detailed a transcription should be is also illustrated by an interview sequence on competition for grades, which in
Denmark is a negative behavior that many pupils hesitate to admit to:

Interviewer: Does it influence the relationship between the pupils
that the grades are there?

Pupil: No, no—no, one does not look down on anyone who gets bad
grades, that is not done. I do not believe that: well, it may be
that there are some who do it, but I don't.

Interviewer: Does that mean there is no competition in the class?

Pupil: That's right. There is none.

At face value, this pupil says that one does not look down on pupils
with low grades and confirms the interviewer's interpretation that
there is no competition for grades in the class. A critical reading may
lead to the opposite conclusion—the boy himself introduces the

phenomenon of looking down on pupils with bad grades, first denies
that it occurs, then repeats the denials with three "no"s and four "not"s
in the few lines of his statement. This many denials of looking down
on other pupils might, with the quantitative increases, suddenly lead
to a qualitative change for the reader, and the statement come to mean
the opposite of what was manifestly said. If the above interview
statement had not been transcribed verbatim, but rephrased into a
briefer form such as "One does not look down on others with low
grades nor compete for grades," the reinterpretation of the manifest
meaning of the statement into its opposite could not have taken place.
The effect of multiple negations canceling each other out is used in
literature, in *Hamlet,* for example:

Hamlet: Madam, how like you this play?
Queen: The lady doth protest too much, methinks. (*Hamlet,* act III,
scene 2)

Ethics. Transcription involves ethical issues. The interviews may
treat sensitive topics in which it is important to protect the *confidentiality* of the subject and of persons and institutions mentioned in the
interview. Along with the necessary and simpler but sometimes forgotten tasks goes the need for secure storage of tapes and transcripts,
and of erasing the tapes when they are no longer of use. In sensitive
cases, it may be advantageous as early as the transcription stage to
mask the identities of the interviewed subjects, as well as events and
persons in the interviews that might be easily recognized. This is
particularly important if a larger research group is involved and several persons will therefore have access to the transcripts.

Some subjects may experience a shock as a *consequence* of reading
their own interviews. The verbatim transcribed oral language may
appear as incoherent and confused speech, even as indicating a lower
level of intellectual functioning. The subjects may become offended
and refuse any further cooperation and any use of what they have said.
If the transcripts are to be sent back to the interviewees, rendering
them in a more fluent written style might be considered from the start.
And if not, consider accompanying the transcripts with information
about the natural differences between oral and written language styles.
Be mindful that the *publication* of incoherent and repetitive verbatim

interview transcripts may involve an unethical stigmatization of specific persons or groups of people.

Those teachers in the grading study who had expressed interest received a draft of the book chapter in which their statements were discussed. A teacher of Danish, who had been quoted extensively, called and asked me to omit or rephrase his statements in the book. The rather off-the-cuff verbatim quotes from his interview showed a very poor Danish used by a teacher of Danish, which he found penible in his profession. At that time I was little aware of the different rules for oral and written language and believed that a verbatim transcription of the interviews was the most loyal and objective transcription. I did, however, respect his request and changed his quotes into a correct written form, which also made them more readable.

Computer Tools for Interview Analysis

During the past decade, computer programs have been developed to facilitate the analysis of interview transcripts. They replace the time-demanding cut-and-paste approach to analysis of often hundreds of pages of paper with "electronic scissors." The programs are aids for structuring the interview material for further analysis; the task and responsibility of interpretation still rest with the researcher.

The computer programs serve as textbase managers, storing the often extensive interview transcripts, and allow for a multitude of analytic operations (for overviews, see Tesch, 1990; Weitzman & Miles, 1995; Miles & Huberman's, 1994, appendix gives a short introduction to choosing among computer programs for qualitative analysis). The programs allow for such operations as writing memos, writing reflections on the interviews for later analyses, coding, searching for key words, doing word counts, and making graphic displays. Some of the programs allow for on-screen coding and note taking while reading the transcripts.

The most common form of computer analysis today is coding, or categorization, of the interview statements. The researcher reads through the transcripts and categorizes the relevant passages; then with code-and-retrieve programs the coded passages can be retrieved and inspected again, with options of recoding and of combining codes.

The potential of some programs to make connections among the categories to develop higher-order conceptual structures is sometimes referred to as theory building.

Computer programs for analyzing interview texts may save the qualitative researcher much of the drudgery of analysis and thereby enable concentration on meaningful and creative interpretations of what was said in the interviews. A further advantage is that the programs force the researcher to make explicit commands to the computer, which when reported can give the readers insight into what often seems like a black-box method of interview analysis. The use of computers in qualitative analysis could, however, reinforce existing trends toward reifying the transcripts and disregarding their basis in a lived social situation. The current emphasis on coding may lead to analyses of isolated variables abstracted from their context in live interpersonal interactions. With the technical ease of coding and of analyzing isolated variables, computer software could further a neglect of the contextual base of interview statements in the narratives of lived conversations.

There are technical developments on the way that may counteract the common infatuation with reified interview transcripts. Today, most analyses of interview conversations are done on the basis of transcripts, and the original tapes are stored somewhere but seldom used during the analysis. In the past few years, however, a new generation of computer programs is being developed that can be used directly on audio- and videotapes, saving the detour of transcribing. The direct listening to and structuring of the original oral speech allows an empathic listening to what was said in the interview interaction.

KIT is a *Windows*-based program that follows and extends the structures from the text analysis program *Textbase ALPHA* (see Tesch, 1990). The new program *KIT* makes transcription redundant by recording and storing the source—interviews and natural speech interactions —on the computer itself in their oral form (*Qualitative Interview and Therapy Analysis,* developed by Carl Verner Skou at the Center of Qualitative Research at the University of Aarhus). The tape recording is transferred to a compact disk, converted into digital form, and stored in the computer. During replay the speech can be coded on the monitor, comments on the passages can be written down, and central passages for later reporting can be transcribed. The coded passages can easily be retrieved for relistening, or recoding and other functions of the analysis program can be conducted—in this case, by working directly with the recorded interview instead of with transcriptions.

KIT's advantages include not only the saving of time and money spent on transcribing all of the interviews, but the speed of retrieval, where the analyst can shift between different passages in, or between, the interviews in less than one second. The many methodical and theoretical problems of transforming oral speech into written texts are simply bypassed when the analyst works directly on recordings of the live conversations. In addition to the current theoretical recovery of oral language from the alienation of written texts, such technical developments in analysis may reclaim the lived interview conversation from the hegemony of transcripts in interview research.

In the next three chapters I address the present state of analysis of interview texts; first by discussing some common questions in interview analysis today (Chapter 10), then by outlining main approaches to analysis (Chapter 11), and finally by providing some examples of interpreting interview statements (Chapter 12).

10

The 1,000-Page Question

One may sometimes receive a question like this when teaching at workshops on qualitative research:

How shall I find a method to analyze the 1,000 pages of interview transcripts I have collected?

This chapter is a reply to this 1,000-page question. It includes some summaries of the stages of an interview investigation that have already been covered and prepares the ground for the analysis stage treated in more detail in the next two chapters.

Dismiss or Interpret the 1,000-Page Question?

A first impulsive reaction to the 1,000-page question is to dismiss it—"Never pose that question!" When an interview project has been conducted in such a way that the 1,000-page question is asked, the question can no longer be answered. A more adequate reply would then be: "Never conduct interview research in such a way that you find yourself in a situation where you ask such a question."

The present approach goes further than merely dismissing the question; the conception of qualitative research implied by the 1,000-page question will be interpreted by taking a closer look at its wording. The question is not only posed too late, it is leading. Yet all questions are leading: They may be opening or closing, productive or counterproductive. In interview research, too much emphasis has been placed on the influence of leading questions in the interview situation, whereas the leading influence of questions put to the interview texts through their analysis has been rather neglected. The 1,000-page question as it is formulated above leads in the wrong direction—it is closing and unproductive.

A lead for the analysis of the question is taken from Antonioni's movie *The Reporter.* In one scene, in which an African shaman is interviewed by the white reporter, the shaman replies something like this to one of the reporter's questions: "I will not answer your question. My answer would tell less about me than your question tells about yourself."

What Does the 1,000-Page Question Mean?

The material for the present analysis is the 17 words of the 1,000-page question as formulated above. The purpose of the analysis is to uncover the meaning of the question, to make explicit its presuppositions and thereby the implicit conceptions of qualitative research it implies. The general interest is prophylactic; it is an attempt to outline modes of conducting interview research so that a researcher never gets into a situation where he or she feels compelled to ask the 1,000-page question. The method of analyzing the question will be discussed in the concluding section. The general form of the analysis is to select 7 key words from the 1,000-page question and analyze them separately:

How (3) shall I find a method (4) to analyze (7) the 1,000 pages (2) of interview transcripts (5) I have (1) collected (6) ?

"HAVE"—TOO LATE!

The answer is simple—the question is posed too late.

Never pose the question of how to analyze transcripts *after* the interviews have been conducted—it is too late to start thinking after the interviewing is done. The answer here parallels that of a statistician: Consult me about the data analysis before you collect your data.

Think about how the interviews are to be analyzed before they are conducted. The method of analysis decided on—or at least considered —will then direct the preparation of the interview guide, the interview process, and the transcription of the interviews. Every stage in an interview project involves decisions that offer both possibilities and constraints in later stages of the project.

The method of analysis should not only be planned in advance of the interviewing. The analysis may also, to varying degrees, be built into the interview situation itself. A clarification of the meaning of what is said may then take the simple form of "I understand that the meaning of what you just said is . . ." Further, the researcher may attempt to confirm or reject his or her hypothesis during the interview, similar to a job interview where the interviewer is continually testing the hypothesis about whether the interviewed applicant is qualified for the job.

In such forms of analysis—interpreting "as you go"—considerable parts of the analysis are "pushed forward" into the interview situation itself. The final analysis then becomes not only easier and more amenable, but will also rest on more secure ground. Put strongly, the ideal interview is already analyzed by the time the tape recorder is turned off. There are social and ethical restraints on how far the analysis of meaning can be undertaken during the interview itself, but this may serve as a methodic ideal for interview research.

An alternative reformulation of the 1,000-page question entails changing the temporal form: *How shall I conduct my interviews so that their meaning can be analyzed in a coherent and creative way?*

"1,000 PAGES"—TOO MUCH!

The answer to this quantitative part of the question is also simple— 1,000 pages of transcripts is too much to handle in a meaningful way.

The precise meaning of the question may depend on its intonation. When posed in a despairing voice, it may indicate a situation of being overwhelmed by an enormous amount of qualitative data, of being completely lost in a jungle of transcriptions. The meaning of the question may then be: Rescue me from my 1,000 pages, I cannot find my way out of the labyrinth.

When posed in a more assertive voice the same question may have another meaning. A diligent young scholar has done his empirical duty and documented his scientific attitude by gathering large amounts of data. He now awaits the expert's praise and advice about how to treat the data. The question may here involve a "reversed positivism"—a quest for scientific respectability by mirroring the positivist emphasis on large quantities of quantitative data with large quantities of qualitative data.

Whether posed in a despairing or in an assertive voice, the formulation of the question leads in the wrong direction. The emphasis is on the quantity—1,000 pages—rather than on the content and the qualitative meanings of what was said.

One thousand pages of transcripts is generally too much to handle. The material is too extensive to overview and to work out the depth of the meaning of what was said. The analysis is too time-consuming and is likely to lead to a superficial product, unfinished due to external time constraints. Should there be definite reasons for needing such a large amount of interview material—1,000 pages correspond to between 30 and 40 hours of interviews—the reasons for the large quantity should be explicitly formulated before the interviews are conducted. It may then turn out that fewer interviews are sufficient, or that the purpose of the investigation is better served by questionnaires.

A rephrasing of the 1,000-page question, involving a change in emphasis from quantity to meaning, could be: *How do I go about finding the meaning of the many interesting and complex stories my interviewees told me?*

"HOW"—ASK "WHAT" AND "WHY" FIRST

Do not pose the question of how to analyze interviews before the answers to the what and the why of an investigation have been given. Content and purpose precede method.

In analyzing an interview, what is not said may be just as important as what is said. In the question analyzed here, the question of "how" is posed without including the "what" and the "why" of the investigation. The term *method* originally meant *the way to the goal*. With no goal stated, it is difficult to show the way to it.

The mode of analysis depends on "what" is analyzed, on the subject matter of the interview, and on the "why," the purpose of the interview. Thus the interpretation of Hamlet's interview rested on a clarification of the topic and purpose of the interview—an exploration of the shapes of clouds or the testing of a hypothesis about Polonius's trustworthiness (Chapter 8, Hamlet's Interview). In general, the theoretical conceptions of what is investigated should provide the basis for making decisions of how—the method to be used for analyzing the content. Thus a psychoanalytic conception of an interview statement as an expression of unconscious forces will involve a different form of analysis than a behavioristic conception of the statement as an element in a chain of stimuli and responses. Further, if a research study purports to test a hypothesis about differences among groups of subjects, then the analysis should be systematic and conducted in the same way for each of the groups in order to test possible differences among them. For explorative purposes it will, on the contrary, be more appropriate to pursue the different interesting aspects of the individual interviews and to interpret them in greater depth.

The specification of the subject matter and the purpose of an interview study could be continued, elaborated further, or made in other ways than suggested here. What is important is that the what and the why of the investigation are clarified before a method of analysis is chosen.

The technical "how to" emphasis of the 1,000-page question can be reformulated to: *How do I go about finding out what the interviews tell me about what I want to know?*

"METHOD" VERSUS KNOWLEDGE

The methodological aspect of the 1,000-page question cannot be answered due to the way the question is formulated. There are no standard methods, no *via regia,* to arrive at essential meanings and deeper implications of what is said in an interview.

The demand for a method may involve an emphasis on techniques and reliability, and a de-emphasis on knowledge and validity. The search for techniques of analysis may be a quest for a "technological fix" to the researcher's task of analyzing and constructing meaning.

There are no standard methods of text analysis that correspond to the multitude of techniques available for statistical analysis. This may be due in part to the relative novelty and the small extent of cross-disciplinary communication about qualitative analysis in the social sciences. The lack of standard techniques of qualitative analysis may, however, also be due to the richness and the complexity of the subject matter. Some general approaches to the analysis of qualitative material—involving different technical procedures—do exist. Five approaches to analyzing the meaning of interviews, to be outlined in the next chapter, are: categorization, condensation, narrative structuring, deeper interpretations, and ad hoc tactics for the generation of meaning.

Method may also be used in the sense of obtaining intersubjectively reliable results. The question then concerns how different readers can arrive at the same meanings when analyzing an interview. This may reflect the common concern that qualitative research leads to as many interpretations as there are researchers. When using a specific method with a specific purpose—for instance, categorization of the subjects' statements in order to compare the attitudes of different groups of subjects toward an issue—then a high intersubjective reproducibility of the categorization is desirable; that is, the results of the comparison should not be influenced by who categorized the answers of the groups. A strict requirement of intersubjective reliability for all forms of interview analysis may, however, lead to a tyranny by the lowest possible denominator: that an interpretation is only reliable when it can be followed by everyone, a criterion that could lead to a trivialization of the interpretations. This may again involve a consensualist conception of truth: that an observation or an interpretation is only considered valid if it can be repeated by everyone, irrespective of the quality of the observation and the argumentation.

The emphasis on method—in the meaning of standardized techniques or of intersubjective reliability—may also involve a disregard of knowledge and expertise during the analysis of the interviews. The question may involve an "externalization" of the interpretation of meaning to fixed rules and criteria, rather than going beyond method and drawing upon the craftsmanship of the researcher, on his or her knowledge and interpretative skills. Psychological research has often placed an empiristic emphasis on naive observers and unprejudiced interpreters as a condition for obtaining objective results. In contrast thereto, the present position emphasizes a knowledge of the subject matter, an expertise in the field studied, as a presupposition for arriving at valid interpretations. The importance of background knowledge for observations is evident in a variety of areas. When analyzing interviews with chess players, the researcher's knowledge of chess at a higher level than that of the interviewees is a precondition for seeing the solutions they did not see. In the psychoanalytical tradition, there has long been an emphasis on the training and the competence of the analyst for making psychoanalytical observations and interpretations.

The alternative to the methodical emphasis of the 1,000-page question is: *How can the interviews assist me in extending my knowledge of the phenomena I am investigating?*

"TRANSCRIPTS"—BEWARE!

Do not conceive of the interviews as transcripts: The interviews are living conversations—beware of transcripts.

The transcripts should not be the subject matter of an interview study, as implied by the 1,000-page question, but rather be means, tools, for the interpretation of what was said during the interviews. Although produced as an oral discourse, the interview appears in the form of a written text. The transcript is a bastard, it is a hybrid between an oral discourse unfolding over time, face to face, in a lived situation —where what is said is addressed to a specific listener present—and a written text created for a general, distant, public.

An emphasis on the transcription may promote a reifying analysis that reduces the text to a mere collection of words or single meanings conceived as verbal data. The originally lived face-to-face conversations disappear in endless transcripts, only to reappear butchered into fragmented quotes. The interviews become closed, they no longer open up to a horizon of possible meanings, to be explored and developed.

An alternative approach toward the transcripts involves entering into a *dialogue* with the text, going into an imagined conversation with the "author" about the meaning of the text. The reader here asks about the theme of the text, goes into the text seeking to develop, clarify, and expand what is expressed in the text. The meanings may be approached as manifestly expressed, or, in line with a "depth herme-neutics," seeking to uncover meanings hidden in the texts.

The alternative to the transcription emphasis in the 1,000-page question is: *How do I analyze what my interviewees told me in order to enrich and deepen the meaning of what they said?*

"COLLECTED" VERSUS COAUTHORED

The interviewee's statements are not collected—they are co-authored by the interviewer.

The inter-view is an inter-subjective enterprise of two persons talking about common themes of interest. The interviewer does not merely collect statements like gathering small stones on a beach. His or her questions lead up to what aspects of a topic the subject will address, and the interviewer's active listening and following up on the answers co-determines the course of the conversation.

There is a tendency to take the results of a social interaction, when first arrived at, as a given, forgetting the original discourse and the social co-construction of the final outcomes. Such a reification may be strengthened by the transcription of the interviews; the fixated written form takes over and the original face-to-face interaction of the interview situation fades away.

A reification of the jointly produced interview into a transcription of collected statements has consequences in both a social and a temporal dimension. Socially, the forgetting of the joint social creation of the interview statements and the neglect of the interviewer's con-structive contributions to the answers produced may lead to a biased view of the interview as merely reflecting the interviewee, with the possible exception of the influence of directly leading questions. The alternative approach of deliberately using the role of the interviewer as a coproducer and a coauthor of the interview, and of reflecting on the social constitution of the interview, is then overlooked.

Temporally, focusing on the transcripts as a collection of statements may freeze the interview into finished entities rather than treat its pas-sages as stepping stones toward a continuous unfolding of the meaning of what was said. In the latter case, the analysis of the transcribed interviews is a continuation of the conversation that started in the interview situation. The interviewee's answers open up to a horizon of possible meanings to be pursued during the later conversational analysis with the interview text. The focus of the analysis moves from what has already been said, goes beyond the immediately given, to what could have been said.

The continued dialogue with the text may lead to a renewed conversation with the interviewee, sharing and developing the zone of possible meanings in the original interview. More often, the analysis will be in the form of an imagined dialogue with the text, unfolding its horizon of possible meanings.

The alternative to the stamp-collecting version of the 1,000-page question is: *How do I carry on the dialogue with the text I have coauthored with the interviewee?*

"ANALYZE" VERSUS NARRATE

Do not let the analysis stage inflate so that it consumes the major portion of time available for an interview project.

The analysis of an interview is interspersed between the initial story told by the interviewee to the researcher and the final story told by the researcher to an audience. To *analyze* means to separate something into parts or elements. The transcription of the conversation and the conception of the interview as a collection of statements might promote a fragmentation of the story told by the interviewee into separate parts, be they single paragraphs, sentences, or words. It is then easy to forget that in open, nondirective interviews the interviewee tells a story, or several stories, to the researcher, and that the transcript itself may then approximate the form of a narrative text.

The structures and functions of the narratives of folktales and literature, as worked out in the humanities, can be used to reflect and analyze the narrative structures employed by the interviewee. A narrative approach to the interview analysis, going back to the original story told by the interviewee and anticipating the final story to be reported to an audience, may prevent becoming lost in a jungle of transcripts. A focus on the interview as a narrative may even make the interview transcripts better reading, in that the original interview is deliberately created in a story form. A narrative conception of interview research supports a unity of form among the original interview situation, the analysis, and the final report.

A narrative alternative to the analysis version of the 1,000-page question then becomes: *How can I reconstruct the original story told to me by the interviewee into a story I want to tell my audience?*

Method of Analysis

A question about interview research was posed in the introduction of this chapter: How can I find a method to analyze the 1,000 pages of interview transcripts I have collected?

The answer given was that the question was posed too late to obtain a satisfactory answer and that its formulation made it difficult to answer. The wording of the question was then analyzed in detail with the purpose of bringing its implicit presuppositions of interview research into the open, and with the general interest of making the question superfluous.

No standardized method of analysis was applied to the question; rather, a variety of approaches were tried in order to bring out the meaning of the question. The general structure was to select 7 key words from the 17-word sentence and analyze them individually. Yet the analysis was not entirely decontextualized; there were continuous overlappings among the meanings developed from the key words that pointed to common threads of meaning underlying the question. By analyzing the separate words, an attempt was made to bring in the context of the question. Guesses were made to find the implied meanings of, for example, vocal intonation—such as whether the emphasis on the "1,000 pages" was in a despairing or an assertive voice. Some brief attempts at an etymological analysis were made, concerning terms as *method* and *analyze.*

The original sentence was rephrased in various forms, leading to different directions of meanings. The alternative rephrasings of the 1,000-page question shifted the focus from what was said to what could have been said, opening up some of the possibilities of meanings that the original formulation of the question closed off. It presupposes a certain background knowledge of interview research to see some of the possibilities the question leads away from. The analysis took the form of an imagined dialogue, an attempt to answer the original 1,000-page question by asking about its possible meanings. The analysis resembled the question-answer sequence of an imagined conversation, resulting in a coauthored story about interview research. The original wording of the 1,000-page question led in unproductive directions. The various rephrasings of the original question attempted to lead the analysis in directions yielding constructive contributions to knowledge.

The deconstruction of the 1,000-page question involved a destruction of the presuppositions of the question and a construction of alternative formulations for enriching interview analysis. The interpretation focused on the tension between what was said and what was not said in the question. This interplay of the said and the not-said did not lead to one, true, objective meaning of the question, but served to keep the conversation going about the meanings the question opens up.

It may be objected that the analysis of the 1,000-page question was too brief and superficial, that it was not comprehensive enough to really develop and go into the complex meanings and presuppositions of the question. I grant that the above analysis could have been extended to include further differentiations of the many issues raised by the question.

The topic of the original question concerned 1,000 pages of interview transcripts of questions and answers, and it was postulated that this was too much material for undertaking a comprehensive analysis. The above interpretation of the 17 words of the 1,000-page question has required around 3,600 words, which makes the quantitative relation of original text to interpretative text 1:212. A corresponding interpretation of the meaning of 1,000 pages would then require 212,000 pages, which amounts to about 1,000 books.

11

Methods of Analysis

Methods exist that can make the interview analysis more amenable than as pictured in the reply to the 1,000-page question. They can be used to organize the interview texts, to condense the meanings into forms that can be presented in a relatively short space, and to work out implicit meanings of what was said. Five main approaches to interview analysis will be outlined: categorization of meaning, condensation of meaning, structuring of meaning through narratives, interpretation of meaning, and ad hoc methods for generating meaning.

In a chapter on methods of analysis some readers may, however, expect to find the magical tool for finally uncovering the treasures of meaning hidden in the many pages of opaque interview transcripts. The following overview of methods will disappoint them—no main roads to the meanings of the interviews are given here. The techniques of analysis are tools, useful for some purposes, relevant for some types of interviews, and suited for some researchers. The central task of interview analysis rests, however, with the researcher, with the thematic questions he or she has asked from the start of the investigation and followed up through designing, interviewing, and transcribing.

Steps of Analysis

The purpose of the qualitative research interview has been depicted as the description and interpretation of themes in the subjects' lived world. A continuum exists between description and interpretation.

Box 11.1 shows six possible steps of analysis. They do not necessarily presuppose each other chronologically or logically (see Giorgi
[1992] and Wolcott [1994] for further treatment of the relation of description and interpretation). The first three steps of description, discover, and interpretation during the interview were discussed earlier
(Chapter 8, Interview Quality). In this chapter I treat the fourth step
of analyzing the transcribed interview, then return to re-interviewing
and action in relation to the discussion of validation as communication
and action (Chapter 13, Communicative Validity, and Pragmatic
Validity).

Approaches to Interview Analysis

Until recently, interview researchers had to rely on the individual
techniques they could come up with: developing their own hunches
or by chance finding some suggestions in the scattered qualitative
literature. Analysis took place through listening to repeated replaying
of the tapes, or by cutting and pasting selections from the transcribed
pages. The analyses more often terminated because of time limits or
exhaustion, rather than with a feeling of having analyzed the material
sufficiently to have worked out its main structures and meanings;
recall the final phases of the emotional hardships of interview inquiries
depicted earlier (see Box 5.1 in Chapter 5).

During the past decade this state of affairs has changed. There are
now several books giving overviews of the different methods of
qualitative analysis (Miles & Huberman, 1994; Silverman, 1993;
Tesch, 1990; Wolcott, 1994). I will differentiate five main approaches
to qualitative analysis and use the term *analysis* for these five approaches in general, and reserve the term *interpretation* for the one
mode of analysis involving a more in-depth interpretation.

Figure 11.1 provides a graphic overview of the size and form of the
outcome of five main approaches to the analysis of the meanings of
interviews. As is evident from the dashes indicating the amount of text,
in all approaches except interpretation the *outcome* of the analysis
requires far less space than the original interview text. In contrast to
the text reduction of the other approaches, interpretation will often
involve a text expansion, with the outcome formulated in far more

Box 11.1

Six Steps of Analysis

A first step is when *subjects describe* their lived world during the interview. They spontaneously tell what they experience, feel, and do in relation to a topic. There is little interpretation or explanation from either the interviewees or the interviewer.

A second step would be that the *subjects themselves discover* new relationships during the interview, see new meanings in what they experience and do. For example, a pupil, describing the effects of grading, comes to think of how the grades further a destructive competition among pupils. The interviewees themselves start to see new connections in their life worlds on the basis of their spontaneous descriptions, free of interpretation by the interviewer.

In a third step, the *interviewer, during the interview, condenses and interprets* the meaning of what the interviewee describes, and "sends" the meaning back. The interviewee then has the opportunity to reply, for example, "I did not mean that" or "That was precisely what I was trying to say" or "No, that was not quite what I felt. It was more like . . ." This dialogue ideally continues till there is only one possible interpretation left, or it is established that the subject has multiple, and possibly contradictory, understandings of a theme. This form of interviewing implies an ongoing "on-the-line interpretation" with the possibility of an "on-the-spot" confirmation or disconfirmation of the interviewer's interpretations. The result can then be a "self-correcting" interview.

In a fourth step, the *transcribed interview is interpreted by the interviewer,* either alone or with other researchers.

(continued)

Box 11.1 Continued

Three parts of this analysis may be discerned; first, *structuring* the often large and complex interview material for analysis. This is usually done today by transcription and by programs for computer analysis of qualitative material. The next part consists of a *clarification* of the material, making it amenable to analysis; for example, by eliminating superfluous material such as digressions and repetitions, distinguishing between the essential and the non-essential. What is essential or non-essential again depends on the purpose of the study and its theoretical presuppositions. The *analysis proper* involves developing the meanings of the interviews, bringing the subjects' own understanding into the light as well as providing new perspectives from the researcher on the phenomena. Five main approaches to the analysis of meaning are condensation, categorization, narrative structuring, interpretation, and ad hoc methods.

A fifth step would be a *re-interview.* When the researcher has analyzed and interpreted the completed interviews, he or she may give the interpretations back to the subjects. In a continuation of a "self-correcting" interview, the subjects get an opportunity to comment on the interviewer's interpretations as well as to elaborate on their own original statements.

A possible sixth step would be to extend the continuum of description and interpretation to include *action,* in that subjects begin to act from new insights they have gained during their interview. The research interview may in such cases approximate a therapeutic interview. The changes can also be brought about by actions in a larger social setting such as action research, where the researcher and the subjects together act on the basis of the knowledge produced in the interviews.

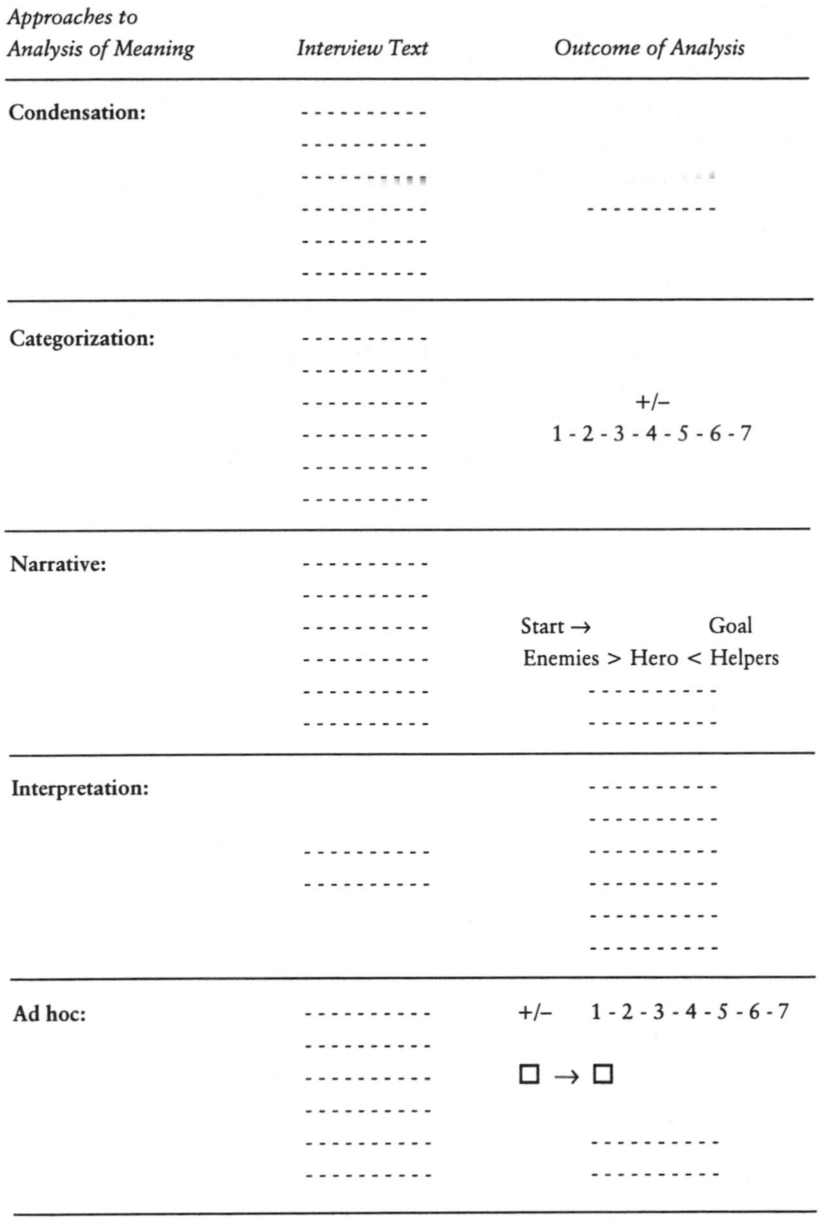

Approaches to Analysis of Meaning	Interview Text	Outcome of Analysis
Condensation:	- ▪▪▪ -	- - - - - - - - - -
Categorization:	- -	+/– 1 - 2 - 3 - 4 - 5 - 6 - 7
Narrative:	- -	Start → Goal Enemies > Hero < Helpers -
Interpretation:	- - - - - - - - - - - - - - - - - - - -	- -
Ad hoc:	- -	+/– 1 - 2 - 3 - 4 - 5 - 6 - 7 □ → □ -

Figure 11.1. Five Approaches to Interview Analysis

words than the interpreted statements; for example, the interpretation of a poem by a literary critic.

The *form* of the results will mainly be in words in meaning condensation, interpretation, and narrative analyses, possibly with some figures for narrative structuring. The outcome of categorization is in numbers, which can be subjected to statistical analysis. The eclectic ad hoc analysis may involve words and figures as well as numbers. An overview of the five approaches will be given before outlining them each in more detail.

Meaning condensation entails an abridgement of the meanings expressed by the interviewees into shorter formulations. Long statements are compressed into briefer statements in which the main sense of what is said is rephrased in a few words. Meaning condensation thus involves a reduction of large interview texts into briefer, more succinct formulations.

Meaning categorization implies that the interview is coded into categories. Long statements are reduced to simple categories such as "+" or "–," indicating occurrence and non-occurrence of a phenomenon; or to a single number on a scale of 1 to 5, for example, to indicate the strength of a phenomenon. Categorization can thus reduce and structure a large text into a few tables and figures. The categories can be developed in advance or they can arise ad hoc during the analysis; they may be taken from theory or from the vernacular, as well as from the interviewees' own idioms.

The present outline of five main methodical approaches to qualitative analysis is in itself a rough categorization of a qualitative diversity of methods of analysis. The perspective here is on how the different methods generate meaning; other perspectives would lead to other categorizations. Thus a focus on whether the analysis leads to qualitative or quantitative data, or whether the analysis is linguistic or psychological, would lead to other categorizations of methodical approaches to interview analysis.

Narrative structuring entails the temporal and social organization of a text to bring out its meaning. It focuses on the stories told during an interview and works out their structures and their plots. If there are no stories told spontaneously, a narrative analysis may attempt to create a coherent story out of the many happenings reported throughout an interview. As with meaning condensation, narrative analysis will generally stay within the vernacular. Structuring through narratives will usually reduce the interview text; it may, however, also expand it by developing the potentialities of meaning in a simple interview story into more elaborate narratives.

Meaning interpretation goes beyond a structuring of the manifest meanings of a text to deeper and more or less speculative interpretations of the text. Examples of meaning interpretation are found in the humanities, such as in a critic's interpretations of a film or a play, and in psychoanalytical interpretations of patients' dreams. In contrast to the decontextualization of statements by categorization, interpretation recontextualizes the statements within broader frames of reference. The context for interpretation of a statement may, for example, be provided by the entire interview or by a theory. In contrast to the text reduction techniques of categorization and condensation, interpretations likely lead to a text expansion, such as in the preceding interpretations of Hamlet's interview (Chapter 8, Hamlet's Interview) and of the 1,000-page question (Chapter 10).

Generating meaning through ad hoc methods is an eclectic approach. A variety of commonsense approaches to the interview text, as well as sophisticated textual or quantitative methods, can be used to bring out the meanings of different parts of the material. The outcome of this meaning generation can be in words, in numbers, in figures and flow charts, and in their combinations.

These five approaches to interview analysis will now be exemplified, while more extensive treatment of the many techniques are found in the literature mentioned above. Meaning condensation will be illustrated by a phenomenological analysis of the interview reported by Giorgi and meaning categorizing by the analysis of the interviews from the grade study. Narrative analysis and ad hoc analysis will be depicted briefly and literature for more extensive treatments referred to. Interpretation of meaning is also described only briefly here: It will be the main topic of Chapter 12.

Meaning Condensation

Giorgi applied a phenomenologically based meaning condensation to the interview on learning reported earlier (Chapter 2, A Research

Interview on Learning). The thematic purpose was "to try to discover exactly what constitutes learning for ordinary people going about their everyday activities and how the learning is accomplished" (Giorgi, 1975, p. 84). The methodological aim of the study was to use phenomenology in the service of qualitative research: "We are interested in demonstrating how rigor and discipline can be applied without necessarily transforming data into quantitative expressions, although the latter has its place. The main point of the study is to demonstrate how one deals systematically with data that remain expressed in terms of ordinary language" (pp. 95-96).

Table 11.1 presents the condensation of the meanings of the first passages from the interview on learning. The "natural meaning units" of the subject's answers are given in the left-hand column and their central themes are presented in the right-hand column. Five steps are involved in this empirical phenomenological analysis: First, the whole interview is read through to get a sense of the whole. Then, the natural "meaning units" as expressed by the subjects are determined by the researcher. Third, the theme that dominates a natural meaning unit is stated as simply as possible. The researcher here attempts to read the subject's answers without prejudice and to thematize the statements from her viewpoint as understood by the researcher.

The fourth step consists of interrogating the meaning units in terms of the specific purpose of the study. The main questions of the study were "What is learning?" and "How was learning accomplished?" The themes of the meaning units were addressed with respect to such questions as, "What does this statement tell me about learning?" In the fifth step, the essential, nonredundant themes of the entire interview were tied together into a descriptive statement. The method thus involves a condensation of the expressed meanings into more and more essential meanings of the structure and style of learning.

Table 11.2 depicts the essential description of the style of learning obtained by answering the researcher's question of "How did learning take place?" The essential description shows structures of learning in everyday situations. These structures were further discussed by Giorgi in relation to the standard psychological theories of learning of the time, which had long neglected the interpersonal context of learning—that learning is a radically inter-human phenomenon.

TABLE 11.1 The Natural Meaning Units and Their Central Themes

Natural Unit	*Central Theme*
1. The first thing that comes to mind is what I learned about interior decorating from Myrtis. She was telling me about the way you see things. Her view of looking at different rooms has been altered. She told me that when you come into a room you don't usually notice how many vertical and horizontal lines there are, at least consciously, you don't notice. And yet, if you were to take someone who knows what's going on in the field of interior decorating, they would intuitively feel there were the right number of vertical and horizontal lines.	1. Role of vertical and horizontal lines in interior-decorating.
2. So, I went home, and I started looking at the lines in our living room, and I counted the number of horizontal and vertical lines, many of which I had never realized were lines before. A beam . . . I had never really thought of that as vertical before, just as a protrusion from the wall. (Laughs).	2. S looks for vertical and horizontal lines in her home.
3. I found out what was wrong with our living room design: many, too many, horizontal lines and not enough vertical. So I started trying to move things around and change the way it looked. I did this by moving several pieces of furniture and taking out several knick-knacks, de-emphasizing certain lines, and . . . it really looked differently to me.	3. S found too many horizontal lines in living room and succeeded in changing its appearance.
4. It's interesting because my husband came home several hours later and I said "Look at the living room; it's all different." Not knowing this, that I had picked up, he didn't look at it in the same way I did. He saw things were moved, but he wasn't able to verbalize that there was a de-emphasis on the horizontal lines and more of an emphasis on the vertical. So I felt I learned something.	4. Husband confirms difference not knowing why.

SOURCE: From Giorgi (1975).

TABLE 11.2 Essential Description of Style of Learning

Learning for S happened when she obtained from a significant other knowledge and
concrete demonstrations of this knowledge that related to a problem that bothered
her for a long time. When S found she could apply this knowledge to her own
situation in her own way, taking into account all the contingencies that the new
situation offered, she felt that learning had been achieved. Thus S learned by being
attentive to another, then applying for herself that knowledge which she received,
with approval from a different significant other.

SOURCE: From Giorgi (1975).

Giorgi also outlines how his empirical phenomenological method
relates to phenomenological philosophy, in particular as this was
developed by Merleau-Ponty (Chapter 3, Phenomenological Description). This concerns fidelity to the phenomena, the primacy of the life
world, the descriptive approach, expressing the situation from the
viewpoint of the subject, treating the situation as the unit of research,
engaged researchers, and the search for meaning. There is here a unity
of content and method, both the interview method and the conception
of learning were based on a phenomenological understanding of the
phenomenon investigated as an intentional meaningful activity in the
daily life of the subject.

In conclusion, this empirical phenomenological method may serve
to analyze extensive and often complex interview texts by looking for
natural meaning units and explicating their main themes. (For further
developments and applications of the method see Fischer & Wertz,
1979; Giorgi, 1985.) It should be noted that meaning condensation is
not limited to a phenomenological approach and has been applied in
other qualitative studies (see Mayring, 1983; Tesch, 1990).

Meaning Categorization

The analysis of the interviews on grades will be used to illustrate
the procedure of categorization. The 30 pupil interviews were categorized in order to test the hypothesis that using grades to measure
learning affects both learning and social relations in school. The transcriptions of the 30 interviews came to 762 pages. Based on educational literature and pilot interviews, a grade perspective on school

Main dimensions	Subcategories

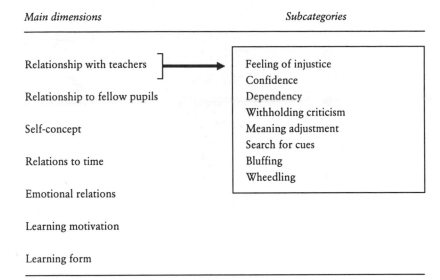

Relationship with teachers → Feeling of injustice
Confidence

Relationship to fellow pupils — Dependency
Withholding criticism

Self-concept — Meaning adjustment
Search for cues

Relations to time — Bluffing
Wheedling

Emotional relations

Learning motivation

Learning form

Figure 11.2. Dimensions and Categories of the Grading Perspective

learning was specified to seven main dimensions, which were themselves differentiated into subcategories.

In Figure 11.2 the seven dimensions of the grade perspective on learning are shown in the left-hand column, and the eight subcategories of one of these dimensions—Relationship With the Teacher—in the right-hand column. For the other six dimensions, corresponding subcategories with content appropriate to each dimension were also made (not included in Fig. 11.2); in all, this came to 42 categories. The categories were taken from previous studies of grading and from pilot interviews in this project. Each category was defined: for example, *Bluffing*—the pupil attempts to give the impression that he knows more than he knows, and with the purpose of obtaining better grades, for example by raising his hand eagerly (cognitive, related to subject matter, acceptable). *Wheedling*—the pupil attempts to win the sympathy of the teacher with the purpose of obtaining better grades (emotional, often unrelated to the subject matter, unacceptable).

Every interview was coded as a whole for each of the 42 categories of attitudes and behaviors in relation to school grades. The categorizations were done as close to the pupil's self-understanding as possible, so that in principle the pupils themselves would accept the

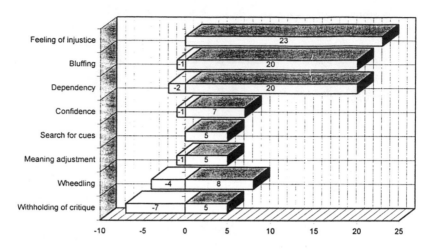

Figure 11.3. Influence of Grades on Pupil's Relationship to Teacher
NOTE: Numbers to the right show how many of the 30 pupils confirmed occurrences of a grading attitude and behavior; negative numbers to the left show how many disconfirmed a grading attitude and behavior. As several pupils had no, or vague, statements regarding a subcategory, the sum of direct confirmations and disconfirmations is less than 30.

categorizations of their statements. The interviews were categorized independently by two coders and their codings were combined. By divergences, a dialogue solution was attempted. In cases where the two coders did not reach a consensus, a third coder was summoned.

Figure 11.3 depicts how many of the 30 pupils confirmed or disconfirmed the eight categories of the dimension—Relationship With the Teacher. The results in general confirmed the hypothesis that grades influence pupils' relationships with their teachers. This varied from 23 of the 30 pupils confirming, and none disconfirming, a feeling of injustice about their grades; to 5 confirming and 7 disconfirming a withholding of critique of their teachers for fear of repercussions on their grades. Similar degrees of support for the grade hypothesis were found for the six other dimensions of the grade perspective. The interviews showed only a weak support for the hypothesis of an increased grade perspective after the introduction of a grade-based, restricted admission to college introduced the year before. In addition to this form of categorization, the grade interviews were also subjected to deeper qualitative interpretations, some examples of which will be discussed in Chapter 12.

The categorization of the meanings of the pupils' statements served several purposes: (a) The categorizations structured the extensive and complex interviews and gave an overview of the occurrence of grading behaviors among the 30 pupils interviewed. Thus in seven tables, as shown in Figure 11.3, the main results of 762 pages of interview transcription regarding the extent of grading attitudes and behaviors could be reported. (b) The categorization made it possible to test the hypothesis that grades influence learning. (c) The quantification of grading behaviors, such as those shown in Figure 11.3, gives readers a background for judging how typical the quotes used in the accompanying qualitative analyses were for the interview material as a whole. (d) The categorization made it possible to investigate differences in grading behavior for different groups among the 30 pupils, such as boys versus girls and pupils with high versus low grades. In this study no significant differences were found. (e) Quantification also made comparisons to other investigations on the effects of grades possible. (f) The categorization could itself be checked for coder reliability and made some checks for interviewer reliability possible; this will be discussed later (see Control of Analysis, below).

The categorization of meanings has long been used for analyzing qualitative material. Categorization is in line with, but not limited to, a positivist emphasis on quantification of facts in the social sciences. Several techniques were developed in the content analysis tradition during World War II to analyze enemy propaganda. The different techniques will not be reviewed here (see, e.g., Miles & Huberman, 1994; Tesch, 1990).

Meaning Structuring Through Narratives

An interview analysis can be treated as a form of narration, as a continuation of the story told by the interviewee. A narrative analysis of what was said leads to a new story to be told, a story developing the themes of the original interview. The analysis may also be a condensation or a reconstruction of the many tales told by the different subjects into a richer, more condensed and coherent story than the scattered stories of the separate interviewees.

The interview used to demonstrate meaning condensation (see Meaning Condensation, above, & Chapter 2, A Research Interview on Learning) started out with a subject's spontaneous story about how she learned the difference between horizontal and vertical lines when decorating a room. Giorgi used the content of the story to develop essential meanings of learning, and he did not analyze the story as narrative.

Mishler's book *Research Interviewing—Context and Narrative* (1986) is a pioneering study of the use of narratives in interview research. He outlines the many interpretative possibilities of treating interviews as narratives, emphasizing the temporal, the social, and the meaning structures of narratives. A narrative contains a *temporal* sequence, a patterning of happenings. It has a *social* dimension, someone is telling something to someone. And it has a *meaning,* a plot giving the story a point and a unity. One of the main social functions of narratives is to maintain social ties: The narratives of a group contribute to constituting the group's identity and to holding the group together (see also Polkinghorne, 1988).

The narrative dimension of interviews is often overlooked. Mishler recounts how, in his study of doctor-patient interaction, there was a long story from a patient about his financial situation. Mishler had initially perceived it as a long digression and disregarded it in the first analysis of the interview. Then, through a closer look from a narrative perspective, the story came to yield essential insight into the nature of doctor-patient interactions. The verbatim and the narrative transcriptions of Leonora's story about her puppy (Chapter 9, Transcription Reliability and Validity, and Table 9.2) were taken from an article by Mishler (1991) in which he discusses the narrative structure of the story and calls attention to the need for linguistic competence to discover and develop narrative structures.

The interview researcher may pay attention to narratives during both interviewing and analyzing, as well as at the reporting stage. When spontaneous stories appear during interviews, the interviewer can encourage the subjects to let their stories unfold. The interviewer may also help the subjects to produce a coherent story, which can be illustrated with an analogy: A small child comes running to his parent, trying to tell about some dramatic event it has experienced, but is too excited by the event itself and needs assistance from someone to create an intelligible story with a sequence understandable to others about what happened. Furthermore, the interviewer can work toward narrative forms during the interview, for example by directly asking for stories and trying together with the interviewee to structure the different happenings recounted into coherent stories.

An author starting on a novel may have a main plot in mind that will be developed on the way. An interview inquiry, too, may be seen as leading to a story the researcher wants to tell, where the key points he or she want to relate to the readers are kept in mind from the start. In both cases the characters may take on their own life during the writing, developing along lines other than those intended by the author, following a structural logic of their own. The result may be a good story, providing new convincing insights and opening new vistas for understanding the phenomena investigated.

During the analysis the researcher may alternate between being a "narrative-finder"—looking for narratives contained in the interviews, and being a "narrative-creator"—molding the many different happenings into coherent stories. In both cases the researcher can employ the concepts and the tools worked out in the humanities for the analysis of narratives, such as the actant model developed by Propp on the basis of Russian fairy tales and Labov's narrative model (see Cortazzi, 1993; Jensen, 1989).

Meaning Interpretation

Although *analysis* and *interpretation* have been used interchangeably throughout this book, I here reserve the latter term for more extensive and deeper interpretations of meaning, inspired by hermeneutical philosophy (Chapter 3, Hermeneutical Interpretation). The researcher has a perspective on what is investigated and interprets the interviews from this perspective. The interpreter goes beyond what is directly said to work out structures and relations of meaning not immediately apparent in a text. This requires a certain distance from what is said, which is achieved by a methodical or theoretical stance, recontextualizing what is said in a specific conceptual context.

The influence of different conceptual frameworks during interpretation is illustrated in Scheflen's article "Susan Smiled: On Explanations in Family Therapy" (1978). It is cast in a story form with a group of therapists watching and commenting on a therapy session. At one point the daughter, Susan, had smiled in an enigmatic way. The discussion among the observers about the meaning of this nonverbal statement, leading to six different interpretations, can also highlight issues of interview interpretation.

One therapist suggested that the smile was sarcastic, thus invoking an expressional paradigm, where a person's actions are attributed to something within the person. Then one member of the group offered a second interpretation by pointing out that Susan had smiled just after her father had turned to her, held out his hands, and said "I think Susan loves us. We certainly love her." The smile is now seen as a response to her father's statement. A further observation led to a third interpretation: After Susan had smiled, her mother turned to her and said: "You never appreciate what we try to do for you." The smile was now interpreted as a provocation, as a stimulus for the mother's reprimand.

In these three explanations Susan's smile was interpreted as an expression, as a response, and as a stimulus. The first focused on Susan in isolation, the second brought up the preceding context and the father-daughter relationship, and the third included the succeeding context and the mother-daughter relationship. A fourth interpretation followed from a closer focus on the interpersonal interaction, noticing that the three members of the family often acted and reacted to each other by withdrawal: When Susan smiled her father turned his face away and fell silent, and when the mother began her reprimand Susan reacted in a similar way. A fifth interpretation followed when the tape was played back and the therapists looked for incidents similar to the sequence in which Susan smiled. There had been two previous exchanges where the father approached, Susan smiled, and the mother reprimanded. This indicated a programmed interaction in this family, the actors following an unwritten script and interacting according to a preexisting scenario. In this interpretation, moving from an individual-centered to a cultural interpretation, Susan smiled because this was the part she was expected to play in the family drama. A sixth interpretation argued that although Susan's smile was a response to her father's approach, it was not a response in kind. In Bateson's language, the smile was meta to the father's statement, her metacommunication derailed her father's offer of involvement.

When discussing the six therapists' interpretations of Susan's smile, Scheflen (1978) does not side with any one model: "These are usually presented as opposing truths in different doctrinal schools, but they are all valid from one point of view or another. And, accordingly, they are all tactically useful at some point or another" (p. 59). The various modes of explanation can be used deliberately as tactics throughout a therapy, can be tactically employed to alter habitual tendencies to deny, ignore, project, and blame: "In the course of family therapy our clients can learn multiple approaches from us and end up with a more flexible and comprehensive strategy for viewing and making sense of their experiences" (Scheflen, 1978, p. 68). The issues of multiple interpretations raised by this case will be addressed again in Chapter 12 and the pragmatic approach to validating interpretations according to their usefulness in Chapter 13.

Interpretations of meaning are sometimes steeped in a mistrust toward the meanings directly expressed. A critical distance in interpretation is found in the form of a "hermeneutics of suspicion" to what a person directly says and a text manifestly expresses, interpreting the meaning to be something else than is directly said, being suspicious of some hidden intention or plot. Thus Hamlet's interview was interpreted earlier as an expression of a pervasive distrust of the words and the acts of others, leading to conversations of "per indirections find directions out" (Chapter 8, Hamlet's Interview). In the social sciences a hermeneutics of suspicion is pronounced in psychoanalysis and Marxism, where the interpreter looks for meanings behind or beneath what is directly expressed—in psychoanalysis as manifestations of unconscious forces, and in Marxism as manifestations of an ideology concealing the basic contradictions of the social and economical forces at work.

Ad Hoc Meaning Generation

The most frequent form of interview analysis is probably an ad hoc use of different approaches and techniques for meaning generation. In contrast to the above condensation and categorization of meanings, in this case no standard method is used for analyzing the whole of the interview material. There is instead a free interplay of techniques during the analysis. Thus the researcher may read the interviews through and get an overall impression, then go back to specific passages, perhaps make some quantifications like counting statements indicating different attitudes to a phenomenon, make deeper interpretations of specific statements, cast parts of the interview into a narrative, work out metaphors to capture the material, attempt a visualization of the findings in flow diagrams, and so on. Such tactics of meaning generation may, for interviews lacking an overall sense at the first reading, bring out connections and structures significant to the research project.

Thirteen such tactics for generating meaning in qualitative texts are discussed and exemplified by Miles and Huberman (1994). They are arranged roughly from the descriptive to the explanatory, and from the concrete to the more conceptual and abstract:

> *Noting patterns, themes* (1), *seeing plausibility* (2), and *clustering* (3) help the analyst see "what goes with what." *Making metaphors* (4), like the preceding three tactics, is a way to achieve more integration among diverse pieces of data. *Counting* (5) is also a familiar way to see "what's there."
>
> *Making contrasts/comparisons* (6) is a pervasive tactic that sharpens understanding. Differentiation sometimes is needed, too, as in *partitioning variables* (7).
>
> We also need tactics for seeing things and their relationships more abstractly. These include *subsuming particulars under the general* (8); *factoring* (9), an analogue to a familiar quantitative technique; *noting relations between variables* (10); and *finding intervening variables* (11).
>
> Finally, how can we systematically assemble a coherent understandable of data? The tactics discussed are *building a logical chain of evidence* (12) and *making conceptual/theoretical coherence* (13). (pp. 245-246)

During the analysis of the grade interviews, several ad hoc techniques were tried out, and one example concerning grades and talkativity will be taken up in Chapter 12.

Issues of Analysis

Some principal issues of analysis will now be raised: the pervasiveness of interpretation, quantitative and qualitative analysis, and theoretical presuppositions.

The Pervasiveness of Interpretation. Analysis is not an isolated stage, but permeates an entire interview inquiry. For the six steps of analysis in Box 11.1, a continuity of description and interpretation was outlined for an entire investigation. The extensiveness of the interpretation was also emphasized for the seven stages of an interview design (Chapter 5) as well as in answering the 1,000-page question (Chapter 10). Meaning clarification and interpretation were suggested throughout the interview situation, and it was postulated that the ideal interview would be interpreted by the end of the interaction (Chapter 8). The transformation from oral speech to written text was depicted as a translation and an interpretation, illustrated by the different transcriptions of the story of Leona's puppy (Chapter 9, Transcription Reliability and Validity, and Table 9.2). The role of interpretation will continue during verification and reporting of the interviews (Chapters 13 & 14). A recognition of the pervasiveness of interpretation throughout an entire interview inquiry may counteract a common overemphasis on methods of analysis as *the* one way to find the meaning of interviews.

Quantitative and Qualitative Analysis. An ideological dichotomization of quantitative and qualitative methods in the social sciences was discussed earlier (Chapter 4, Qualitative and Quantitative Research). During the concrete analyses of the grading interviews, multiple interactions of quantitative and qualitative approaches took place. Three instances will be mentioned: qualitative development of categories for quantification, qualitative differentiation of categories through quantification, and the problem of quantification of a complex phenomenon as denials.

It was a presupposition for the quantification of the grading behaviors that the categories had been developed qualitatively on the basis of previous literature and pilot interviews. The requirement that the interview statements be coded in an "either/or" manner required precise definitions of the categories. When testing the categories in pilot interviews, this led to further qualitative differentiations of grading behaviors, such as dividing "competition" into refined categories with clearly different meanings for the pupils, such as "comparison oriented," "grade jealousy," "sportsmanlike competition," and "destructive competition." This quantitative scoring procedure presupposed a qualitative development of the categories, and it contributed to a qualitative differentiation of these categories. The very development and differentiation of categories is mainly a qualitative endeavor, and the creation of appropriate categories may be just as significant a contribution of knowledge as the number of observations made for the different categories.

From a purely quantitative viewpoint, one might expect that the more frequently a form of grading behavior was confirmed or disconfirmed the more certain the categorization would be. In some cases, however, problems with such a quantitative approach to coding could arise, such as with the interpretation of many denials of competition as possibly meaning a confirmation (Chapter 9, Transcribing Interviews). Following the categorization procedure based on the level of the pupil's self-understanding, this statement was coded as indicating non-occurrence of competition. With a deeper interpretation, leading to a confirmation of competition, this example points to a principal limitation of the quantification of qualitative interview material. It would be foolhardy to give an exact quantitative measure of how many "nos" are needed before they can come to mean "yes." Deciding when a quantitative increase in negation turns around and becomes a confirmation requires a critical qualitative interpretation of the linguistic style, the pauses, and the intonation of the statement. For such complex, ambiguous, and contradictory interview statements an exact quantitative scoring is in principle impossible; it is not feasible to give an exact quantitative criterion of how many denials are required before the denials become an involuntary confirmation.

Theoretical Presuppositions. The theoretical basis of an investigation provides the context for making decisions about how interviews will be analyzed. Different techniques of analysis are means for answering different thematic questions. The analyst's theoretical conceptions of the subject matter influence how he or she analyzes the interviews. The analysis of the interviews may be part of generating a theory, as well as an application or a testing of theories.

In the grounded theory approach developed by Glaser and Strauss, there is an attempt through the analysis of the data to develop a theoretical interpretation of what is seen and heard (Strauss & Corbin,

1990). The field studies here involve observations as well as informal or formal interviews. There is a continual coding and recoding of the observations, as the researcher's insight grows during an investigation, working toward an empirically grounded theory.

In the present discussion of design the example of teasing was used to illustrate how different theoretical conceptions would lead to different forms of questioning (Chapter 5, Designing), a issue taken up again with the demonstration interview about grades (Chapter 7, An Interview About Grades). Freudian, Rogerian, and Skinnerian approaches to the understanding of such phenomena as teasing and grades will likewise lead to different forms of analysis of the interview texts, emphasizing different aspects and contexts of the phenomena.

On a metatheoretical level there are contrasting conceptions of the meanings to be reported through analysis, such as with the postmodern, hermeneutical, phenomenological, and dialectical perspectives to interview research discussed in Chapter 3. This includes meaning finding versus meaning construction, as indicated by the miner and the traveler metaphors of interview research. In the miner approach, the analyst uncovers and purifies the meanings more or less buried in the interviews. In the traveler approach, the analyst co-creates with the subjects the meanings he or she reports, and through interpretation constructs elaborate stories.

Control of Analysis

Control is a key issue for the analysis of large amounts of complex interview material. In contrast to the readers of a critic's analysis of a poem, the readers of an interview report will not have access to the tape recordings and the often many hundreds of pages of interviews that the researcher's interpretations are based on. Nor do the interview texts pose the same amount of resistance to the interpreter as a patient would do in a therapy situation. The reader of an interview study has to depend on the researcher's selection and contextualization of interview statements. Two approaches to control the interview analysis will be mentioned here: the use of multiple interpreters and the explication of procedures.

Multiple Interpreters. The analysis of interviews is often undertaken by the researcher alone, and the reader is left with little material for evaluating the influence of the researcher's perspective on the outcome of the analysis. By using several interpreters for the same interviews, a certain control of haphazard or biased subjectivity in analysis is possible. Several coders are frequently used for categorization and could be used more often for interpretations of the deeper meanings of the interviews.

When categorizing the interviews in the grade study, both a dialogical and an arithmetical approach to intersubjective agreement were included (Chapter 4, Objectivity in Qualitative Research). *Coder reliability* was checked on a sample of the interviews; here the two coders independently had the same scorings for 39% of the instances and different scorings for 61%. For the latter, the two coders reached agreement through discussion for 60%, and for the remaining 1% a third coder was called in to have the final word. The intersubjective agreement obtained by the categorizations indicates that other coders, using the same coding procedure, would be likely to arrive at the same categorizations of the interviews. A further check was made to see if I, the project leader, would more often get my own categorizations accepted instead of those of the paid student assistants. This was found not to be the case.

Furthermore, the categorization made some checks on *interviewer reliability* possible—whether the pupils' descriptions of the effects of grading were influenced differently by the four interviewers in the study. A significant difference was found between two interviewers on amount of grading behaviors reported. A check revealed that one had followed the interview guide very conscientiously and taken care to have the pupils cover the many themes in the interview guide, whereas the other had more often pursued the many interesting leads that came up during the interviews.

When different meanings are found by different analysts, they may be worked together into a dialogue leading to an intersubjective agreement. Or the different meanings found can be reported side by side, accompanied by the reasons for the divergent interpretations, such as by the majority and minority votums in official committees. The use of several analysts may not only serve as a control of a random or prejudiced subjectivity, it may also lead to an enrichment of the analysis by including multiple perspectives. The discussions about the different interpretations can lead to a conceptual clarification and refinement of the issues in question, such as in the interpretation of Susan's smile (see Meaning Interpretation, above).

Explication of Procedures. An alternative or a supplement to a multiple interpreter control of analysis is that the researcher present examples of the material used for the interpretations and explicitly outline the different steps of the analysis process. In Giorgi's phenomenological analysis, the researcher's "cards" were put on the table for inspection. The readers could then retrace and check the steps of the analysis. Giorgi (1975) acknowledges that another investigator, looking at the data differently, could write a different general description, though hardly wholly different:

> Consequently, the control comes from the researcher's context or perspective on the data. Once the context and intention becomes known, the divergence is usually intelligible to all even if not universally agreeable. Thus the chief point to be remembered with this type of research is not so much whether another position with respect to the data could be adopted (this point is granted beforehand), but whether a reader, adopting the same viewpoint as articulated by the researcher, can also see what the researcher saw, whether or not he agrees with it. That is the key criterion for qualitative research. (p. 96)

In the next chapter I will attempt to "lay my cards on the table" through the interpretation of interview statements on grades, in order to make it possible for the reader to follow the steps of the interpretative process.

12

The Plurality of Interpretations

One approach to interview analysis will now be treated in some detail
—extensive and critical interpretations of the meanings of interview
statements—and supplemented by some ad hoc techniques. First a
plurality of interpretations and the hermeneutic primacy of the question will be discussed. Then interview reports about grades are interpreted with respect to different questions and contexts, and validation
of the multiple interpretations will be related to the questions raised
and to the communities of validation. In conclusion, a modern quest
for meaning is contrasted with a postmodern deconstruction of sub-
stantialized meanings.

The Primacy of the Question

A common objection to interview interpretations goes like this:
"Different interpreters find different meanings in the same interview,
the interview is thus not a scientific method."

Dissimilar interpretations of the same interview passages do occur,
though probably less than is commonly assumed. The above objection
involves a demand for objectivity in the sense that a statement has only
one correct and objective meaning, and the task of interpretation is to
find this one and only true meaning. Contrary to such a requirement
of unequivocality, hermeneutical and postmodern modes of understanding allow for a legitimate plurality of interpretations (see Chapter
3, Hermeneutical Interpretation; and Postmodern Construction).

There are multiple questions that can be posed to a text, with different questions leading to different meanings of a text. A hermeneutic question-answer dialectic is not only a matter of the questions the reader poses to a text, but also of an openness to the questions with which the text confronts the reader.

An interpreter's presuppositions enter into the questions he or she poses to a text. These questions codetermine what meanings can be found in the text. Some hermeneutic distinctions of types of questions to texts now follow. A first question concerns the relation of the author's and the reader's meaning. Is the purpose of a text interpretation to get at the *author's intended meaning* of the text—what Ibsen really meant to say with his play *Peer Gynt*—or does it concern the *meaning the text has for us* today? The interpretation of an interview involves a related distinction—is the purpose to analyze, for example, interviews about grades in order to arrive at the individual pupils' understanding of their grades? Or is the aim for the researcher to develop, through the pupils' descriptions, a broader interpretation of the meaning of grades in the educational system?

Another issue in interpretation concerns whether it is the *letter of the text* or *its "spirit"* that is to be interpreted in, for example, a legal text. Is what matters to get at the expressed meaning or at the intended meaning? In interview studies, this becomes a question of the level on which the interpretations should take place: Should the interviews be analyzed on a manifest level? Or is the purpose to get at latent meanings that are not explicitly conscious for the subject, as in the "depth hermeneutics" of psychoanalysis?

A third issue implies the principal question of whether there exists *one correct interpretation* of a literary text or of a Bible story; or whether there is a *legitimate plurality of interpretations*. Can the gospels of the New Testament thus be said to have one correct interpretation, or are they essentially ambiguous, open to different interpretations? If the principle of a legitimate plurality of interpretations through interview analyses is accepted, it becomes meaningless to pose strict requirements of interpreter consensus. What then matters is to formulate explicitly the evidence and arguments that enter into an interpretation, so that the interpretation can be tested by other readers.

A fourth issue involves the question of what aspects of a theme should be interpreted, and in what larger context. Hermeneutical text

interpretations, psychoanalytical studies, and also psychological interview investigations, have often involved an individualistic and idealistic focus on the experiences and intentions of individuals. There has
been a neglect of the *social and material context* the persons live in;
see Sartre's (1963) critique of the "psychoanalyzing" of Robespierre's
reasons for his political behavior (Chapter 3, Dialectical Situating).
The interview method as such does not, however, need to be idealistic
or individualistic. It is mainly the contexts in which it has been used
that have given the interview method this characteristic.

In current interview research the variety of interpretations is not
the main problem, but rather the lack of explicit formulation of the
research questions to a text. We may distinguish between a biased and
a perspectival subjectivity by differences of interpretation (see also
Chapter 4, Objectivity in Qualitative Research). A *biased subjectivity*
simply means sloppy and unreliable work; researchers noticing only
evidence that supports their own opinions, selectively interpreting and
reporting statements justifying their own conclusions, overlooking any
counterevidence. A *perspectival subjectivity* appears when researchers
who adopt different perspectives and pose different questions to the
same text come up with different interpretations of the meaning. A
subjectivity in this sense of multiple perspectival interpretations is a
specific strength of interview research. When the readers' different
perspectives on a text are made explicit, the different interpretations
should also become comprehensible (see Giorgi's criterion of qualitative research in Chapter 11, Control of Analysis). With an explication
of the perspectives adopted toward an interview text and a specification of the researchers' questions posed to an interview passage,
several interpretations of the same text will not be a weakness, but a
richness and a strength of interview research.

When different interpretations appear arbitrary, this may in part
be because the questions asked of a text are not explicitly stated. The
issue is here not only that of making the researcher's questions to a
text explicit, but also of what questions can legitimately be put to a
text. In interpretations of legal texts this may be of vital interest, such
as whether it is justifiable in the interpretation of a law to ask about
the intentions of the original lawmakers, or whether it is only the letter
of the law as it stands today that can be taken into account when
deciding a case. Decisions about what questions to a text are allowable,

codetermining the range of answers, is in the final analysis an issue of power. In law it is the politically appointed Supreme Court that has the final decision about the legitimate context for the interpretation of a legal text.

Questions Posed to an Interview Text

The relationship between questions posed to, and answers from, a text will be illustrated with interpretations of interview statements about grades. One question concerns the context of interpretation. Another question is whether the interviewee is considered an informant or a representative. A third question concerns interview statements in which the information is empirically invalid, but that may provide valuable knowledge about production and consequences of the invalid knowledge.

THREE CONTEXTS OF INTERPRETATION

I know that somebody will say that it is wheedling ("apple polishing") if one seems to be more interested in a subject matter than is usual and says: "This is really interesting," asks a lot of questions, wanting explanations. I don't think it is . . .

In religious instruction, where we get grades (from the teacher), but do not have an examination at the end of the school year, there is plenty of time to talk about anything else. Well, people do their homework during these lessons, and then we sometimes, perhaps two or three of us, discuss something interesting with the teacher. And then, afterwards, it sometimes happens that someone remarks: "Well, well, somebody seems to be wheedling."

(*Later on in the interview, about other pupils*): Sometimes we don't know whether they do it in order to wheedle or not, but at other times it seems very opportunistic. (*In a tense voice*) It's rather unpleasant . . . It isn't easy to figure out whether people wheedle or whether they're just interested.

This high school girl's statement is rich in information about grading's influence on the relationships between teachers and pupils. It is, however, not quite clear what her remarks mean. In order to explicate their meaning, several types of questions will be asked of the

TABLE 12.1 Contexts of Interpretation and Communities of Validation

Contexts of Interpretation	Communities of Validation
Self-understanding	The interviewed subject
Critical commonsense understanding	The general public
Theoretical understanding	The research community

statement. A first line of inquiry addresses the meaning of the text in three different interpretational contexts: self-understanding, a critical commonsense understanding, and a theoretical understanding.

Contexts of interpretation are presented in the left-hand column in Table 12.1, and the corresponding communities for validation in the right-hand column. I will first interpret the statement about wheedling in the three contexts of self-understanding, a critical commonsense understanding, and theoretical understanding and thereafter bring up the corresponding communities of validation.

Self-Understanding. The interpreter here attempts to formulate in a condensed form what the subjects themselves understand to be the meanings of their statements. The interpretation is more or less confined to the subjects' self-understanding: a rephrased condensation of the meaning of the interviewees' statement from their own viewpoints as these are understood by the researcher. The meaning condensation used by Giorgi, and also the categorization of the grade interviews, took place within the context of the subject's self-understanding (Chapter 11, Meaning Condensation; and Meaning Categorization).

This pupil is interested in religion and enjoys discussing it with the teacher, but she experiences that other pupils may regard this as wheedling. In other situations, she has difficulty determining whether the other pupils wheedle or whether they are actually interested in the subject matter. She experiences this ambiguity as rather unpleasant.

Critical Commonsense Understanding. The interpretation here goes beyond reformulating the subjects' self-understanding—what they themselves experience and mean about a topic—while remaining within the context of a commonsense understanding. The interpretations may include a wider frame of understanding than that of the subjects themselves, be critical of what is said, and may focus on either the content of the statement or on the person making it. The interpretation of the statement with the denials of competition mentioned earlier (Chapter 9, Transcribing Interviews; Chapter 11, Issues of Analysis) thus went beyond the pupil's self-understanding to include a critical commonsense reading of the many denials as possibly meaning a confirmation.

By including general knowledge about the *content* of the statement it is possible to amplify and enrich the interpretation of a statement. For the question "What does the statement express about the phenomenon of wheedling?" the girl's statement may be interpreted as a manifestation of a basic ambiguity in the teacher-pupil relationship created by grading. Within a dominating grade perspective, the subject matter and the human relationships in school are "instrumentalized": They become mere means toward the goal of the highest possible grade point average. In the classroom it may appear ambiguous whether an expressed interest in a topic is genuine, or whether it is just a means to "twist" the teacher in the interest of improving one's grades.

The questions put to the text may also center on the *person,* asking what a statement expresses about the interviewed subject. Thus in the earlier interpretation of Hamlet's interview the question to the interaction was changed from the manifest content, that is, the shape of a cloud, to the person of Polonius and his trustworthiness (Chapter 8, Hamlet's Interview). In the pupil's statement above, the question "What does it express about the pupil's own relation to wheedling?" may lead to an interpretation that this girl employs two standards: The same activity of talking interestedly with the teacher is evaluated more positively when conducted by herself than when carried out by others. The topic involves a conflict for her; her voice is tense, and a speculative interpretation might be that she belongs to that group of pupils whom the others accuse of wheedling.

Theoretical Understanding. In a third context, a theoretical frame for interpreting the meaning of a statement is applied. The interpretations are then likely to go beyond the subject's self-understanding and also to exceed a commonsense understanding, such as when incorporating a psychoanalytic theory of the individual or a Marxist theory of society.

In a somewhat speculative interpretation, the psychoanalytical concept of "projection" may be used: At an unconscious level the pupil projects her own nonacceptable wheedling behavior onto other pupils, while denying it for herself.

In a Marxist theory about the school as socializing to wage labor, with grades as the currency of the school system (Bowles & Gintis, 1976; Kvale, 1972), the statement about apple polishing may be interpreted as an expression of learning at school having a "commodity character." The pupils learn—through the grading of their learning—how to distinguish between the use value and the exchange value of their work. Their questions to the teacher may be led by a utility interest in obtaining a better understanding of the knowledge presented. The questions may also be part of an instrumental exchange relation; the knowledge about which they ask interested questions has no intrinsic use value for the pupils, the questions only serve the purpose of making a positive impression on the teacher—an impression that can be exchanged for a higher grade. At school the pupils thus learn to subordinate the use value of their work to its exchange value.

Interrelatedness of Interpretational Contexts. The three interpretational contexts derive from different explications of the researcher's perspective and lead to different interpretations. The contexts may be further differentiated, and they may also merge into each other. The instrumental attitude toward learning—knowledge as a mere means to high grades—which was discussed above in a commonsense context, also follows from sociological and Marxist theories about education. At the same time, this means-ends thinking may be part of the everyday consciousness of school. For some of the Danish pupils, such an instrumental attitude was an open part of their self-understanding:

> My interests have taken me very far from that which takes place at high school. I go here with the explicit purpose of getting as good an examination as possible, with the least possible effort.

The contexts of interpretation suggested above serve to make explicit the questions posed to a statement. One pupil's description of wheedling has given rise to a number of interpretations. The various interpretations are, according to the present perspective, not haphazard or subjective, but follow as answers to different questions to the text. Not only the questions to the interviewees, but also the questions to the interview texts co-constitute the answers obtained.

THREE COMMUNITIES OF VALIDATION

Different communities of validation correspond to the three interpretational contexts outlined above—the interviewed subject, the general public, and the research community.

The Interviewee. When the interviewee's own understanding of a statement is asked for, the validity of the researcher's interpretations is, in principle, decided by the subject. The pupil's "yes" or "no" to the interpretation that she herself does not wheedle but believes that other pupils maybe do, is here the criterion for validity. Within the context of self-understanding applied by the categorization of the grade interviews, the girl's statement was cautiously classified as not confirming an occurrence of wheedling. It is seldom possible in the actual analysis of many interviews to present every single interpretation to the interviewees for confirmation or disconfirmation. The researcher then tries to keep his or her interpretations within the interviewee's context of understanding as seen by the researcher.

The General Public. The interpretation is made within the understanding of a general public. The deliberations of a jury in court is one example of a critical common sense of understanding. The criterion for validity is then whether a consensus may be obtained that an interpretation is reasonably documented and logically coherent. The statement on wheedling was interpreted above as an expression of a basic ambiguity in the teacher-pupil relationship due to grading. It is here up to lay readers to judge whether the interpretation is reasonably documented and argued. The validity of interpretation does not, in this case, depend on the acceptance of the subject interpreted, but upon the fact of whether the documentation and the argumentation are convincing to members of the general public.

The Theoretical Community. When a statement is interpreted within a theoretical context, the validity of the interpretation will depend on whether the theory is valid for the area studied, and whether the specific interpretations follow logically from the theory.

An evaluation of the validity of a theoretical interpretation presupposes a specific theoretical competence. Thus, in contrast to a lay jury testing the validity of critical commonsense interpretations, theoretical interpretations are validated by a community of researchers.

The validity of the interpretation of wheedling—as an expression of the commodity character of schoolwork—will thus depend on a judgment of whether Marx's economic commodity theory is still valid today, whether it can be generalized from the economics domain to the field of education, and whether the specific interpretation involves a reasonable use of the commodity categories. The validity of the interpretation will, in this case, depend on a dialogue among theoretically competent persons with a knowledge of the current position of Marxist theory.

INTERPRETATION OF CONTENT OR OF PERSON

Until now I have focused on the validity of the researcher's interpretation of the interviewee's statement. Validity also pertains to the content of the subjects' statements. What the subjects tell may be true or false, they can be a reliable or unreliable witness about their own behavior and that of others.

As one approach to the validity of a subject's statement, a distinction between two perspectives toward the interviewee will be made: as an *informant,* a subject, a witness; or as a *representative,* as an object of analysis. Hamlet's interview of Polonius may again be used (Chapter 8, Hamlet's Interview). From an informant's perspective on what the cloud looks like, the content of Polonius's answers is, due to Hamlet's leading questions, worthless. From a representative perspective, the indirect message about Polonius's credibility is for Hamlet a matter of life or death.

In the interview by Socrates and the one reported by Giorgi, the subjects were regarded as informants, providing conceptual knowledge on love and beauty and empirical knowledge of the nature of learning, respectively (Chapter 2). In the therapeutic interview reported by Rogers, the content of the client's accusations of the therapist hating her were likely distorted (Chapter 2). The probably false accusations represented, however, something important about the client making the accusations, which she, assisted by the therapist's reflections of her statements, eventually realized herself.

The pupils participating in the grade interviews were, from one viewpoint, informants: They provided information about the influence of grades on the learning and work situations at high school. The pupils were witnesses—"observer substitutes"—of the classroom interaction. Their task was to report as reliably as possible what they had experienced about the grades' influence on their own and other pupils' behavior. In this first perspective, which involves a *veridical* reading of the statements, the focus is on the content of the subjects' observations and experiences. In a second perspective involving a *symptomatical* reading, the subjects' own relations to the phenomena they describe are the topic of interest. The pupils interviewed are representatives of pupils in general, they are objects subjected to the effects of grading, their statements represent the effects that grades have on pupils. In this approach the pupils' own relationships to the phenomena are of interest, such as resistance toward talking about specific aspects of grading, hesitance when describing wheedling, denial of grades' influence on the school situation, or a distinct exaggeration of the grades' influence.

The different questions of validity raised by a veridical or a symptomatical reading can be illustrated in relation to the following statement:

> Grades are often unjust, because very often—very often—they are only a measure for how much you talk and for how much you agree with the teacher's opinion.

The interview context for this statement was presented earlier (Chapter 1, Conversation as Research). In a veridical reading of the statement above, the pupil gives a rather precise formulation of two beliefs: Grades are very often only a measure for (a) how much you talk, and (b) how much you agree with the teacher's opinion.

Both assertions can, in principle, be empirically verified or falsified. A "triangulation" may be used here. This means that the same phenomenon is investigated from different angles to determine its exact location, in the present context by including different informants and methods to determine its precise meaning and validity. Concerning "informant-triangulation," several other pupils when interviewed also pointed to a connection between amount of speech and grades obtained, as well as that an adaptation to the teacher's opinions led to higher grades. When the two assertions were presented in a questionnaire to a larger sample of pupils, a majority confirmed the first assertion and rejected the latter (see Box 5.4 in Chapter 5). Both beliefs were rejected by the teachers interviewed. The assertions are not new; for example, one or both have been put forward earlier by another "informant"—the rector at the University of Copenhagen, Ludvig Holberg, who in a speech in 1736 criticized the university's examinations for primarily rewarding the students' verbal fluency.

By applying an ad hoc "method-triangulation," an indirect support for the veridicality of the first talkativity statement was found. When reading through the interviews from the 30 pupils it was striking how the interviews varied in number of pages, even though one school hour had been set aside for each interview. Following a hunch, I ranked the interviews according to number of pages, then correlated that to the pupils' grade point averages. The resulting correlation was 0.65, with a chance probability of $p < .001$. There is thus a significant connection between how much the pupils talked during the interviews and their grade point averages. The connection, however, is open to several interpretations: Do the pupils get high grades because they generally talk a great deal? Or are pupils who get high grades more reflected on the issues of grading, and more at ease with talking with an interviewer about grades?

In the present method context it may be noted that an ad hoc approach to meaning generation led to a significant quantitative relationship, which raises questions for further qualitative interpretations. To conclude from an informant perspective, an informant and a method triangulation provide some, but not conclusive, support for the empirical validity of the pupil's assertion of a connection between talkativity and grades.

Even if the statement in a veridical reading had been strongly falsified on an empirical level, it could, in a symptomatic reading, represent important knowledge about the effects of grading on the pupils. Two questions for a symptomatic reading, going in different temporal directions, are: (a) How does a partly invalid understanding of the basis for grading arise, how is it produced? (b) What are the consequences of a partly invalid understanding of the basis for grading for everyday life at school?

PRODUCTION OF AN INVALID UNDERSTANDING

In the grade interviews there were several statements that—in a veridical reading—had to be incorrect in content. In the passage on wheedling quoted above, the other pupils, but not the interviewee, wheedled. Of the 30 pupils interviewed, no one said that they themselves wheedled, but 8 reported directly, included in Figure 11.3, and 8 others indicated that other pupils wheedled. From an informant viewpoint, the pupils' reliability as witnesses on the presence of wheedling must thus be questioned, because a large number of the statements were obviously invalid, either in their reports about others or about themselves.

Yet in a symptomatic reading the empirically incorrect statements on wheedling may provide important knowledge about the psychological situation in which the pupils are placed by the grading system—why they were led to produce a distorted understanding. Wheedling appears to Danish high school pupils to be an unacceptable behavior that they would rather not recognize in themselves, but that some believe is necessary to achieve high grades. It refers to a basic ambiguity in the teacher-pupil relationship; the pupils may experience the same activities in themselves as a genuine interest in the subject matter and in the others as a deliberately calculating exchange attitude in order to maximize grades. In this situational analysis, grade behavior is deindividualized and interpreted as the pupils' subjective attempts to solve the contradictory demands of a school situation where their learning is graded.

The symptomatic reading concerns the origin of an invalid understanding in the conditions of the subject's life world that produce and sustain an inadequate conception of social reality. In his development of psychoanalysis, Freud was shocked to discover that a number of the patients' stories about being exposed to sexual seduction in childhood, which he had regarded as valid, turned out to be imaginary according to new information. The false stories about sexual seductions had been an important basis of a sexual theory on the origin of neuroses. The discovery that many of the patients' stories were empirically false led to a crisis of psychoanalytic theory, until Freud performed a "Copernican reversal": the decisive point for the development of a neurosis was not the sexual events themselves, but the fantasies about the sexual events.

A related reversal from a veridical to a symptomatic reading of distorted stories is found in an English study by Hagan (1986). Mothers who lived in slum areas were interviewed about their experiences with the social welfare system. They had many stories of humiliating encounters with social workers. By including other evidence, Hagan found that some of the episodes told about harsh and degrading treatment by the staff had to be exaggerated and distorted. Her first reaction was to reject the interview method, as it provided unreliable information about the staff's behavior. She adopted another perspective, however, and read the biased accounts as expressions, symptoms, of the mothers' degrading life situations. Their self-respect was strongly threatened by having to live on welfare. The distortion of their interaction with the welfare personnel could be seen as one means of sustaining the welfare clients' self-respect vis-à-vis the interviewer and possibly also for themselves.

None of the above interpretations are definitive. Thus Freud's retraction of the childhood seduction theory of neurosis has later been criticized by feminist scholars. They see his reinterpretation as a flight from his earlier provocative discoveries of sexual abuse in a Victorian society and toward a more innocuous theory of fantasies more acceptable to a bourgeois society.

THE CONSEQUENCES OF AN INVALID UNDERSTANDING

Empirically false interview statements can have real consequences for the subjects' behavior. In the following statement, the number 8 stands for the average grade on the Danish grading scale:

> You might take 8 as the average grade in a class. And then, if you want more than 8, you have to make yourself more noticed by the teacher than the other pupils. So, in order to deserve a higher grade, it almost unavoidably has to be done at the expense of others.

This pupil and several others were convinced that there had to be a certain grade average in a class and that the teacher then had only a limited number of high grades to distribute among all the pupils. If one pupil got a higher grade, then another pupil in the class must automatically get a lower grade in order to maintain the assumption of a class average of 8. The pupils' belief is invalid according to the official Danish rules on grading, and also according to the teachers interviewed.

Although the pupils' belief—that there has to be a given grade average in a class—in all likelihood is empirically false, it is part of their social reality and may have consequences for their actions at school. Several pupils reported that the belief that the class was graded on the curve led to a destructive competition ranging from passive omission of helping others to active attempts at obstructing other pupils, for fear of others improving their grades with the consequence of one's own position on the grade scale deteriorating.

Although the content of the statement about a fixed grade average is in a veridical reading likely to be invalid, it provides in a consequential reading important knowledge about the background for such pupil behaviors as a destructive competition for grades. In sociology, the phenomenon that empirically false beliefs may have real social consequences is termed the Thomas theorem—if people believe ideas are real, they are real in their consequences.

QUESTIONS PUT TO TEXTS

I have shown above how different questions put to interview texts lead to different answers. Thus one type of question led to an *experiential* reading of the pupils' statements, clarifying the understanding the pupils themselves had of grading. Another type of question led to a *veridical* reading, investigating the validity of the pupils' information about the effects of grades, here regarding the pupils as witnesses or informants. The questioning also involved a *symptomatic* reading, focusing on the pupils themselves and their reasons for making a certain statement. There was finally a *consequential* reading, addressing the consequences of the pupils' beliefs about grading for the school situation. The questions drew on different contexts of interpretation in which the validation of the answers involved different communities, such as the interviewed pupils themselves, the general public, and the research community.

A first point to be made here is the length of the analysis; the interpretations fill more than 10 times as many pages as the pupil's original statements; see also the earlier interpretations of Hamlet's interview and of the 1,000-page question. These analyses entail an expansion of the original interview text, which is hardly feasible for every one of several hundred pages of interview texts. In the present case, the many hundred remaining pages served as a background context for the above interpretations of selected statements on wheedling, instrumental motivation, talkativity and grades, and competition.

A second point is that the interview quotes selected here are not typical of the interviews as a whole, but contain particularly poignant and complex descriptions of phenomena reported less vividly by other pupils. They were selected from a theoretical perspective in that they point to key issues for the understanding of the impact of grading for the pupils.

A third point is that several of these theoretically interesting statements were very difficult to categorize unequivocally with respect to their meaning. The vagueness, ambiguities, and contradictions of such statements were sources of error in the attempt to obtain categorizations with a high intersubjective reliability, yet from an interpretational perspective they point to essential aspects of the phenomena studied.

A fourth point is that different interpretations of the same interview passage need not be the result of haphazard or biased subjectivity, but result from different research questions. What then becomes important is to formulate explicitly the questions put to a text, and in some cases also to argue the relevance and legitimacy of these questions. In the above interpretation this concerns, for example, the legitimacy of applying an economic commodity perspective to school learning.

A fifth point is that the questions posed to the pupils' statements, and the distinctions made, do not belong to some fixed interpretational scheme. They were developed during the analysis of the grade interviews and are content and context specific. They arose from the nature of the interview topic—the social context of grading—as well as from a hermeneutical approach to meaning interpretation and from the specific theoretical perspectives adopted. The questions posed here to the grading interviews may be relevant for interpretations of other types of interviews, but likely in other forms that are adapted to their specific research topic and research questions.

The Quest for "The Real Meaning"

A common question asked of interview researchers goes something like "How do you know you get to know what the person really means?" A tempting reply: "What do you really mean by 'really means'?" will probably not lead anywhere

Guessing at the meaning of "the 'real meaning' question" suggests a belief in the existence of some basic meaning nuggets stored somewhere, to be discovered and uncovered, uncontaminated, by the objective techniques of an interviewer understood as a miner digging up precious buried metals. The "real meaning" question is a leading question, in this case leading to endless pursuits of an undefined and fictitious entity. The quest for real, true meanings came to an end in philosophy some years ago. Interview researchers might still go on wild goose chases, hunting the real meanings of their subjects' experiences. Psychotherapists might still be digging for real meanings in the deep interior of their patients' unconscious psyches. Both conceive of truth as found, not as made.

A meaning storage conception involved in the question of real meanings raises issues of where the meanings are stored and also of who owns the meanings of a statement. An imagined dialogue can illustrate the issue of ownership of meanings:

A: Did you really mean that?

B: No, that is not what I said.

A: Oh yes, you said it and you did mean it!

B: I know what I wanted to say, and I know that I did not mean what you say I meant!

A: I know you, and I know what you really mean!

In this interchange, two things are disputed: the true meaning of a statement is explicitly disputed, and, somewhat more implicitly, who has the right and the power to determine the real meaning of the statement—the speaker of the original statement or the interpreting partner. An interrelational approach would regard the meanings of the conversation as belonging to neither, but existing between the subjects, in their inter-action. An interrelational interpretation of the conversation sees the interchange as a power game, a contest for who in the relationship possesses the right to attribute the definite meaning to a statement.

A miner metaphor of interview research entails a belief in the world as objectively given in meanings or numbers to be uncovered by scientific research. The search for real-meaning nuggets leads to a reification of the subjective rather than to an unfolding, a differentiation, and an enrichment of the subjective. In an interrelational conception, the interviewer is a traveling reporter who reports stories in which meanings are created through conversational interactions.

A postmodern approach forgoes the search of true fixed meanings and emphasizes descriptive nuances, differences, and paradoxes. There is a change from a substantial to a relational concept of meaning, with a move from the modern search for the one true and real meaning to a relational unfolding of meanings. Different interpreters constructing different meanings of an interview story is then not a weakness, but a strength of the interview method. Meanings and numbers are constructions of a social reality. The interview gives no direct access to unadulterated provinces of pure meanings, but is a social production of meanings through linguistic interaction: The interviewer is a co-producer and coauthor of the resulting interview text. In this interrelational conception the interviewer does not uncover some preexisting meanings, but supports the interviewees in developing their meanings throughout the course of the interview.

From a postmodern perspective, Lather (1995) has discussed the interrelational construction of meaning during the reading of texts. We read within a range of conventions, and she addresses the question of how we can learn to read our own ways of reading. Rejecting any simple analytical frame, her goal is to proliferate, juxtapose, and create disjunctions among different ways of reading, working toward a multilayered data analysis. Inspired by van Maanen's (1988) accounts of different ethnographic genres in *Tales of the Field* (see Chapter 14, Writing as Social Construction), Lather outlines different readings of the same text. Although her portrayal of reading styles pertains to a textbook, the styles may well be transposed to the reading of interview texts. In a *realist* reading there is a search for the "native's" point of view and of finding the text's essence and truth. The reader assumes an observational and descriptive role, adopting a "god's eye point of view." A *critical* reading demystifies via a hermeneutics of suspicion; it seeks deeper truth underlying the hegemonic discourse of the texts. The reader assumes the role of the emancipator of self and/or other, seeking a truth beyond ideologies and false consciousness. The reader calls attention to larger social, political, and economical issues, assuming an advocatory role, with the danger of attempting to speak for others, of saying what they want and need. A *deconstructive* reading proliferates, destabilizes, and denaturalizes. The text is read as documentation for its unconscious silences and unspoken assumptions. A deconstructive reading makes use of drawing, artistry, literary practices, and blurs the fact/fiction distinction. These different readings suggested by Lather (1995) involve different questions posed to the text and lead to different answers about the meaning of the text.

With a transition from an individual storage conception of meaning to an interrelational constitution of meaning in the original interview conversation—and in the readers' conversations with the interview text—the social and power relationships of subject and researcher become more obvious. Does the interviewer own the meanings constructed in and on an interview, interpreting it within his or her selected contexts? Or should the original "authors" of the interview statements have their say in the interpretation and communication of their stories? This is not only an issue of validity of interpretation, but of ethics and power, of the right and the power to attribute meaning to the statements of others.

In the imagined meaning dialogue above, the partners appeared to be on an equal social level, while contesting who was in power. If the meaning interpreter had the status of a professional expert, the original speaker might more humbly have accepted the "real" meanings attributed to him or her. The expert might, as "the great interpreter," appropriate the meaning from the subject's world and recontextualize the original interrelational meanings in his or her theoretical schemes. These can be meaningful and legitimate as new stories told by the interpreter, but if reified as the real meaning of the interview subject, or as the real unconscious meaning of the patient, they become more problematic. Interview research involves the danger of an "expertification" of meanings where the expert expropriates the meanings from the subjects' lived world and reifies them into his or her categories to express some more basic reality. It should here not be overlooked that the implicit, or unconscious, meanings attributed to interviewees and patients may often simply be the explicit and conscious theories of the expert interpreter.

Eco (1990, 1992) has addressed the vicissitudes of interpretation in academic texts and in his novels. *The Name of the Rose* (1984) can be read as a parody of the modern meaning hunters; as a critique of the modern quest for true and objective meanings, of "an insane passion for truth" expressed in the intellectual dogmatism of the scholastic disputes at the university of Paris; as well as of the empiricist protagonist "detective" searching for the objective truth while attempting to solve a mystery that turns out to be very much of his own making.

In his later novel *Foucault's Pendulum* (1989), the caricatures are turned toward the relativism of the New Age, with its unlimited interpretations where everything can mean everything, as in the following passage on the interpretation of quantitative measurements:

"Truths?" Aglie laughed ... "Still, amid all the nonsense there are some unimpeachable truths. Gentlemen, would you follow me to the window?"

He threw open the shutters dramatically and pointed. At the corner of the narrow street and the broad avenue, stood a little wooden kiosk, where, presumably, lottery tickets were sold.

"Gentlemen," he said, "I invite you to go and measure that kiosk. You will see that the length of the counter is one hundred and forty-nine centimeters—in other words, one hundred-billionth of the distance between the earth and the sun. The height at the rear, one hundred and seventy-six centimeters, divided by the width of the window, fifty-six centimeters, is 3.14. The height at the front is nineteen decimeters, equal, in other words, to the number of years of the Greek lunar cycle. The sum of the heights of the two front corners and the two rear corners is one hundred and ninety times two plus one hundred and seventy-six times two, which equals seven hundred and thirty-two, the date of the victory at Poitiers. The thickness of the counter is 3.10 centimeters, and the width of the cornice of the window is 8.8 centimeters. Replacing the numbers before the decimals by the corresponding letters of the alphabet, we obtain C for ten and H for eight, or $C_{10}H_8$, which is the formula for naphthalene."

"Fantastic," I said. "You did all these measurements?" (Eco, p. 288).

13

The Social Construction
of Validity

I now turn to the issue of how to get beyond the extremes of a subjective relativism where everything can mean everything, and an absolutist quest for the one and only true, objective meaning.

Verification of knowledge is commonly discussed in the social sciences in relation to the concepts of reliability, validity, and generalizability. The main emphasis in this chapter will be on validation, treating the interdependence of philosophical understandings of truth, social science concepts of validity, and the practical issues of verifying interview knowledge. Classical conceptions of truth will be included as well as a postmodern approach leading to validity as social construction. The ensuing practical consequences for interview research involve an emphasis on the quality of the craftsmanship of research and on communicative and pragmatic forms of validation.

The Trinity of Generalizability,
Reliability, and Validity

In modern social science the concepts of generalizability, reliability, and validity have reached the status of a scientific holy trinity. They appear to belong to some abstract realm in a sanctuary of science far removed from the interactions of the everyday world, and to be worshipped with respect by all true believers in science.

As an introduction to the multiple contexts and discourses of verification and the social construction of knowledge, I will start with a history of my own encounters with the concept of validity. As a student of psychology in Norway in the 1960s, I read heavy texts on the importance of validity, reliability, and generalizability in scientific research. I tried to memorize the definitions of predictive validity, concurrent validity, content validity, and face validity, and struggled to understand the concept of construct validity. The very terms *validity* and *reliability* did not belong to the Norwegian vernacular, but were foreign English-Latin terms. The psychometric discussions of validity appeared abstract and esoteric, as if belonging to some distant philosophical universe together with Kant's transcendental a prioris and the like.

As a student I dared to ask some natural scientists on campus about these fundamental scientific concepts, and was somewhat bewildered to find that the very terms of the methodological holy trinity of psychological science were often unfamiliar to natural scientists. The concepts were, however, very real to us students of psychology; generalizability, validity, and reliability were frequently used as examination topics to differentiate between students who had, and those who had not, pledged allegiance to the scientific trinity of psychology.

When later traveling in the United States I learned other meanings for the terms *validity* and *reliability;* for example, when told while cashing a check in the supermarket that my European driver's license was not valid as identification, or in an academic discussion that my argument was not valid. Or that the information about the used car I was looking at was not reliable, the car dealer was known to be an unreliable person. Here the terms *valid* and *reliable* belong to the vernacular, important to the ongoing interactions of everyday life.

When I became engaged in qualitative research, the positivist trinity emerged again, now employed by mainstream researchers to disqualify qualitative research. The stimulus "qualitative research interview" appeared automatically to trigger conditioned responses like: "The results are not reliable, they are produced by leading interview questions"; "The interview findings cannot be generalized, there are too few interview subjects"; and "The results are not valid, they are only based on subjective interpretations."

Some qualitative researchers have a different attitude toward questions of validity, reliability, and generalizability. These are simply ignored or dismissed as some oppressive positivist concepts that hamper a creative and emancipatory qualitative research. Other qualitative researchers—Lincoln and Guba (1985), for instance—have gone beyond the relativism of a rampant antipositivism and have reclaimed ordinary language terms to discuss the truth value of their findings, using concepts such as trustworthiness, credibility, dependability, and confirmability.

From a postmodern perspective issues of reliability, validity, and generalizability are sometimes discarded as leftovers from a modernist correspondence theory of truth. There are multiple ways of knowing and multiple truths, and the concept of validity indicates a firm boundary line between truth and nontruth. In contrast hereto, Lather (1995), from a feminist post-structural frame valorizing practice, addresses validity as an incitement to discourse, a fertile obsession, and attempts to reinscribe validity in ways that use the postmodern problematic to loosen the master code of positivism.

I will return to external critiques of the trustworthiness of interview findings in the book's conclusion, Chapter 15. In the present chapter I will attempt to conceptualize generalizability, reliability, and validity in ways appropriate to qualitative research. The discussion represents a rather moderate postmodernism; although rejecting the notion of an objective universal truth, it accepts the possibility of specific local, personal, and community forms of truth, with a focus on daily life and local narrative (Kvale, 1992; Rosenau, 1992). The present approach is not to reject the concepts of reliability, generalizability, and validity, but to reconceptualize them in forms relevant to interview research. The understanding of verification starts in the lived world and daily language where issues of reliable observations, of generalization from one case to another, of valid arguments, are part of everyday social interaction.

Generalizability

A persistent question posed to interview studies is whether the results are generalizable. In everyday life we generalize more or less spontaneously. From our experience with one situation or person we anticipate new instances, we form expectations of what will happen in other similar situations or with similar persons. Scientific knowledge also lays claim to generalizability; in positivist versions, the aim of social science was to produce laws of human behavior that could be generalized universally. A contrasting humanistic view implies that every situation is unique, each phenomenon has its own intrinsic structure and logic. Within psychology, universal laws of behavior have been sought by natural science-oriented schools such as behaviorism, whereas the uniqueness of the individual person has dominated in humanistic psychology. In a postmodern approach the quest for universal knowledge, as well as the cult of the individually unique, is replaced by an emphasis on the heterogeneity and contextuality of knowledge, with a shift from generalization to contextualization.

Forms of Generalizability. The issue of qualitative generalization has been treated particularly in relation to case studies. Stake (1994) provides this definition: "Qualitative case study is characterized by the main researcher spending substantial time, on site, personally in contact with activities and operations of the case, reflecting, revising meanings of what is going on" (p. 242). Three forms of generalizability will be outlined based on Stake's discussion of generalization from case studies—naturalistic, statistical, and analytic.

Naturalistic generalization rests on personal experience: It develops for the person as a function of experience; it derives from tacit knowledge of how things are and leads to expectations rather than formal predictions; it may become verbalized, thus passing from tacit knowledge to explicit propositional knowledge.

Statistical generalization is formal and explicit: It is based on subjects selected at random from a population. With the use of inferential statistics the confidence level of generalizing from the selected sample to the population at large can be stated in probability coefficients. When the interviewees are selected at random and the interview findings quantified, the findings may be subjected to statistical generalization. Thus for the correlation found between talkativity and grade point average it was possible to state that there was only 1/1,000 probability that this was a chance finding limited to the 30 randomly chosen pupils of the grade study (Chapter 12, Questions Posed to an Interview Text).

More often, interview subjects are not selected at random but by other criteria, such as typicality or extremeness, or simply by accessibility. For example, an interview sample of women who have turned to a help center for victims of violence are a self-selected and not a random sample from the population. Their strong motivation for help may lead to valuable knowledge on the nature of being subjected to violence. The findings of the self-selected sample cannot, however, be statistically generalized to the population at large.

Analytical generalization involves a reasoned judgment about the extent to which the findings from one study can be used as a guide to what might occur in another situation. It is based on an analysis of the similarities and differences of the two situations. In contrast to spontaneous naturalistic generalization, the researcher here bases the generalization claims on an assertational logic. There are several forms of assertational logic, such as the legal form of argumentation in court and arguments for generalization based on theory. By specifying the supporting evidence and making the arguments explicit, the researcher can allow readers to judge the soundness of the generalization claim (see also Yin, 1994, on inductive generalization).

In her article, "Generalizing From Single Case Studies" in system evaluation, Kennedy (1979) argues for establishing rules for drawing inferences about the generality of qualitative findings from a case study, rules of inference that reasonable people can agree on. Whereas the scientist tends to study specific cases in order to draw inferences about the general case, the practitioner draws on knowledge of the general case to form interpretations of and actions in the specific case. As one point of departure, Kennedy turns to practical situations in the legal and the clinical fields.

In case law it is the most analogous preceding case, the one with the most attributes similar to the actual case, that is selected as the most relevant precedent. The validity of the generalization hinges on the extent to which the attributes compared are relevant, which again rests upon rich, dense, thick descriptions of the case. Kennedy outlines criteria for relevant attributes of comparison in legal and clinical cases, the latter instance encompassing precision of description, longitudinal information, and multidisciplinary assessment.

In case law, the court decides whether a previous case offers a precedent that can be generalized to the case being tried:

Thus it is the receiver of the information who determines the applicability of a finding to a new situation. . . . Like generalizations in law, clinical generalizations are the responsibility of the receiver of information rather than the original generator of information, and the evaluator must be careful to provide sufficient information to make such generalizations possible. (Kennedy, 1979, p. 672)

Researcher and Reader Generalization. There is an issue here of who should conduct the analytical generalization from the qualitative research case—the researcher or the reader and the user? How much should the researcher formalize and argue generalizations or leave the generalizing to the reader? In science, it has commonly been the researcher who builds up and argues for the generality of his or her findings—through statistical procedures or by an assertational logic. For the legal and the clinical cases discussed by Kennedy, it is the judge or the clinician who makes the judgment of whether a previous case was sufficiently analogous to be used as a precedent for the present case. In both instances it is paramount that sufficient evidence is provided by the researcher for the analytic generalizations to be made. An example of a reader generalization that can be mentioned is Freud's therapeutic case stories, where his descriptions and analyses have been so vivid and convincing that readers today still generalize many of the findings to current cases.

Targets of Generalization. Schofield (1990) has suggested three targets for generalization. The first is studying *what is*—attempting to establish the typical, the common, the ordinary. One seeks to maximize the fit between the research case and what takes place more broadly in a society. A second target is *what may be*—here the aim of generalizing is not what is, but what may be. Schofield mentions a study of the use of computers in school that did not select average representative schools, but schools at the leading edge of integrating computers in teaching. This was done on the assumption that the most advanced cases might provide findings generalizable to the future role of computers in schools. A historical example may be added here—at the time when Marx analyzed the situation of the wage laborers and the contradictions of the use versus the exchange value of labor, wage laborers made up only a small percentage of the working population. Decades later, wage labor became the dominating form of labor, whereby Marx's analysis of wage labor became increasingly generalizable to the situation of workers at large.

A third target of generalization is *what could be*—locating situations that we believe are ideal and exceptional and studying them to see what goes on there. As examples, Schofield mentions school classes with unusual intellectual gains and also well-functioning racially desegregated schools. In constructivist and postmodern approaches the emphasis on the "could be" is extended from preconceived ideals to more open forms. Donmoyer (1990) thus advocates the use of case studies to teach readers to envisage possibilities, to expand and enrich the repertoire of social constructions available to practitioners and others. We may here add the interest in ethnographic studies as cases demonstrating the rich varieties of human behavior, also indicating possible ranges for our own society. Gergen (1992) depicts the construction of new worlds as one potential of a postmodern psychology. Rather than "telling it like it is," the challenge is "to tell it as it may become." A "generative" theory is designed to unseat conventional thought and thereby open new and desirable alternatives for thought and action. Rather than mapping only what is, or predicting future cultural trends, research becomes one means of transforming culture.

Reliability and Validity of Interviews

Throughout this book I have emphasized that issues of verification do not belong to some separate stage of an investigation, but should be addressed throughout the entire research process. As an introduction to conceptual issues of validity and truth, some concrete issues of the reliability and validity of interview inquiries from previous chapters will be briefly recapitulated.

Reliability. Reliability pertains to the consistency of the research findings. Issues of reliability during interviewing, transcribing, and analyzing have been treated in the previous chapters. Interviewer reliability was in particular discussed in relation to leading questions, which—when they are not a deliberate part of an interviewing technique—may inadvertently influence the answers, such as in the example of different wordings of a question about car speeds leading to different answers (Chapter 8, Leading Questions). Interviewer reliability in the grade study was discussed on the basis of the categorizations of the subjects' answers (Chapter 11, Control of Analysis). Under transcription of interviews, an example was given of the intersubjective reliability of the transcripts when the same passage was typed by two different persons (Chapter 9, Transcription Reliability and Validity). During categorization of the grading interviews, percentages were reported for the intersubjective agreement between two coders for the same interviews (Chapter 11, Control of Analysis). Though increasing the reliability of the interview findings is desirable in order to counteract haphazard subjectivity, a strong emphasis on reliability may counteract creative innovations and variability.

Validity. Although validation is treated in this chapter as a separate stage, it concerns all seven stages of an interview investigation. In the present approach, the emphasis on validation is moved from inspection at the end of the production line to quality control throughout the stages of knowledge production.

Box 13.1 gives an overview of validity issues throughout an interview investigation. Before turning to conceptual issues of validity, including validation as social construction, a brief outline of generalization by qualitative studies will be given.

Validity in Modern and Postmodern Contexts

Ascertaining validity involves issues of truth and knowledge. I will first discuss some meanings of validity, then include classical conceptions of truth, and thereafter discuss postmodern conceptions of knowledge. The practical implications for interview research are then treated with respect to validity as craftsmanship in research, as communication and action.

In ordinary language dictionaries, *validity* refers to the truth and correctness of a statement. A valid argument is sound, well grounded, justifiable, strong, and convincing. A valid inference is correctly derived from its premises. In social science textbooks one finds both a narrow and a broad definition of validity. In a positivist approach, scientific validity became restricted to measurements: for instance,

Box 13.1

Validation at Seven Stages

1. *Thematizing.* The validity of an investigation rests on the soundness of the theoretical presuppositions of a study and on the logic of the derivations from theory to the research questions of the study.

2. *Designing.* The validity of the knowledge produced depends on the adequacy of the design and the methods used for the subject matter and purpose of the study. From an ethical perspective, a valid research design involves beneficence—producing knowledge beneficial to the human situation while minimizing harmful consequences.

3. *Interviewing.* Validity here pertains to the trustworthiness of the subject's reports and the quality of the interviewing itself, which should include a careful questioning as to the meaning of what is said and a continual checking of the information obtained as a validation in situ.

4. *Transcribing.* The question of what constitutes a valid translation from oral to written language is involved in the choice of linguistic style for the transcript.

5. *Analyzing.* This has to do with whether the questions put to an interview text are valid and whether the logic of the interpretations is sound.

6. *Validating.* This entails a reflected judgment as to what forms of validation are relevant to a specific study, the application of the concrete procedures of validation, and a decision on what the appropriate community is for a dialogue on validity.

7. *Reporting.* This involves the question of whether a given report is a valid account of the main findings of a study, as well as the role of the readers of the report in validating the results.

"Validity is often defined by asking the question: Are you measuring what you think you are measuring?" (Kerlinger, 1979, p. 138). Qualitative research is then invalid if it does not result in numbers. In a broader concept, validity pertains to the degree that a method investigates what it is intended to investigate, to "the extent to which our observations indeed reflect the phenomena or variables of interest to us" (Pervin, 1984, p. 48). Within this wider conception of validity, qualitative research can, in principle, lead to valid scientific knowledge.

Textbook presentations have been based on positivist epistemological assumptions with a correspondence theory of truth. The standard definitions of validity have been taken from the criteria developed for psychological tests as formalized by Cronbach and Meehl in 1955. In psychology, validity became linked to psychometrics, where the concurrent and predictive validity of the psychological tests were declared in correlation coefficients, indicating correspondence between test results and some external criteria. These psychometric tests, such as intelligence tests, have frequently been applied to predict school success. The external criterion was here simple—grade point average in later schooling. With a further questioning about what the school grades measure, the issue becomes more complex. Grades have been found to predict later grades in school, but success after graduation to a lesser extent. The issue of predictive validity is here not merely an empirical issue, but raises such normative questions as what should the criteria of success be—position in the occupational hierarchy, income, contributions to the community?

The issue of what is valid knowledge involves the philosophical question of what is truth. Within philosophy, three classical criteria of truth are discerned—correspondence, coherence, and pragmatic utility. The *correspondence* criterion of truth concerns whether a knowledge statement corresponds to the objective world. The *coherence* criterion refers to the consistency and internal logic of a statement. And the *pragmatic* criterion relates the truth of a knowledge statement to its practical consequences.

Although the three criteria of truth do not necessarily exclude each other, they have each obtained strong positions in different philosophical traditions. The correspondence criterion has been central within a positivist social science where the validity of knowledge is expressed as its degree of correspondence with an objective reality. The coherence criterion has been strong in mathematics and hermeneutics. The pragmatic criterion has prevailed in pragmatism and to a certain extent in Marxist philosophy. The three truth criteria can be regarded as abstractions from a unity, where a comprehensive verification of qualitative research findings will involve observation, conversation, and interaction.

The belief in an objective world has been the basis of a modernist understanding of truth and validity. In a positivist philosophy, knowledge became a reflection of reality: There is only one correct view of this independent external world, and there is ideally a one-to-one correspondence between elements in the real world and our knowledge of this world. In a postmodern era, the foundations of true and valid knowledge in a medieval absolute God or a modern objective reality have dissolved. The conception of knowledge as a mirror of reality is replaced by knowledge as a social construction of reality. Truth is constituted through a dialogue; valid knowledge claims emerge as conflicting interpretations and action possibilities are discussed and negotiated among the members of a community.

In science the decisive point is the conversation in the community of researchers about the relation among the methods, the findings, and the nature of the phenomena investigated. The move from knowledge-as-observation to knowledge-as-conversation was illustrated in a recent television program on the development of the natural sciences. After showing the newest technical advances in microscopes for cell studies and giant telescopes for the investigation of space, the camera suddenly shifted to a room with elegant 18th-century furniture. The transition was accompanied by a voice saying something to the effect that: It is not by the techniques of these instruments and the resulting observations that the truth of the new scientific knowledge is determined, but through discussions about the observations among the scientists, such as in this room of the British Royal Society of Sciences.

The social construction of valid knowledge is brought out in the concept of construct validity, which was originally introduced by the psychometricians Cronbach and Meehl for psychological tests. It pertains to the measurement of theoretical constructs—such as intelligence and authoritarianism—by different measures; construct validity involves correlations with other measures of the construct and logical analysis of their relationships. Cronbach (1971) later extended the concept of construct validity to qualitative summaries as well as numerical scores; it is an open process in which to validate is to investigate—"validation is more than corroboration; it is a process for developing sounder interpretations of observations" (p. 443).

Cherryholmes (1988; see also Tschudi, 1989) has argued that construct validity is a discursive and rhetorical concept. A construct and its measurement are validated when the discourse about their relationships is persuasive to the community of researchers. A constructive conception of validity goes beyond the original discourse of psychological testing and experimental design, and opens in Cherryholmes's analysis to multiple discourses, such as phenomenological, interpretative, critical, and deconstructive analyses. This radicalization of construct validity brings it close to a postmodern emphasis on the social construction of knowledge.

Some implications of the above discussion for validation of qualitative research will now be discussed. First, when giving up a correspondence theory of truth as the basis for understanding validity, there is, following Popper, a change in emphasis from verification to falsification. The quest for absolute, certain knowledge is replaced by a conception of defensible knowledge claims. Validation becomes the issue of choosing among competing and falsifiable interpretations, of examining and providing arguments for the relative credibility of alternative knowledge claims (Polkinghorne, 1983). Validation here comes to rest on the *quality of craftsmanship* in research.

Second, a modern belief in knowledge as a mirror of reality recedes and a social construction of reality, with coherence and pragmatic criteria of truth, comes to the foreground. Method as a guarantee of truth dissolves; with a social construction of reality the emphasis is on the discourse of the community. *Communication* of knowledge becomes significant, with esthetics and rhetorics entering into a scientific discourse.

Third, with a modern legitimation mania receding, there is an emphasis upon a *pragmatic* proof through action. The legitimation of knowledge through external justification by appeals to some grand systems, or meta-narratives, and the modern fundamentalism of securing knowledge on some undoubtable, stable fundament, lose interest.

Justification of knowledge is replaced by application, knowledge becomes the ability to perform effective actions. Criteria of efficiency and their desirability become pivotal, raising ethical issues of right action. Values do not belong to a realm separated from scientific knowledge, but permeate the creation and application of knowledge.

Implications of the above discussion for interview research will now be addressed in relation to validation as craftsmanship, as communication, and as action. This does not lead to new, fixed criteria replacing the psychometric concepts of validity, nor does it secure unambiguous knowledge. Rather, it extends the frames of reference for asking about the validity of knowledge in social research—"Post-modern social science presumes methods that multiply paradox, inventing ever more elaborate repertoires of questions, each of which encourages an infinity of answers, rather than methods that settle on solutions" (Rosenau, 1992, p. 117).

Validity as Quality of Craftsmanship

I will here attempt to demystify the concept of validity, to bring it back from philosophical abstractions to the everyday practice of scientific research. With an alternative concept of validity—going from correspondence with an objective reality to defensible knowledge claims—validity is ascertained by examining the sources of invalidity. The stronger the falsification attempts a proposition has survived, the more valid, the more trustworthy the knowledge. Validation comes to depend on the quality of craftsmanship during investigation, continually checking, questioning, and theoretically interpreting the findings.

The concept of validity as quality of craftsmanship is not limited to a postmodern approach, but becomes pivotal with a postmodern dismissal of an objective reality against which knowledge is to be measured. The craftsmanship and credibility of the researcher becomes essential. Based on the quality of his or her past research in the area, the credibility of the researcher is an important aspect of fellow researchers ascribing validity to the findings reported. Validity is not only a matter of the methods used; the person of the researcher (Salner, 1989), including his or her moral integrity (Smith, 1990), is critical for evaluation of the quality of the scientific knowledge produced. Three aspects of validation as investigation will now be outlined— checking, questioning, and theorizing the knowledge produced.

To Validate Is to Check. The researcher adopts a critical outlook on the analysis, states explicitly his or her perspective on the subject matter studied and the controls applied to counter selective percep- tions and biased interpretations, and in general plays the devil's advocate toward his or her own findings.

Various modes of checking the findings have been suggested by writers on qualitative research. An investigative concept of validation is inherent in the grounded theory approach of Glaser and Strauss (1967). Validation is here not some final verification or product control; verification is built into the research process with continual checks on the credibility, plausibility, and trustworthiness of the findings. Miles and Huberman (1994) emphasize that there are no canons or infallible decision-making rules for establishing the validity of qualitative research. Their approach is to analyze the many sources of potential biases that might invalidate qualitative observations and interpretations; they outline in detail tactics for testing and confirming qualitative findings. These tactics include: checking for repre- sentativeness and for researcher effects, triangulating, weighing the evidence, checking the meaning of outliers, using extreme cases, following up on surprises, looking for negative evidence, making if-then tests, ruling out spurious relations, replicating a finding, check- ing out rival explanations, and getting feedback from informants (p. 263).

Runyan (1981) discussed the validation of multiple interpretations in psychobiography in relation to the episode of van Gogh cutting off his left ear and giving it to a prostitute. More than a dozen explana- tions of this act have been proposed in the literature, ranging from inspiration by newspaper accounts of Jack the Ripper, to visits to bullfights in Arles, to aggression turned inward and a reawakening of Oedipal themes. Runyan discusses in detail the credibility and strength of the different interpretations. This includes checking the empirical evidence for and against an interpretation, examining the theoretical coherence, and critically evaluating and comparing the relative plausi- bility of the different interpretations given for the same act. In general, the more attempts at falsification an interpretation has survived, the stronger it stands.

To Validate Is to Question. When ascertaining validity, the questions of "what" and "why" need to be answered before the question of "how". The content and purpose of an investigation precedes the method. Discussing the question "Do photographs tell the truth?" Becker (1979) makes the general question "Is it true?" specific in "Is this photograph telling the truth about what?" And to decide what a picture is telling us the truth about, he suggests that we should ask ourselves what questions it might be answering.

A common critique of research interviews is that their findings are not valid because the subjects' reports may be false. This is a possibility that needs to be checked in each specific case (see Dean & Whyte, 1969). The issue of validity again depends on the "what" of the researcher's questions. In hermeneutical interpretations, the questions posed to a text become all-important. In the grading study, the primacy of the question posed to an interview statement was demonstrated by the interpretations of pupils' statements about competition, talkativity, and wheedling (Chapter 12, Questions Posed to an Interview Text). Different questions posed to interview texts led to different answers. Thus one type of question led to an *experiential* reading of the pupils' statements. Another type of question led to a *veridical* reading, regarding the interviewees as witnesses or informants. The questioning also involved a *symptomatic* reading, focusing on the interviewees themselves and their reasons for making a given statement. The forms of validation differ for the different questions to the interview texts. In the grade study they varied from a critical follow-up in the interview of the pupils' statements, to statistical analysis to verify a pupil's postulated connection between talkativity and grades, to the coherence of interpretations about the production and the consequences of beliefs about grading.

Richardson (1994) has taken issue with the geometrical concept of triangulation, which was applied above in the validation of a veridical reading of a pupil's postulate of a connection between talkativity and grades (Chapter 12, Questions Posed to an Interview Text). Richardson rejects the use of a rigid, fixed, two-dimensional triangle as a central image for validity for postmodern texts, because it contains assumptions of a fixed point or object that can be triangulated: "Rather, the central image is the crystal, which combines symmetry and substance with an infinite variety of shapes, substances, transmutations, multidimensionalities, and angles of approach" (p. 522). She then outlines how crystallization by means of postmodern mixed-genre texts provides us with a deepened, complex, and partial understanding of the topic. The multiple questions to, and readings of, the pupils' statements about grades may be seen as crystallizations opening to continual transformations of the meaning of grades.

To Validate Is to Theorize. Validity is not only an issue of method. Pursuing the methodological issues of validation generates theoretical questions about the nature of the phenomena investigated. Deciding whether a method investigates what it intends to investigate involves a theoretical conception of what is investigated. In the terms of grounded theory, verifying interpretations is an intrinsic part of the generation of theory.

The inconclusive results in the grade study of the attempts at an informant-triangulation of a pupil's belief in a connection between talkativity and grades need not merely indicate a problem of method; it also raises theoretical questions about the social construction of school reality. Pupils and teachers may live in different social realities with regard to which pupil behaviors lead to good grades. It is possible that pupils, in a kind of "superstitious" behavior, believe in a connection where there is none; or it may be that teachers overlook or deny a relation that actually exists. Ambiguity of the teacher's bases for grading, and contradictory beliefs by pupils and teachers about which behaviors lead to good grades, appear to be essential aspects of the social reality of school. The complexities of validating qualitative research need not be due to an inherent weakness in qualitative methods, but may on the contrary rest on their extraordinary power to picture and to question the complexity of the social reality investigated.

Communicative Validity

Communicative validity involves testing the validity of knowledge claims in a dialogue. Valid knowledge is constituted when conflicting knowledge claims are argued in a dialogue: What is a valid observation is decided through the argumentation of the participants in a discourse. In a hermeneutical approach to meaningful action as a text, Ricoeur (1971) rejects the position that all interpretations of a text are equal; the logic of validation allows us to move between the two limits of dogmatism and skepticism. Invoking the hermeneutical circle and criteria of falsifiability, he describes validation as an argumentative discipline comparable to the juridical procedures of legal interpretation. Validation is based on a logic of uncertainty and of qualitative probability, where it is always possible to argue for or against an interpretation, to confront interpretations and to arbitrate between them.

A communicative approach to validity is found in several approaches in the social sciences. In psychoanalysis the validity of an interpretation is worked out in a dialogue between patient and therapist. It is also implied in evaluation studies of social systems; House (1980) has thus emphasized that in system evaluation, research does not mainly concern predicting events, but rather whether the audience of a report can see new relations and answer new but relevant questions. Cronbach (1980) has advocated a discursive approach where validity rests on public discussion. The interpretation of a test is going to remain open and unsettled, the more so because of the role that values play in action based on tests; the aim for a research report is to advance sensible discussion—and, "The more we learn, and the franker we are with ourselves and our clientele, the more valid the use of tests will become" (p. 107). In a discussion of narrative research, Mishler (1990) has conceptualized validation as the social construction of knowledge. Valid knowledge claims are established in a discourse through which the results of a study come to be viewed as sufficiently trustworthy for other investigators to rely upon in their own work.

When conversation is the ultimate context within which knowledge is to be understood, as argued by Rorty (Chapter 2, Interviews in Three Conversations), the nature of the discourse becomes essential. There is today a danger that a conception of truth as dialogue and communicative validation may become empty global and positive undifferentiated terms, without the necessary conceptual and theoretical differentiations worked out. Some specific questions concerning the how, why, and who of communication will now be raised.

How. Communication can involve persuasion through rational discourse or through populist demagogy. The forms of persuasion about the truth of knowledge claims will be different in the harsh logical argumentation of a philosophical dialogue, in the juridical proceedings and legal interpretations in a courtroom, in a narrative capturing an audience, and in a humanistic therapy encounter based on positive feelings and reciprocal sympathy.

Philosophical discourses, such as the dialogues of Socrates, are characterized by a rational argumentation. The participants are obliged to test statements about the truth and falsity of propositions on the basis of argued points of view, and the best argument wins. This discourse is ideally a form of argumentation where no social exertion of power takes place, the only form of power being the force of the better argument.

Why. The question here concerns the purpose of a discourse about true knowledge. What are the aims and criteria of arriving at true knowledge? Habermas's (1971) discourse theory implies a consensual theory of truth: The ideal discourse aims at universally valid truths as an ideal. Eisner (1991) has advocated qualitative research as art, based on connoisseurship and criticism, accepting the personal, literary, and even poetic as valid sources of knowledge. The aim is here consensus: "Consensual validation is, at base, agreement among competent others that the description, interpretation, evaluation, and thematics of an educational situation are right" (p. 112). From a postmodern perspective, Lyotard (1984) has argued that consensus is only a stage in a discussion, and not its goal, which he posits as paralogy—to create new ideas, new differentiations, new rules for the discourse. To Lyotard, discourse is a game between adversaries rather than a dialogue between partners.

Who. The concept of communicative validity raises the question of who communicates with whom. Who is a legitimate partner in a dialogue about true knowledge? Three interpretative communities were brought in by the validation of the interviews of grading. The member of the interpretative community validating an interpretation could be the *subject* interviewed, the *general public* interpreting within a critical common sense understanding analogous to a jury, or the *scientific community* of scholars possessing methodical and theoretical competence in the specific area. Taking a lead from the use of "reflecting teams" in psychotherapy, where the one-way mirror is reversed and the family in treatment views the therapeutic team's discussions of their interpersonal interaction (Andersen, 1987), we might also reverse the direction in research and have the subjects listen to and comment on the researchers' conversations about their interviews.

Validation through negotiations of the community of scholars is nothing new; in the natural sciences the acceptance of the scientific community has been the last, ultimate criterion for ascertaining the truth of a proposition. What is relatively new in qualitative research in the social sciences is the emphasis on truth as negotiated in a local context, with extension of the interpretative community to include the subjects investigated and the lay public. Communicative validation approximates an educational endeavor where truth is developed in a communicative process, with both researcher and subjects learning and changing through the dialogue.

A heavy reliance on intersubjective validation may, however, also imply a lack of work on the part of the researcher and a lack of confidence in his or her interpretations, with an unwillingness to take responsibility for the interpretations. There may be a general populist trend when leaving the validation of interpretations to the readers, as in reader response validation, with an abdication to the ideology of a consumer society: "The customer is always right."

Power and Truth. Different professional communities may construct knowledge differently, and conflicts may arise about which professions have the right to decide what is valid knowledge within a field, such as health, for example. Furthermore, there is the specific issue of who decides who is a competent and legitimate member of the interpretative community. The selection of members of the community to make decisions about issues of truth and value is considered crucial for the results in many cases, such as in the selection of members of a jury, or of a committee to examine a doctoral candidate, or of an academic appointment committee.

Habermas's consensus theory of truth is based on the ideal of a dominance-free dialogue, which is a deliberate abstraction from the webs of power relationships within real-life discourses, and again in contrast with Lyotard's postmodern understanding of a scientific con-

versation as a game of power. More generally, scientists are not pur-
chased to find truth, but to augment power: "The games of scientific
language become the games of the rich, in which whoever is wealthiest
has the best chance of being right. An equation between wealth,
efficiency and truth is thus established" (Lyotard, 1984, p. 45).

Pragmatic Validity

Pragmatic validation is verification in the literal sense—"to make
true." To pragmatists, truth is whatever assists us to take actions that
produce the desired results. Knowledge is action rather than observation, the effectiveness of our knowledge beliefs is demonstrated by the
effectiveness of our action. In the pragmatic validation of a knowledge
claim, justification is replaced by application. Marx stated in his
second thesis on Feuerbach that the question of whether human
thought can lead to objective truth is not a theoretical but a practical
one. Man must prove the truth, that is, the reality and power of his
thinking in practice. And his 11th thesis is more pointed; the philosophers have only interpreted the world differently, what matters is
changing the world.

A pragmatic concept of validity goes farther than communication;
it represents a stronger knowledge claim than an agreement through
a dialogue. Pragmatic validation rests on observations and interpretations, with a commitment to act on the interpretations—"Actions
speak louder than words." With the emphasis on instigating change,
a pragmatic knowledge interest may counteract a tendency of social
constructionism to circle around in endless interpretations and a
plunge of postmodern analyses into infinite deconstructions.

A pragmatical knowledge interest in helping patients change is
intrinsic to the therapeutic interview, where communication of interpretations serves to instigate changes in the patient. For naturalistic
inquiry, Lincoln and Guba (1985) have gone farther than consensual
validation and pointed to action-oriented quality criteria for qualitative research, such as an inquiry enhancing the level of understanding of the participants and their ability to take action, empowering
them to take increased control of their lives. Action research goes from
descriptions of social conditions to actions that can change the very

conditions investigated. Also, system evaluation goes beyond the correspondence criterion to include pragmatic validity: "The ultimate tests of the credibility of an evaluation report is the response of decision makers and information users to that report" (Patton, 1980, p. 339).

We may discern between two types of pragmatic validation— whether a knowledge statement is accompanied by action, or whether it instigates changes of action. In the first case, validation of a subject's verbal statement is based on supporting action that *accompanies* the statement. This concerns going beyond mere lip service to a belief, to following it up with action. Thus in investigations of racial prejudice, comprehensive inquiries go beyond a subject's mere verbal statements against racial segregation and investigate whether the statements are also accompanied by appropriate supportive actions.

The second, stronger, form of pragmatic validation concerns whether interventions based on the researcher's knowledge may *instigate* actual changes in behavior. Freud did not rely on the patient's self-understanding and verbal communication to validate therapeutic interpretations; he regarded neither the patient's "yes" nor "no" to his interpretations as sufficient confirmation or disconfirmation; the "yes" or "no" could be the result of suggestion as well as of resistance in the therapeutic process. Freud recommended more indirect forms of validation, such as observing the patient's reactions to an interpretation, for example in the form of changes in the patient's free associations, dreams, recall of forgotten memories, and alteration of neurotic symptoms (Freud, 1963, p. 279). Spence (1982) has followed up on the emphasis on the pragmatic effects of interpretations: Narrative truth is constructed in the therapeutic encounter, it carries the conviction of a good story, and it is to be judged by its aesthetic value and by the curative effect of its rhetorical force.

In collaborative action research, investigators and subjects together develop knowledge of a social situation and then apply this knowledge through new actions in the situation, thus testing the validity of the knowledge in praxis. Reason (1994) describes a study of health workers that was based on participatory inquiry with a systematic testing of theory in live-action contexts. The topic was stress that came from hidden agendas in their work situation, such as suspicions of drug taking and of child abuse in the families the health workers visited. The coresearchers first developed knowledge through discussions among themselves, by role playing, and thereafter by raising their concerns directly with their client families. Reason discusses the validity in this cooperative inquiry, and emphasizes the need to get beyond a mere consensus collusion where the researchers might band together as a group in defense of their anxieties, which may be overcome by a continual interaction between action and reflection throughout the participatory inquiry.

How. The forms of pragmatic validation vary: There can be a patient's reactions to the psychoanalyst's interpretation of his or her dreams, or a client's responses to a behavior therapist's interventions to change the reinforcement contingencies of his or her problem behavior. There are the reactions of an audience to a system evaluation report, and the cooperative interaction of researcher and subjects in action research.

Why. A scientific discourse is, in principle, indefinite; there is no requirement of immediate action; new arguments that could alter or invalidate earlier knowledge can always appear. In contrast to the uncoerced consensus of the scientific discourse, practical contexts may require actions to be undertaken and decisions to be made that involve a coercion to consensus. This includes the proceedings of a jury, the negotiations of a dissertation committee, decisions about therapeutic interventions, and decisions about institutional changes in action research.

A pragmatic approach implies that truth is whatever assists us to take actions that produce the desired results. Deciding what the desired results are involves values and ethics. The moral normative aspect of validation is recognized in system evaluation, where "the validity of an evaluation depends upon whether the evaluation is true, credible, and normatively correct" (House, 1980, p. 255). The importance of values in validation follows through a change of emphasis in social research from primarily mapping the social world with respect to *what is,* to changing the focus to *what could be.* Thus Gergen's (1992) postmodern conception of generative theory (see Generalizability, above) involves research that opens new possibilities of thought and action as a means of transforming culture.

Who. The question of "who" involves the researcher and the users of the knowledge produced. Patton (1980) emphasizes the credibility of the researcher as an important criterion of whether a research report is accepted or not as a basis for action. The question of "who" also involves ethical and political issues. Who is to decide the direction of change? There may be personal resistance to change in a therapy as well as conflicting vested interests in the outcome of an action study. Thus, regarding audience validation in system evaluation, who are the stakeholders that will be included in the decisive audience: the funding agency, the leaders of the system evaluated, the employees, or the clients of the system?

Power and Truth. Pragmatic validation raises the issue of power and truth in social research: Where is the power to decide what the desired results of a study will be, or the direction of change; what values are to constitute the basis for action? And, more generally, where is the power to decide what kinds of truth seeking are to be pursued, what research questions are worth funding? Following Foucault we should here beware of localizing power to specific persons and their intentions, and instead analyze the netlike organization and multiple fields of power-knowledge dynamics.

Validity of the Validity Question

I have argued here for integrating validation into the craftsmanship of research, and for extending the concept of validation from observation to also include communication about, and pragmatic effects of, knowledge claims. The understanding of validity as craftsmanship, as communication and action, does not replace the importance of precise observations and logical argumentation, but includes broader conceptions of the nature of truth in social research. The conversational and pragmatic aspects of knowledge have within a positivist tradition been regarded as irrelevant, or secondary, to obtaining objective observations; in a postmodern conception of knowledge the very conversation about, and the application of, knowledge become essential aspects of the construction of a social world. Rather than providing fixed criteria, communicative and pragmatic validation refer to extended ways of posing the question of validity in social research.

I have further attempted to demystify the concept of validity, maintaining that verification of information and interpretations is a normal activity in the interactions of daily life. Even so, a pervasive attention to validation can be counterproductive and lead to a general invalidation. Rather than let the product, the knowledge claim, speak for itself, validation can involve a legitimation mania that may further a corrosion of validity—the more one validates, the greater the need for further validation. Such a counterfactuality of strong and repeated emphasis on the truth of a statement may be expressed in the folk saying, "Beware when they swear they are telling the truth."

Ideally, the quality of the craftsmanship results in products with knowledge claims that are so powerful and convincing in their own right that they, so to say, carry the validation with them, like a strong piece of art. In such cases, the research procedures would be transparent and the results evident, and the conclusions of a study intrinsically convincing as true, beautiful, and good. Appeals to external certification, or official validity stamps of approval, then become secondary. Valid research would in this sense be research that makes questions of validity superfluous.

14

Improving Interview Reports

When the understanding of validation and generalization is extended to include communication with readers, the writing of reports takes on a key position in an interview inquiry. Reporting is not simply re-presenting the views of the interviewees, accompanied by the researcher's viewpoints in the form of interpretations. The interview report is itself a social construction in which the author's choice of writing style and literary devices provide a specific view on the subjects' lived world. The writing process is one aspect of the social construction of the knowledge gained from the interviews, and the report becomes the basis for the research community to ascertain the validity of the knowledge reported. The current focus on conversation and rhetorics in social research, as well as what is termed a crisis of representation, leads to an emphasis on the presentation of research findings.

Interview reports are often boring to read. Some ways of improving standard modes of reporting interviews will be outlined and some ethical issues of reporting interviews pointed out. Finally, after discussing writing as a social construction, modes of enriching interview reports are suggested.

Boring Interview Reports

Some three thousand years ago, Odysseus returned to Greece from his research inquiry in distant countries. Homer's oral tale of the voyage, later written down, was cast in a form that still engages today. Freud's soon hundred-year-old therapeutic case stories still provoke heated controversies. Current interview studies may not be that long lived; reports need to be read to have a life after publication. Some impressions from reading current interview reports will be offered.

Tiresome Interview Findings. Interview studies are often tedious to read: They are often characterized by long, obtuse, verbatim quotes, presented in a fragmented way, with primitive categorizations, and not seldom at inflated length. Hundreds of pages with quotes from the interview transcripts, interspersed with some comments and a few tables with numbers from categorizations, seldom make interesting reading. The subjects' often exciting stories have—through the analyzing and reporting stages—been butchered into atomistic quotes and isolated variables.

This style of reporting interviews may have been influenced by a qualitative hyperempiricism, with the many interview quotes made to serve as basic facts. Extensive verbatim transcripts are regarded as rock-bottom documentation of what was really said in the interviews. The different rhetorical forms of oral and written language are overlooked in the construction of verbatim interview transcripts, with their tiresome repetitions, fillers, and incomplete sentences.

After having endured the reading of a series of interview reports, one may long for some dramatic therapeutic case histories with narratives that can both be entertaining and carry provocative new insights. One may even look forward to reading about laboratory experiments with their neat logical rigor, elegant designs, clear presentations, and stringent discussions of the findings and considerations of possible sources of error that could invalidate the findings.

Dreary impressions of qualitative reports are not new:

> For 30 years, I have yawned my way through numerous supposedly exemplary qualitative studies. Countless numbers of texts I have abandoned half read, half scanned. I'll order a new book with great anticipation—the topic is one I'm interested in, the author is someone I want to read—only to find the text boring. (Richardson, 1994, pp. 516-517)

There may be several reasons for colorless interview reports. The writer may be so overwhelmed by the extensive and complex interview texts that any personal perspective on the interviews is lost. The researcher may strongly identify with the interview subjects, "go native" and be unable to retain a conceptual and critical distance from the subjects' accounts. The fear of subjective interpretations may lead to reports that consist of a tiresome series of uninterpreted quotes, refraining from theoretical interpretations as if from some dangerous form of speculation. The page inflation of interview reports may simply be due to researchers not knowing what story they want to tell, and they therefore are not able to select the main points they want to get across to their audience. Without knowing the "what" and the "why" of the story, the "how"—the form of the story—becomes problematic.

Method as a Black Box. If readers actually find the interview results of interest, they may want to know about the design and the methods that have produced this intriguing knowledge. They are then likely to encounter a black box. The readers will have to guess about the social context of the interview, the instructions given the interviewees, the questions posed, and the procedures used during transcribing and analyzing the interviews. For a reader who wants to evaluate the trustworthiness of the findings, to reinterpret or apply the results, information on the methodic steps of an investigation is mandatory. In interview reports, however, the link between the original conversations and the final report is often missing.

Qualitative interviews can contain detailed descriptions of the subjects' life situations, their experiences and actions, but may be virtually devoid of descriptions of the interview situation and of the researcher's actions used to obtain the information reported about the subjects. Though the strengths of qualitative studies are their detailed descriptions and the use of the researcher as an instrument, depictions of the researcher's own activities while producing the knowledge are conspicuously absent.

One reason for the neglect of method may be that an interview study hardly follows discrete, formal procedures; much is left to improvisation and the intuition of the interviewer and interpreter. A further reason may be that there are no established common conventions for reporting qualitative studies. Rather than leading to a silence on method, the unique nature of an interview study should in fact pose a challenge to the researcher to describe as precisely as possible the specific steps, procedures, and decisions taken in the specific study.

A possible reason for the neglect of method in interview reports may be as a counterreaction to the positivist idolatry of methods that equated science with formalized bureaucratic procedures. We may further speculate that the interview researcher has a bad methodic conscience—that his or her study does not live up to established canons of social science research. This methodic insecurity may then lead to omitting any mention of method—the procedures applied are simply swept under the carpet. Freely applying psychoanalytic defense mechanisms, one may invoke a repression of method due to anxiety and guilt from not living up to the ruling method ideals.

Investigating With the Final Report in Mind

The aim of a report is to inform other researchers and the general public of the importance and the trustworthiness of the findings. The report should contribute new knowledge to the development of a field, and be cast in a form that allows the conclusions to be checked by the reader. The interview report is the end product of a long process; what is worth communicating to others from the wealth of interview conversations is to be conveyed in the limited number of pages of an article or a book, presenting the main aims, methods, results, and implications of an interview inquiry. The writing of the report is here presented as the last of the seven method stages of an interview study.

As one approach to making interview reports more readable, I will suggest taking the final report into consideration from the very start of an inquiry. In the story of the five hardship phases of an interview project, reporting was depicted as the final phase of exhaustion (Chapter 5, Openness and Emotions in Interview Studies). As a countermeasure it was recommended that an interview project be directed from the start toward the final report; that the researcher keep in mind throughout the stages of the investigation the original vision of the story he or she wants to tell the readers. In Box 14.1, a consistent directedness toward the final report is envisaged throughout the seven stages of an interview study.

Box 14.1

Investigating With
the Final Report in Mind

1. *Thematizing.* The earlier and clearer that researchers keep the end product of their study in sight—the story they want to tell—the easier the writing of the report will be.

2. *Designing.* Keep a systematic record of the design procedure as a basis for the method section of the final report. Have the final form of the published interviews in mind when designing the study, including the ethical guideline of informed consent with respect to later publication of the subjects' stories. Under the ethical ideal that research should serve to enhance the human situation, communicating the findings to the scientific and general communities is of prime importance.

3. *Interviewing.* The ideal interview is in a form communicable to readers at the moment the tape recorder is turned off.

4. *Transcribing.* The readability of interviews that will be published should be kept in mind during transcription, as well as the protection of the subjects' confidentiality.

5. *Analysis.* In a narrative analysis, the analyzing and reporting of an interview merge and result in a story to be told to the readers. In other forms of analysis, too, the presentation of the results should be kept in mind, with the analysis of the interviews becoming embedded in the writing of the findings.

6. *Verification.* With a conception of validation as communication and action, how a study is reported becomes a key issue.

7. *Reporting.* Working toward the final report from the start of an interview study should contribute to a readable report of methodologically well-substantiated, interesting findings.

Writing for the Readers

Until recently there has been little interest in how to communicate the results of interview studies. The writing of an interview report has often been regarded as merely re-presenting what was done and found, with little regard for the readers and their use of the report.

In contrast thereto, researchers in system evaluation and market research have been well aware of the effects of the form of their reports on their intended audiences—such as the length of a report or the differential impact of quantitative and qualitative data. Patton (1980) thus mentions that an extensive, well-documented, and formally elegant evaluation report may end up in the recipient's waste basket. A face-to-face communication, perhaps including a few pages of report summaries, may have a far stronger impact on the recipients and their decision making.

For market research, it has been posited that lower-level managers often want extensive quantitative data in order to legitimize their decisions and thereby give them an alibi if things should go wrong. Upper-level managers, who are responsible for the future of the company, may be more open to qualitative methods with creative and new interpretations: "Those who really want the help of an investigation in order to solve concrete issues are more susceptible to consider a qualitative investigation, whereas the 'alibi-seekers' rather choose quantitative studies" (Osiatinsky, 1976, p. 58).

The closeness of interview studies to ordinary life, with their often lively descriptions and engaging narratives, makes an interview report potentially interesting to the general public. In some cases, this may entail a conflict between the demands of the scientific and the general communities, between presenting the results in a scientifically documented and controllable form or in an illustrative and engaging popular form. The dilemma of presenting captivating stories versus formal documentation of method and findings may be envisaged by two contrasting scenes for the report—the art gallery and the court room.

In *art* it is the end product—a painting or a sculpture—that is essential, and not the methods of the production process. The painting techniques employed may be of interest to fellow artists and to art historians, but the techniques are not the reason for taking a piece of art seriously. A painting carries its own message, it convinces through its expression and style. In literature, the content and form of Shakespeare's dramas still capture us today, while little is known about the dramas' origins or of Shakespeare's methods of writing.

In contrast, in a report to a *court,* say from interviews by a psychologist about child abuse, eloquence and style are not essential to the report. There will be an intense cross examination from the prosecution and the defense, critically trying to find weak points in the interviews and their interpretations. The procedures will be under scrutiny and attempts made to undermine the reliability of witnesses; of the forms of interrogation, such as the influence of leading questions; and the logic of the interpretations drawn.

An interview report should ideally be able to live up to artistic demands of expression as well as to the cross-examination of the court room. Before turning to possible ways to improve interview reports with regard to scientific criteria of rigor and artistic criteria of elegance, some moral issues involved in publishing interviews will be addressed.

Ethics of Reporting

The publication of a research report raises moral questions about what kinds of effects a report leads to. Thus psychological research should ideally both produce scientific knowledge and contribute to ameliorating the human condition (see Chapter 6). This involves communicating the findings in a form that is both scientifically sound and readable to the potential users of the knowledge reported. The publication should further be in line with the ethical guidelines of informed consent, confidentiality, and consequences.

Informed Consent. As discussed earlier, care should be taken before the interview situation to have a clear understanding with the interviewees about the later use and possible publication of their interviews, preferably with a written agreement (Chapter 6, Ethical Guidelines; Chapter 8, The Ethics of Interviewing).

Confidentiality. In order to protect the subjects' privacy, fictitious names and sometimes changes in subjects' characteristics are used in the published results. This requires altering the form of the information without making major changes of meaning. Yet disguising subjects is not without hazards.

A misleading camouflage can be illustrated by an interview study of refugees' adaptation to the Danish culture. At the suggestion of her advisor, myself, a student had changed the names as well as the nationalities of the refugees she had interviewed and quoted at length in her master's thesis. The external examiner pointed out a serious lack of understanding in the thesis's analysis of the social and psychological situation of a refugee from Chile. On closer examination it turned out that the "Chilean" refugee was a disguised Polish refugee. The student, herself an immigrant, had not taken into account that Polish refugees in Denmark in the 1970s tended to be strongly anticommunist and Chilean refugees to be equally strongly socialist or communist. Disguising names and nationality had brought about marked changes in the meaning of the social situations and identity of the subjects, whereby several of the interpretations made little sense. The example points out the problems of concealing information without substantially changing its meaning, a decision that requires an extensive knowledge of the phenomena investigated.

The particular problems of privacy in the writing stage of a qualitative inquiry have been discussed by Glesne and Peshkin (1992), who mention several well-known social science studies in which, despite the use of fictitious names and the like, reporters and others have been able to track down the actual persons. Among the more easily resolved issues of confidentiality are the interviewees who do not want to be anonymous subjects: They have engaged themselves strongly in a project and want to be responsible for their statements with full names.

Consequences. It may be difficult for a researcher to anticipate the potential consequences of an interview report. One unintended consequence of the grade study will be mentioned. A teacher of French, who had received a copy of the chapter containing the results from his interview, called and asked me not to use his statements in my book. In high school, French was an unpopular subject for many pupils and this teacher was keenly aware of and eloquent about his use of grades to motivate his pupils to learn French. His statements were highly illustrative of the use of grades as a motivational device and would be easily grasped by the readers. At the time of publication, however, a public discussion had started about the relevance of keeping French as a subject in Danish high schools. The teacher now feared that his descriptions of using grades to motivate his pupils to learn the unpopular French could be used in the public debate as an argument for omitting French as a school subject. The negative consequences did not directly concern the teacher himself, but rather his profession with regard to the public image of French as a school subject. I concurred with his request and changed "French" to "English" in his statements—and thereby lost some of their expressive value.

Other decisions about whether to change a report due to anticipated consequences may not be so easily solved. Glesne and Peshkin (1992) raise a general question:

> What obligations does the researcher have to research participants when publishing findings? If the researcher's analysis is different from that of participants, should one, both, or neither, be published? Even if respondents tend to agree that some aspect of their community is unflattering, should the researcher make this information public? (p. 119)

The intended result of the grade study was to document the effects of grading in contrast to official Danish curricular goals, such as promoting the pupils' independence and their creativity, cooperation, and interest in lifelong learning. I had believed that this would have an emancipatory effect through leading to public knowledge about, and possible changes in, the new grade-based restricted admission to the universities. The study had no such consequence: By the time the book was ready for publication, public interest in the issue had waned. Furthermore, the book was written in an academic style, heavily documented with quotations, and contained extensive methodical discussions. I had attempted to refrain from interesting but more speculative interpretations in anticipation of the common critiques of qualitative interview research. The result was that the lived reality of the pupils' school situation was lost, and the book had no appeal to either the pupils or the general public. There were a few reviews of the book: Those in conservative newspapers were critical of the results, maintaining that they were based on too few subjects, may have been provoked by leading questions, and that the speculative interpretations were biased by the author's leftist views.

Improving Standard Modes of Reporting

Readers of an interview report can adopt a multitude of perspectives to the text: Are the results interesting, do they give new knowledge, novel insights, provoke new perspectives on the topic of the study? What are the theoretical implications of the findings? Does the new knowledge support or go against current theories in the area? From a methodic stance questions also arise: How trustworthy are the findings? What is the methodical base for the results reported? And from a practical viewpoint still other questions arise: What are the practical consequences of the study? Are the findings sufficiently trustworthy to act on? In this section standard formats for reporting interviews will be outlined, and in a later section modes of enriching the interview reports will be suggested.

STANDARD STRUCTURE OF A REPORT

In Box 14.2, the seven stages of an interview investigation are placed under the standard headings of a scientific report: introduction, method, results, and discussion (see, e.g., American Psychological Association, 1989). The reporting of the methods and the results of interview studies will now be treated in more detail.

METHOD

The reader of an interview report needs to know the methodical procedures in order to evaluate the trustworthiness of the results. Knowledge of specific details of method may also be required for a reinterpretation or for an application of the findings of a study. And, in rare cases, the reader may be interested in the method for replicating or extending the original study. Box 14.3 lists some of the information that a reader not satisfied with a black box in the method section can look for.

RESULTS

In contrast to a critic's interpretation of a literary text—where the poem or novel will either be known by or available to the reader—the interview interpreter will have to select and condense the interpreted

---

Box 14.2

Structuring an Interview Report

I. **Introduction:** *Thematizing*

The general purpose of the study is stated, the conceptual and theoretical understanding of the investigated phenomena is outlined, a review of the relevant literature on the research topic is provided, and the specific research questions for the investigation are formulated.

II. **Method:** *Designing, Interviewing, Transcribing, and Analyzing*

The methods applied throughout the study are described in sufficient detail for the reader to ascertain the relevance of the design for the topic and purpose of the investigation, to evaluate the trustworthiness of the results, and, in principle, to be able to replicate the investigation.

III. **Results:** *Analysis and Verification*

The results are reported in a form that gives a clear and well-structured overview of the main findings, and with the reliability, validity, and generalizability of the findings critically evaluated.

IV. **Discussion**

The overall implications of the results are discussed. This involves the relevance of the findings to the original research questions and the theoretical and practical implications of the findings.

---

texts for the reader. In contrast to engaging and well-structured, rich, and "eminent" literary texts, some interviews may be boring to read, trivial, redundant, with little inner connections or deeper significance. It is up to the researcher to provide the perspectives and contexts that render the interviews engaging to the reader.

Box 14.3

Reader Questions About Methods

Design: Were subjects selected at random, by accessibility, by self-selection, or by theoretical sampling? Such information is a precondition for decisions about applying statistical analysis upon the results, and for the reader to draw generalizations from a study.

Interview Situation: What information was given to the subjects before the interview? What was the social and emotional atmosphere like, the degree of rapport during the interview? What questions were posed? How was the interview guide organized? Such information is essential for interpreting the meaning of what is said in an interview.

Transcription: What instructions were given to the transcribers, particularly with respect to verbatim versus edited transcripts? Such information is especially relevant for linguistic analyses and for psychological interpretations.

Analysis: What were the steps of the analysis? Was the analysis a personal intuitive interpretation, or were formal procedures applied? If categorizations were undertaken, how were they done, by whom, and how were the categories defined?

Verification: What checks were conducted of the reliability of interviewing, transcribing, and analyzing? What controls were made for counteracting biased and selective interpretations? What are the arguments for the validity of the findings?

There are no standard modes of presenting the results of interview studies. There are standard ways to present quantitative data. For example, in Figure 11.3 on grading behaviors (see Chapter 11), a simple computer program provided eight graphic options for presenting the numbers. Even though there are no comparable standard forms for presenting qualitative interview studies, there are several options available. The usual mode of presenting interview findings in the form of quotations will be treated here, and modes of enriching reports will be suggested later.

Interview Quotations. The common mode of presenting the findings of interview inquiries is through selected quotes. The interview quotes give the reader an impression of the interaction of the interview conversation and exemplify the material used for the researcher's analysis. Box 14.4 suggests some guidelines for improving readability when quoting interview statements.

'The Number of Pages. Quantity appears to be a persistent problem for qualitative researchers: they seem to feel that the sheer number of pages will justify their studies not having quantitative data; and they can have too many pages of interview material and too few pages for reporting the findings. Interview researchers sometimes complain that it is impossible to report the rich findings of their studies in short articles or even in books of normal size. In particular, they may want to include many pages of transcripts as documentation for their conclusions. They may also point out that it is easier to report in short form the neat designs of experimental and questionnaire studies with their quantitative data presented in simple tables and figures. The response of the editor of a Norwegian medical journal to such demands for extra pages by qualitative researchers was simple: "Everyone is special." Thus experimental researchers want more space to present the elaborate design and the sophisticated new equipment of a study, statisticians need extra space to develop the mathematical presuppositions of the statistical computations presented, and so forth.

Qualitative investigations in themselves need not require extra space—several of the qualitative studies used in the present book are in the form of short articles (e.g., Giorgi, 1975; Runyan, 1981; Scheflen, 1978). Psychotherapists may be able to present provoking findings in brief case studies, and also by means of short examples (see Laing, 1962). One reason may be therapists' long experience in

Box 14.4

Guidelines for Reporting Interview Quotes

1. The quotes should be related to the general text.

The researcher should provide a frame of reference for understanding the specific quotes and the interpretations given. Frames can vary from the lived world of the subjects to the researcher's theoretical models.

2. The quotes should be contextualized.

The quotes are fragments of an extensive interview context, which the researcher knows well but which is unknown to the reader. It will be helpful to render the interview context of the quote, including the question that prompted an answer. The reader will then know whether a specific topic was introduced by the interviewer or by the subject, and whether in a way leading to a specific answer.

3. The quotes should be interpreted.

The researcher should state clearly what viewpoint a quote illuminates, proves, or disproves. It should not be up to the reader to guess why this specific statement was presented and what the researcher might have found so interesting about it.

4. There should be a balance between quotes and text.

The quotes should not make up more than half of the text in a chapter. When interview quotes come from several subjects, each with their particular style of expression, many quotes with few connecting comments and interpretations can appear chaotic and produce a linguistic flicker.

5. The quotes should be short.

The maximum length of an interview quote is ordinarily half a page. Readers can loose interest if quotes are too long, often because these long interview passages contain several different dimensions, which makes it difficult for

Box 14.4 Continued

the reader to find a connecting thread. If longer passages are to be presented, they may be broken up and connected with the researcher's comments and interpretations. The exception to this is lively narrative interview passages, which may be read as stories of their own.

6. Use only the best quote.

If two or more interview passages illustrate the same point, then use only the best, the one that is the most extensive, illuminating, and well-formulated statement. For documentation it is sufficient to mention how many other subjects expressed the same viewpoints. If there are many different answers to a question, it will be useful to present several quotes, indicating the range of viewpoints.

7. Interview quotes should be rendered in a written style.

Verbal transcriptions of oral speech, with its repetitions, digressions, pauses, "hms", and the like, are difficult to grasp when presented in a written form. Interview excerpts in a vernacular form, in particular in local dialects, provide rough reading. To facilitate comprehension, the subject's spontaneous oral speech should in the final report be rendered into a readable, written textual form. The exception is when the linguistic form itself is important to the study, for example, for sociolinguistic interpretations.

8. There should be a simple signature system for the editing of the quotes.

The interview passages presented in the final report are more or less edited. Names and places that violate confidentiality will have to be altered. In order that the reader will know about the extent of editing of the quotes, the principles for editing should be given, preferably with a simple list of symbols for pauses, omissions, and the like.

SOURCE: These guidelines are taken from Borum and Enderud (1980) and have been edited and extended here.

listening to patients, becoming experts in attending to and selecting the essential aspects of the many stories they hear. In contrast, interview researchers who are novices in relation to their subject matter and the interview method, may have difficulty in developing a critical and selective distance from what they hear.

Art contains highly condensed and eloquent depictions of the manifold human condition. The quality and impact of a work of art are not enhanced by increasing its size. The short stories of Hemingway would hardly be more telling if they had been twice as long, nor would Leonardo da Vinci's *Mona Lisa* be more intriguing if painted on a double-sized canvas.

Writing as Social Construction

Current developments in the social sciences have promoted an interest in the writing of research reports. A postmodern movement from knowledge as corresponding to an objective reality to knowledge as a social construction of reality involves a change in emphasis from an observation of, to a conversation and interaction with, a social world. When validation is conceptualized as a social construction of knowledge, with a communal negotiation of its meaning, communication of the findings becomes a focal part of a research project. There is today a renewed interest in rhetorics (Simons, 1989), and there is an emphasis on audience reception in media research.

With an epistemological crisis in the representation of knowledge, with a disbelief in an objective world to be copied and re-presented in a objective form, the question arises: How can a researcher tell his or her story? Three approaches to the crisis of representation in reporting social research will be presented. These are van Maanen's (1988) *Tales of the Field,* from ethnography; Richardson's (1990) explicit, postmodern *Writing Strategies;* and Eisner's (1993) artistic approach to representing educational research.

Van Maanen (1988) has addressed the narrative conventions in ethnography for presenting the social reality of the cultures studied; they are mentioned above in Lather's discussion of different ways of reading a text (Chapter 12, The Quest for "The Real Meaning"). From his own studies of police departments, van Maanen depicts and illustrates three kinds of tales from the field—realistic, confessional, and impressionistic.

A *realistic* tale is narrated in a dispassionate, third-person voice, with the author absent from the text. The author is "the distant one" in a realistic tale based on an assumed "Doctrine of Immaculate Perception." The natives' point of view is produced through the quotes that characterize realistic tales; the quotes render a story authentic while the many technical and conceptual issues of constructing a transcription from an oral conversation are bypassed. With the ethnographer having the final word on how the culture is interpreted, he or she takes on an interpretative omnipotence.

The *confessional* tale, narrated in the first person, is highly personalized and self-absorbed. Mini-melodramas of hardship in the field endured and overcome, with accounts of what the fieldwork did to the ethnographer, are prominent features of confessional tales.

The realistic tale focuses on the known, and the confessional tale on the knower, a third tale—the *impressionistic*—attempts to bring together the knower and the known by focusing on the activity of knowing. Impressionistic tales present the doing of the fieldwork rather the doer or the done. The impressionistic tale is self-conscious and, as in impressionistic painting, it focuses on an innovative use of techniques and styles, highlighting the episodic, complex, and ambivalent realities studied. The impressionistic tale unfolds event by event, suggesting a learning process.

Van Maanen's (1988) goal in outlining the different styles of writing is not to establish one true way of writing ethnography, but to make ethnographers aware of the classic uses of rhetoric, such as voice, style, and audience, and from this knowledge to select consciously and carefully the voice most appropriate for the tales they want to tell.

Richardson (1990) addresses the issue of how to write a research report with the postmodern realization that all knowledge is socially constructed: "Writing is not simply a true representation of an objective reality, out there, waiting to be seen. Instead, through literary and rhetorical structures, writing creates a particular view of reality" (p. 9). This raises questions of criteria for evaluating a text, such as scientific soundness, aesthetic resonance, and ethical rightness.

With a crisis of representation there is an uncertainty about what constitutes reality. Richardson (1990) takes issue with a modernist belief in the externality of facts and the belief in a neutral, transparent language, where scientific writing lets the reader see the external world as it is. She goes on to discuss how writing up what the researcher has learned is itself a central theoretical and methodological problematic, with the writing itself imparting value: "Language is not simply 'transparent,' reflecting a social reality that is objectively out there. Rather language is a *constitutive* force, creating a particular view of reality" (p. 12). The grammatical, narrative, and rhetorical structures of the language we use bestow meaning and value on the topics of our writing, in poetry and in science.

The author is a narrator, a person who speaks on behalf of others:

> Because writing is always value constituting, there are always the problems of authority and authorship. . . . Narrative explanations, in practice, mean that one person's voice—the writer's—speaks for that of the others. . . . These practices, of course, raise postmodernist issues about the researcher's authority and privilege. For whom do we speak and to whom do we speak, with what voice, to what end, using what criteria? (pp. 26-27)

Going beyond a modernist disregard of the rhetorics of scientific writing, Richardson discusses, on the basis of her own interviews with "the other woman," strategies for shaping qualitative research into texts for different kinds of readers—trade, professional, and mass circulation—and outlines the use of literary devices such as different narratives and metaphors in writing the voices and lives of her interviewees.

In his presidential address to the American Educational Research Association, Eisner (1993) approached the representation of qualitative research from an artistic point of view. "The battle that once ensued to secure a place for qualitative research in education has largely been won. . . . Now the question turns to just what it is that different forms of representation employed within the context of educational research might help us grasp" (p. 8). Representation, in Eisner's use of the term, does not refer to the "mental representation" of cognitive science, but to "the process of transforming the contents of consciousness into a public form so that they can be stabilized, inspected, edited, and shared with others" (p. 6). The act of representation is also an act of invention; representational forms provide the means through which meaning is made:

> Stories and narratives by no means exhaust the ways in which the processes of education in and out of schools can be studied or described. Film, video, the multiple displays made possible through computers, and even poetically crafted narrative are waiting in the wings. I believe that we won't have to wait long before they are called to center stage. (p. 8)

These forms, as well as more propositionally formulated descriptions of events, all have the potential to reveal aspects of the world. The different forms of representation are appropriate to different topics, require different skills of the researcher, as well as different competencies for those who are to evaluate the visual, narrative, or poetic forms of representation. Eisner even goes as far as not ruling out the possibility of accepting a novel as a dissertation at the Stanford School of Education.

Enriching Interview Reports

Going beyond the standard requirements for scientific reports, I will now outline some ways of enhancing the readability of reports of interview studies. Such devices become preeminent in the representation of interviews when writing an interview report is conceived as a social construction of knowledge.

JOURNALISTIC INTERVIEWS

One way of reporting interviews is simply as interviews. The social science researcher may here take a lead from journalists, who from the start of each of their interviews will have a specific audience in mind, a limited amount of space, and a nonnegotiable deadline.

The journalist, and also the radio reporter, will in a portrait interview try to build the situation and the interpretations into the interview itself. The local context and social situation may be introduced through the interviewer's questions, for instance: "We are now sitting in the living room of the house you built when you retired, with a view through the birch forest to the fjord. Could you tell me about . . . ?" The main points and interpretations can develop from the subjects' replies to the journalist's questions, or be suggested by the journalist for confirmation or disconfirmation by the subject. Thus the contextualization and interpretation can be built into the conversation, with both journalist and interviewee more or less having the intended audience in mind. The journalist may later edit the sequence of the statements in order to provide continuity in the interview. The oral form is usually changed into a written form appropriate to the subjects' own linguistic style. The guiding line throughout the interview, the transcribing, and the editing will be to assist interviewed subjects to tell their stories as eloquently as possible to an anticipated audience. Finally, there is the ethical consideration of allowing the subjects to hear or see their edited interview before it is published.

There are exceptions to the above idealized journalistic portrait interview, such as critical demasking interviews. Social science is not the same as journalism, one difference being the responsibility of the researcher to make explicit the procedures used for editing and analyzing the interview. The journalist also has a right to protect his sources, which goes counter to the principle of scientific control of evidence. Yet when it comes to the presentation of results, research interviewers can still learn from good journalism.

DIALOGUES

Interviews can also be reported in the form of dialogues. Again, the information is conveyed by the interview interaction, but formalized and stylistically edited.

Socrates' conversations with his philosophical opponents are classical examples of a philosophical discourse: All of the information is included in the dialogue, with few subsequent interpretations by the reporter—Plato. Historians of philosophy have different views on the extent to which Socrates' dialogues were direct accounts of philosophic disputes that actually took place, or whether they were mainly or entirely constructions by Plato. Independent of their status as verbatim reproductions or literary constructions, the content of the philosophical dialogues continues to interest us today with the critical questions they pose as to the nature of truth, goodness, and beauty. Socrates' dialogues have an eminently artistic form; librarians may today have problems with whether to categorize them according to their content as philosophy or according to their artistic form as literature.

THERAPEUTIC CASE HISTORIES

A free and reflective approach to conversations and narratives can be found in reports of therapeutic interviews. Freud's clinical case stories are one illustration of an engaging and artistic presentation of conversations: He received the Goethe Prize for his writing. The works of Laing (1962) also show that it is possible through the careful use of brief conversations—theoretically interpreted from double-bind theory, psychoanalytic theory, and existential philosophy—to communicate radically new ways of understanding therapy in a simple understandable form.

In scientific psychology journals a more impersonal, formal style has generally been required. For a personal narrative of experimental studies one has to go to an exception such as Skinner's "A Case Study in Scientific Method" (1961; see also Chapter 5, Openness and Emotions in Interview Studies).

The case study is an exemplar. In the present understanding, the use of exemplars is not a mere popularization of theoretical points or putting some "flesh on the statistical bones" of a study. Rather, the case has its own value as an exemplar: It can serve as a vehicle for learning, as in Løvlie's discussion of ethics (Chapter 6, Ethical Theories). Donmoyer (1990) has pointed to the use of stories in teaching as a halfway house between tacit personal knowledge and formal propositional knowledge. Case stories also serve as a basis for generalization in the legal and clinical fields (Chapter 13, Generalizability).

The relational and tacit aspects of the interview situation are difficult to present in explicit verbal form. The oral knowledge gained from therapy is not easily transformed into written texts. Important facets of therapeutic knowledge are best communicated by anecdotes, case stories, narratives, and metaphors (Polkinghorne, 1992). Therapists' formulation of their experiential knowledge as case stories and narratives become a link between the singular and the general. Such forms of transmission come closer to craftsmanship and art than to the standard norms of formal scientific reporting.

NARRATIVES

While case stories may contain reports of spontaneous stories, the interview report can also be systematically structured with regard to narratives. In the therapeutic tradition, Spence (1982) has applied narrative forms in both the process and the presentation of therapy. Scheflen's (1978) article on the interpretations of Susan's smile (Chapter 11, Meaning Interpretation) was cast in the narrative form of a therapeutic team watching a video recording of a family therapy session, with the therapists in turn contributing new interpretations, and with the narrator, Scheflen, weaving the threads of interpretation into a fabric.

Narratives can serve as a mode of structuring an interview during analysis (Chapter 11, Meaning Structuring Through Narratives). The interview report itself may also have the form of a narrative rendering subjects' spontaneous stories, or their stories as structured into specific narrative modes, or as recast into new stories. In the latter case, the stories are reconstructed with regard to the main points the researcher wants to communicate. In a narrative approach the interviewer may conceive of his or her investigation as storytelling from beginning to end. The narrative interviewer will encourage subjects to tell stories, assist them in developing and clarifying their stories, and during the analysis work out the narrative structures of the interview stories and possibly compose the stories to be told in the final report.

"Narrative is both a mode of reasoning and a mode of representation. People can apprehend the world narratively and people can tell about the world narratively" (Richardson, 1990, p. 21). Narratives provide a powerful access to the temporal dimension of human existence, and Richardson discusses the use of different forms of narrative reporting from everyday life, autobiography, biography, and in cultural and collective stories.

METAPHORS

Novelists surpass qualitative researchers in communicating a complex social reality: "Their appeal is that they dramatize, amplify, and depict, rather than simply describe social phenomena. The language itself is often figurative and connotative, rather than solely literal and denotative. Part of this has to do with the use of metaphors, analogies, symbols, and other allusive techniques of expression" (Miles & Huberman, 1984, p. 221). A study's main points may be more easily understood and remembered when worked into vivid metaphors. Through a metaphor, one kind of thing is understood in terms of another. Psychoanalysis is replete with metaphors, often taken from myths and literature, such as the Oedipus and the Electra complexes. Metaphors also, though often unnoticed, permeate mainstream social scientific writing with terms like theory-"building," knowledge as "enlightening," and so on (see Richardson, 1990).

Miles and Huberman (1994) advocate the use of metaphors in reporting qualitative studies. A metaphor is richer, more complete than a simple description of the data. Metaphors are data-reducing and pattern-making devices. Miles and Huberman thus found in a school improvement study that a remedial reading room felt like an "oasis" for the students sent there. The metaphor "oasis" pulls together separate bits of information: The larger school is harsh and resource-thin, like a desert, and some resources are abundant in the pupils' remedial room, like the water in an oasis.

VISUALIZING

Although interview data are of a verbal nature, the possibilities of presenting the results in visual form should not be overlooked. Quantitative data are today often presented visually in the form of graphs and figures. A comparative choice of standard visual modes of presentation does not exist for qualitative inquiries. There are, however, several options, such as a tree graph of the main categories and their subcategories, diagrams with boxes and arrows showing the main sequences of a story, and the like.

If the researcher has artistic abilities, interview results may be presented as drawings. Going to a different field, a Danish professor of architecture found that he could not convey to his students through lectures or writing what he found essential about modern and postmodern architecture. He then resorted to collages, where he, through his placing of buildings in unexpected contexts, from new angles, such as an opera house under the sea, was better able to comment on the current situation of architecture than through words (Lund, 1990). The collages attained an aesthetic value of their own, and are now being displayed in art galleries.

MODES OF PRESENTATION IN THE PRESENT BOOK

Different forms of writing about interview research have been tried throughout this book. Interview *quotes* were used as illustrations, such as in different forms of transcribing the same statements. Quotes were also used as material in the interpretation of the meaning of grading behaviors as competition and wheedling. Larger sequences of interviews on learning and on grading, as well as therapeutical and philosophical conversations, have been reproduced as *exemplars* of specific forms of interviewing. The grading study has been used throughout the book as a *case* to depict some of the pitfalls and the potentialities of interview research.

There have been some attempts at a *narrative* form, such as the personal account of five emotional phases of an interview project, and a more formal course of an interview investigation was pictured as going through seven stages. The answer to the 1,000-page question was in the form of a *deconstructive tale* where the presuppositions of the question were destructed and alternative constructions for enriching the interview analysis were put forth. A short *imagined conversation* was constructed to illustrate controversies over ownership of meaning. *Metaphors* have been used to condense and profile certain meanings, such as the miner and traveler metaphors of research interviews and the Scylla and Charybdis dilemma of therapeutic inquiries. The figure of two profiles forming the outline of a vase was an attempt to *visualize* the interrelational nature of interview research.

In keeping with a traveler metaphor of interview research, the present book can be read as a travel report about interview inquiries. It has outlined a travel route through seven stages from an original idea to the finished report. Practical advice for other travelers in the field has been offered, real and imagined conversations taking place on the way have been reported, and reflections on the events encountered have been provided.

When interview travelers return home from their conversations with the people they met, their tales may enter into new conversations with the research community and the general public. The next, concluding, chapter is introduced by two conversations constructed to illustrate contrasting receptions of travel reports about interview inquiries.

PART
IV

CONCLUSION

Throughout this book I have treated interviews and interview research as forms of conversation. Interviews have been regarded literally as inter views. The interview researcher was depicted in the first chapter as a traveler in a foreign country, learning through his or her conversations with the inhabitants. When the traveler returns home with tales about encounters in the distant land, he or she may discover that listeners react rather differently to these stories. In the concluding chapter I turn from the interviewers' original conversations with their subjects to their conversations with others about the interviews.

15

Conversations About Interviews

It is sometimes easier for interview researchers to carry out conversations with their subjects, than to enter into conversations with colleagues about the conversations with their subjects. This final chapter goes beyond conversations with the interviewees to include conversations about the interviews within the research community, and also within the general community. I first discuss standard external objections to interview research and then some internal challenges to the use of qualitative research interviews. Finally, the investigation of the human conversation through interview conversations is addressed.

Reception of Interview Studies

In the introduction, an ambiguous illustration of a vase and two faces was used to depict a dual approach to interview conversations, the viewer alternatively focusing on the interaction of interviewer and interviewee or on the knowledge constructed through their interaction (Chapter 1, Overview of the Book).

In Figure 15.1, the ambiguous vase figure is extended from the interview conversation to encompass as well the researcher's conversations with other researchers about his or her interviews. I will outline here how different conceptions of knowledge and research lead to different forms of conversations about the value and the truth of the knowledge generated by the interviews.

Interviewee   Interviewer/Researcher   Fellow Researcher

Figure 15.1. Knowledge Construction Through the Interview and the Research Conversation

Two different conversational communities for an interview story will be discussed. The first consists of modern social scientists with affinities to the miner metaphor of interview research. Ten standard objections, in line with a conception of the interviewer as a miner unearthing nuggets of meaningful facts by applying standard methods, will be outlined. The other conversational community consists of researchers in the qualitative field and the humanities and is in congruence with the traveler metaphor of interviewing, closer to a postmodern perspective. Some less standard internal objections to interview research are discussed from this position, in which an interview inquiry is conceived of as close to a craft and an art.

The two conversations about interviews will be given in an idealized form, abstracted from the complex and real social and power webs they are embedded in—as when presenting a qualitative dissertation for defense at a university. In another study I have treated the social and power contexts of examination discourses and dissertation defenses as situations in which the valid and authoritative knowledge of a discipline is constituted (Kvale, 1993b). I will conclude this chapter by discussing potentialities of interview research as conversations about the human conversation.

Before turning to general forms of conversations about interviews, a extreme case will be presented in Box 15.1. The reception of this study highlights some conversations that an interview report can elicit from its readers, some of the specific arguments encountered, and the issue of what the appropriate social context is for judgments of the quality of a study.

Ten Standard Objections
to Interview Research

Reports of qualitative interview studies have tended to evoke rather standardized objections from the mainstream of modern social science. Though the wording and tone may vary, there are about 10 basic responses to the same stimulus—"a qualitative research interview." They may follow nearly automatically, even before the findings and methods of a specific interview study have been presented.

In Box 15.2, 10 of the more frequent objections to interview research are listed; some point to real problems inherent in the use of the interview method, whereas others arise from an inadequate understanding of the use of conversations as research. A genuine conversation about research interviews requires that both parties are open to what the other tries to say and also open to questioning their own presuppositions. In cases where this is not possible, a rhetorical defense may be necessary; some suggestions for responding to the 10 standard objections are discussed below. They are mainly summaries of arguments presented in earlier chapters, which are indicated in parentheses.

The present focus on external critiques of interview research is a double-edged sword. It can support an already strong trend toward external legitimation of qualitative research, or it can be conducive to an internal improvement of its quality. The aim of the following discussion is to prepare novice researchers for the most predictable external responses to their interview inquiries. With a preknowledge of the standard critiques to be expected, the qualitative researcher can decide whether they pertain to his or her study. If the objections are considered valid to the specific study, they can be taken into account

Box 15.1

Sex, Violence, Religion, Feminism, and Interviews

Interview researchers sometimes feel that their reports do not receive the attention they deserve. One case of audience reception will be mentioned as an exception: a dissertation accepted at the University of Bergen in Norway—*Whom God Loves He Chastises*—part of which appeared in book form (Lundgren, 1985).

Twenty-two women from a local religious sect were interviewed about sexual abuse in marriage. Their detailed descriptions of the sexual abuse, often in sadistic forms, in their marriages are tough reading. Moreover, the men, according to the women, justified the violence by a theology of subjugation, invoking St. Paul's dictum that a woman shall be subordinate to man in all matters. In the charismatic religious sect's interpretation, this meant that man represents the authority of God and objections to discipline are indications that women are carriers of Satan's rebellion.

The book instigated a lively public debate, and the researcher was interviewed on national television. The study had touched on a series of controversies—sex and religion, feminist research, and quantitative versus qualitative research. A religious newspaper, *Dagen,* wrote under the headline "Not Serious Research": "The way this is presented is not science, but falls within a pregiven dismal ideological pattern." The researcher was offended and she filed a libel suit against the newspaper for damaging her scientific reputation. The suit went to trial, and university professors were summoned to testify on the scientific quality of the study.

Box 15.1 Continued

Some of the arguments voiced by the witnesses in court and in the newspaper discussion can be mentioned. The findings were read by many as quantitative conclusions and generalizable; for instance that the study showed that abuse of women was just as prevalent in religious groups as in non-religious groups. In fact, the women interviewed were self-recruited and therefore the results were not generalizable; although this had been stated by the researcher in her report, it was lost in the public debate. There were objections of too few subjects, that the methods and procedures of selection had not been sufficiently accounted for, and that the questioning techniques were suspected of steering toward specific types of knowledge. Alternative interpretations of the sexual abuse than the theology of subjugation were not sufficiently considered, and the distinction between this theology being the cause or the justification of the abuse not sufficiently worked out. Other feminists took issue with the "conservative, male, researchers with tenure" for disqualifying qualitative feminist research.

The court verdict was Solomonic. The newspaper was acquitted: It was entitled, according to freedom of speech and the divergent scientific opinions, to voice its harsh criticisms. Regarding the plaintiff's work, the court found that it satisfied strong criteria for scientific research. Both parties accepted the verdict as supporting their position. Several professors regretted that the case had come to court, because it should not be up to a court of law, but to the university to make judgments about the scientific quality of research. The interviews later provided the basis for a play performed at a local theater.

SOURCES: Bergen Byrett [city court], Bergen, Norway: verdict September 8, 1985; articles in the newspapers *Dagen* and *Bergens Tidende,* September and October, 1985.

Box 15.2

Ten Standard Reactions
to Qualitative Interviews

The qualitative research interview is *not:*

1. scientific, but only reflects common sense

2. objective, but subjective

3. trustworthy, but biased

4. reliable, it rests upon leading questions

5. intersubjective, different readers find different
   meanings

6. a scientific method, it is too person-dependent

7. scientific hypothesis testing, only explorative

8. quantitative, only qualitative

9. generalizable, there are too few subjects

10. valid, it relies on subjective impressions

---

when designing an interview investigation, and thereby serve to improve the quality of the research. If the objections are regarded as invalid, the arguments for this can be presented in the report.

The following discussion will remain on a general level, outlining a conceptual framework for addressing the standard objections. The discussion may save novices some of the time and energy often used for external defense. This can leave more resources for internal improvement of the quality of the knowledge produced by interviews, and for facing new challenges intrinsically relevant to the potentials of interview research, which will be discussed in the next section.

> 1. *The qualitative research interview is not scientific, but reflects only common sense (Chapter 4, The Scientific Status of the Interview).*

As pointed out earlier, there is no single authoritative definition of science, according to which the interview can be unequivocally categorized as scientific or unscientific. A working definition of science as the methodical production of new, systematic knowledge was suggested. The question of scientific or not again depends on the understanding of the key terms in this definition, such as *methodical, new, systematic,* and *knowledge* in relation to the specific investigation.

The research interview is a specific development of the common conversations of daily life. Rather than dismissing commonsense understanding as unscientific, the conversations of daily life have here been regarded as the context from which the more specialized scientific conversations are developed and to which they return. Systematic reflection on common sense understanding and on ordinary language conversations may contribute to a refined understanding of a human world understood as a conversational reality.

> 2. *The qualitative research interview is not objective, but subjective (Chapter 4, Objectivity in Qualitative Research).*

The basic terms of the question are ambiguous. Some of the many meanings of objectivity were discussed earlier, with one conclusion being that if the meaning of objectivity is understood as intersubjective agreement, then objectivity appears to be a rather subjective concept. The objectivity of interview research needs to be discussed separately for different meanings of objectivity in relation to the interview inquiry in question. With regard to three key meanings of objectivity— as free of bias, as intersubjective, and as reflecting the nature of the object investigated—the interview can, in principle, be an objective method. With the object of the interview understood as being within a linguistically constituted and interpersonally negotiated social world, the qualitative research interview obtains a privileged position regarding objective knowledge of the social world.

A discursive conception of truth goes beyond the polarization of subjective and objective—valid knowledge is sought through a rational argument by participants in a discourse. The basic medium of this discourse is language, which is neither objective nor subjective, but inter-subjective.

---

3. Interview results are not trustworthy, they are biased.

The answer needs to be specific—to ask who cannot be trusted and in what sense. Bias may be on the side of the interviewee or of the interviewer. Experimental studies have demonstrated how expectancies of both subjects and researchers may unintentionally influence the results of the experiments. With the interpersonal interaction in the interview having a decisive impact on the results, the potential influence of interviewee and interviewer bias deserves careful attention.

Unacknowledged bias may entirely invalidate the results of an interview inquiry. A recognized bias or subjective perspective, may, however, come to highlight specific aspects of the phenomena investigated, bring new dimensions forward, contributing to a multiperspectival construction of knowledge.

---

4. Might not the interview results be due to leading questions?
(Chapter 8, Leading Questions).

The leading effects of leading questions are well documented. They can, however, not only elicit biased answers, but be used deliberately in professional interviews, for example by lawyers and by clinical psychologists; their use depends on the topic and purpose of the investigation. The qualitative interview is well suited to systematically using leading questions to check the reliability of the interviewees' answers. Rather than being used too much, deliberately leading questions are today probably too little applied in research interviews.

While the technical issue of leading questions in interviews has been rather overemphasized, the leading effects of the research questions of a project have received less attention. The decisive issue—for interview questions and research questions—is not whether to lead or not to lead, but where the questions do lead, whether they lead in important directions that yield new and worthwhile knowledge.

> 5. *The interpretation of interviews is not intersubjective; different readers find different meanings (Chapter 4, Objectivity in Qualitative Research; Chapter 11, Control of Analysis; Chapter 12).*

Different interpretations of the same verbatim interview texts definitely occur, though probably less often than commonly believed. In current interview research there are too few rather than too many interpretations.

We may here distinguish between a biased subjectivity, to be avoided, and a perspectival subjectivity. Through the latter, readers who adapt different perspectives and pose different questions to the same text come out with different interpretations of the meaning of the text. When different interpretations appear arbitrary, this may be because the questions posed to a text, and their presuppositions, are not made explicit. With a clarification of the perspectives adopted toward an interview text several interpretations of the same text will not be a weakness but a richness and a strength of interview research.

> 6. *The interview is not a scientific method, it is too person-dependent (Chapter 2, The Mode of Understanding in the Qualitative Research Interview; Chapter 5, From Method to Craftsmanship).*

A common worry is that different interviewers will come up with different interviews. A research interview is flexible, sensitive to context, and dependent on the personal interaction of the interviewer and interviewee.

Rather than attempt to eliminate the personal interaction of interviewer and interviewee, we might take a lead from therapeutic interviews and regard the person of the interviewer as the primary methodological tool, with the relevant data created by the unique interaction between the interviewer and interviewee. The importance of interviewers as instruments for obtaining knowledge puts strong demands on their craftsmanship, their empathy, and their knowledge.

> 7. *Qualitative interviews do not test hypotheses; they are only explorative and thus not scientific (Chapter 4, Qualitative and Quantitative Research; Chapter 5, Thematizing and Designing).*

Contrary to this objection, interview studies may be used for testing of hypotheses about differences among groups, and a single interview may be designed as a process of continual hypothesis testing—the interviewers' questions here serve to test hypotheses, employing an interplay of questions, counter-questions, leading questions, and probing questions.

Testing of hypotheses is, however, not a necessary criterion or goal for social research. Exploratory and descriptive studies are important parts of scientific inquiry in fields as diverse as geography, zoology, anatomy, and linguistics. The nuanced descriptions of the phenomena studied have intrinsic value and constitute one of the strengths of the qualitative research.

> 8. *Interviews are not quantitative, only qualitative (Chapter 4, Qualitative and Quantitative Research).*

In the modern social sciences, quantification has often been considered the very criterion of science, and, when not taken as self-evident, is legitimated by referring to the natural sciences. This argument overlooks the role of qualitative descriptions in fields such as botany, zoology, and geology, as well as the qualitative analyses in chemistry. In the practice of research, qualitative and quantitative approaches interact; in published social science reports, however, there has been a tendency to downplay the qualitative aspects of the research process.

Despite an interweaving of the qualitative and quantitative aspects of social research, a dichotomized conception with a hegemony on the quantitative side may still prevail. This could well have less to do with the practice of science than with a fundamentalist belief in the natural, and the social, world as a basically mathematically ordered universe.

> 9. *Interview findings are not generalizable; there are too few*
> *subjects (Chapter 5, Designing; Chapter 13, Generalizability).*

A quest for generalizability has loomed heavily over the social sciences, accompanied by a demand for a large number of subjects on which to base the generalizations. The number of subjects necessary will depend on the purpose of a study, such as predicting a national election, testing the differences among groups, or investigating the biography of one person. In addition to common statistical generalizations, there are analytical generalizations in qualitative case studies, where the researcher presents evidence and arguments for the claims of generalizable knowledge.

There is also the question of why there is such a strong emphasis on generalization. In postmodern approaches to the social sciences, the goal of universal generalizability is being replaced by an emphasis on contextuality and heterogeneity of knowledge.

> 10. *Interviewing is not a valid method, it depends on subjective*
> *impressions (Chapter 13).*

We may here distinguish between a practical and a theoretical approach to the validity of interview findings. A practical approach based on good craftsmanship in research departs from an understanding of validity as referring to the strength and credibility of an assertion. Validation becomes investigation: a continual checking, questioning, and theoretical interpretation of the findings.

With a postmodern move away from knowledge as correspondence with an objective reality toward knowledge as a social construction of reality there is a change of emphasis from observation of, to conversation and interaction with, the social world. By going beyond a correspondence theory of truth, which is at the root of the older psychometric validity concepts, to conceive validation as communication with and action on the social world, the research interview based on conversation and interaction attains a privileged position.

* * * * *

Some comments on this formalized conversation about interviews will be put forth. First, the above standard objections to qualitative interviews are not independent, they can be traced to a *positivist* conception of social research, depicted earlier (Chapter 4, Positivism). They correspond to a miner metaphor of interview research (Chapter 1, The Interviewer as a Miner or as a Traveler), conceiving of knowledge as nuggets of objective meaning-data to be uncovered, uncontaminated by the human researcher, a conception that I have attempted to replace with a traveler metaphor for interview conversations.

Second, the standard objections contain global and *ambiguous concepts,* such as objectivity and validity. They need to be discussed and defined as precisely as possible. It should furthermore be clarified which objections involve general problems of research, such as investigator bias, and which raise interview-specific issues, such as the impact of leading questions. The levels at which the objections are raised also need to be specified; the issue of leading questions may involve practical interview techniques as well as the philosophical issue of a neutral access to an objective empirical world.

Third, not only is the content of the objections to qualitative research rather standardized, but so is their polarized form as *dichotomies:* objective versus subjective, quantitative versus qualitative, and so on. The very form of the objections, or questions, is itself leading: They are based on a dichotomized presupposition of the nature of knowledge as either true or false. Each part of the posited dichotomy may then serve as a tribal banner for competing groups; at the start fueling a heated controversy, gradually replaced by an insight that the controversy may have been constructed on a pseudo issue. The field is then left and replaced by a new controversy under a different banner, still retaining the dichotomized form, as well as some old themes and supporters on each side. There appears to be a "dichotomy of the decade" in modern social science: in the 1960s, natural science versus the humanities; in the 1970s, quantitative versus qualitative; in the 1980s, objective versus subjective; and in the 1990s, universal versus local knowledge. The way out is to go beyond the dichotomized thinking of either/or categories by emphasizing description and dialogue about the qualitative nuances and differences of the issues raised.

Finally, in a *reinterpretation,* the standard critiques can be reversed and read as pointing to the power of qualitative interview research. The very strength of the interview is its privileged access to the common understanding of subjects, the understanding that provides their worldview and the basis for their actions. The deliberate use of the subjective perspective need not be a negative bias; rather, the personal perspectives of the subjects and the interpreter can provide a distinctive and sensitive understanding of the phenomena of the everyday life world. A controlled use of leading questions may lead to well-controlled knowledge. The plurality of interpretations opens to the richness of meanings of the human life world, the person of the researcher is the most sensitive instrument available to investigate human meanings. The explorative potentialities of the interview can open to qualitative descriptions of new phenomena. Generalizing from and validating interview findings open up alternative modes of evaluating qualitative research, with an emphasis on communication of and action on the findings.

The above 10 critiques of qualitative interviews may be seen as challenges to the advancement of interview research. They may lead to improving the methodic craftsmanship of interview inquiries, and they may further a conceptual clarification of the mode of understanding in the interview as one form of conversational research. I will now turn to alternative critiques of interview inquiries that imply that the very power and potentials of conversation as research have not been realized in its current use.

Internal Critiques of Interview Research

Critiques in a different vein than the above standard objections may be heard from audiences sympathetic to the idea of qualitative research, such as scholars in the humanities and professionals such as therapists. Their various critiques are closer to an understanding of the interviewer as a traveler returning home with tales from conversations in a new country.

The internal critiques depicted in Box 15.3 are pertinent to much current interview research. Suggestions for overcoming some of these

---

Box 15.3

Ten Internal Critiques
of Interview Research

Current interview research is:

- *individualistic,* it focuses on the individual and neglects a person's embeddedness in social interactions

- *idealistic,* it ignores the situatedness of human experience and behavior in a social and material world

- *intellectualistic,* it neglects the emotional aspects of knowledge, overlooks empathy as a mode of knowing

- *immobile,* the subjects sit and talk, they do not move or act in the world

- *cognitivist,* it focuses on thoughts and experiences at the expense of action

- *verbalizing,* it makes a fetish of verbal interaction and transcripts, neglects the bodily situatedness of the interview

- *alinguistic,* although the medium is language, linguistic approaches to language are ignored

- *atheoretical,* it entails a cult of interview statements, and disregards theories of the field studied

- *arhetorical,* published reports are boring collections of interview quotes, rather than convincing stories

- *insignificant,* it produces trivialities, and hardly any new knowledge worth mentioning

---

critiques have been put forth in previous chapters. Some instances will be reviewed below to demonstrate that the criticized features do not necessarily pertain to interview inquiries, but rather to what have been common modes of applying and understanding interviews in research.

Most interview research today is carried out as individual interviews; the use of group interviews may well bring up lively *interpersonal dynamics* and show the social interactions leading to the interview statements. Interviews can be used to obtain descriptions of the cultural and the historical, the social and the material context of subjects' lives. Anthropological interviews focus on the respondent's culture, and interviews are employed in recording oral history (Yow, 1994). Some instances of interview studies that include the *material and social situations* of the subjects have been mentioned earlier, such as Oscar Lewis's descriptions of Mexican peasants' life situation (1964), Becker-Schmidt's (1982) tracing of the contradictions in the interviews of women industrial workers to conflicts between their work and home situations, Hagan's (1986) analysis of the situation of mothers on welfare, and my own attempts to link the effects of learning for grades to the requirements of wage labor. The use of therapeutic interviews for research shows the possibilities of applying *empathy and emotional interaction* to obtain significant knowledge of the human situation. In recent feminist qualitative research there is an emphasis on the knowledge potentials of feelings and empathy in human interaction, including research interviews.

Though most interview research today is chair-bound, researchers might learn from radio and TV interviewers who walk around with their subjects in the subjects' natural surroundings, such as their workplace or home. *Conversations integrated in the subjects' natural activities* of their daily world provide a more comprehensive picture of their background situation than the office-based views. There are trends today toward giving the knowledge obtained through interviews back to the participants in the social situation in which the knowledge was developed. This pertains to the use of interviews in system evaluation; and in *action research* and feminist research particularly, the knowledge acquired through interviews is utilized to change the situations investigated.

The verbal fixation of interview research may to a certain extent be counteracted by videotaped interviews and thereby retaining access to the *bodily expressions* and interpersonal dynamics of the interaction. The development of computer programs for directly analyzing the audiotape and videotape recordings allows a move from the alienation of transcripts to listening to conversations. Parallel with the trends toward including nonlinguistic aspects of interview conversations, is a trend toward going beyond the naive use of language in social science interviewing by an orientation toward *sociolinguistics*. This includes an increasing awareness of the differences between the oral speech of the interviews and the written texts analyzed. Postmodern analyses of the linguistic construction of the social world have contributed to this attention to the pivotal role of language in interview research.

The impact of Glaser and Strauss's grounded theory (see Strauss & Corbin, 1990) in current qualitative research shows the possibility of formulating *theories* grounded on empirical interviewing. Within the psychoanalytical tradition, the development of innovative theories on the basis of patient interviews has not been limited to Freud's original contributions at the turn of the century, but has continued with theories originating with therapeutic interviews about the authoritarian personality in the 1930s and 1940s, and the narcissistic personality in the 1970s and 1980s. The *communication of qualitative studies* has come to the fore in the past few years, drawing on narrative approaches, the rhetorical tradition, and also through experiments with artistic forms of reporting interview studies.

It remains to be seen whether the use of research interviews will yield *significant knowledge* of the human situation. Perhaps one hindrance to the development of comprehensive and penetrating knowledge has been the often individualistic and practical topic-centered approach to many interview studies, rather than using interviews in larger, common research projects guided by theory.

Although the above internal critiques in my view characterize many current interview studies, the brief responses should indicate that they do not necessarily pertain to interview research. The qualitative research interview is a specific form of conversation, however, and there are other approaches more appropriate to some of the concerns raised above. Comprehensive understandings of cultural situations are better acquired through field studies and participant observation than interviews. For obtaining practical knowledge about changing behavior, action research is more adequate. Deeper knowledge of a person's fantasies and feelings may only be methodically and ethically accessible through intensive therapeutic interviews. It should further be pointed out that the present book gives a rather "puristic" view of the interview as a method used in isolation. Interviews are often used in combination with other research methods, such as the above, which will provide a more multifaceted view of the phenomena investigated.

There are current trends that could make much of the above internal critique obsolete—an increasing methodological sophistication in interview research and new ways of conceiving of interview research. Throughout this book philosophical perspectives congenial to the mode of understanding in the qualitative research interview have been included: such as phenomenology, hermeneutics, dialectics, and postmodernism. In particular, postmodern and feminist thought today has an impact on how qualitative research is conceived (see, e.g., Denzin & Lincoln, 1994).

In an earlier chapter, therapeutic research was depicted in a dichotomized either/or version as a dangerous voyage through a narrow strait between two monsters—a no-method Charybdis and an all-method Scylla—producing a long history of shipwrecked dissertations (Chapter 4, Psychoanalytical Knowledge Production). In the present context, qualitative research may be depicted as a voyage through an archipelago of friendly islands—the humanities, therapy, action research and feminist research, and art—each offering the interviewer-traveler different genres and scenarios for the voyage.

Conversations About Conversations

In conclusion, I will return from alternative genres to the knowledge potentials of interviews as human conversations. In current philosophy there is an emphasis on validity of knowledge to be constructed through a discourse. In this view, conversation in social science research is not limited to explorative interviews as preparation for the "real" scientific studies, but rather conversation permeates the entire process of social science inquiry. Research is conceived as conversation, with the subjects of a study, with the scientific community, and with a wider public. Social research becomes one mode of expanding the historical conversation of humankind.

The entire interview inquiry is in a broad sense a conversation. In the first, thematizing stage of an investigation there is a conversation with the literature of tradition, with its theories and findings. The interview situation is a direct conversation, and interpretation is seen as a dialogue with the text produced by the interview. Verification involves a conversation with different communities, with a focus on validation as communication and action. Reporting was seen as invoking an imagined dialogue with a potential audience, a dialogue that can become real through the publication of the findings.

The *inter view* is a situation of knowledge production in which knowledge is created between the views of the two partners in the conversation. In preceding chapters the focus has been on knowledge production through the interaction of the interviewer and the interviewee. The construction of knowledge is not completed by the interaction of the researchers and their subjects, but continues with the researchers' interpretations and reporting of their interviews, to conversations with other researchers about their findings. In this chapter, two formalized dialogues with different audiences were depicted in line with a miner and a traveler metaphor, respectively, of the interviewer. The nature of knowledge presupposed by the one audience consisted of isolated objective facts; by the other, of knowledge as interrelational, constituted by conversational interaction.

An interview inquiry is not above the social world, it is not a neutral conversation allowing us to decide about the true nature of the social world, or—more modestly—to decide objectively among competing knowledge claims. The interview conversation is part of the social world studied, and as was shown by the two formalized conversations about interviews, a controversial means for obtaining knowledge of the social world.

In order to clarify the nature of the research interview we need to extend our understanding of the nature of the conversational realities studied by the interview conversations. We know about the cultural world through our own conversations and by reading the conversations of others. The cultural world we are conversing about is again a conversational world in which meaning has been constituted through negotiations of interpretations. We exist in a conversational circle, where our understanding of the human world depends on conversation and our understanding of conversation is based on our understanding of the human world. This is not a vicious circle, but in a hermeneutical sense a *circuluous fructuoisi*. The problem is not to get out of the conversational circle, but to get into it in the right way.

Rather than trying to escape the conversational circle—as was attempted by positivist approaches to the modern social sciences with the scientist as an external observer, ideally a visiting man from Mars —the challenge is to expand our understanding of the human world through a dialogue within the human conversational reality.

Discussions of qualitative research, including the major part of the present book, have tended to remain within a methodological and epistemological context. There has been relatively little questioning about the relation of the interview to the nature of the subject matter investigated, which involves a theory of the social world. Perhaps one major contribution of the current interest in qualitative interview research will be an impetus to address the conversational nature of the social world studied by the social sciences. This involves not only addressing the hermeneutics of the conversation, but also bringing in the broader social contexts of an interview—something that has been little treated in this book—such as the embeddedness of conversations in contexts of power, economy, and politics.

Throughout this book the research interview has been discussed in relation to three different forms of conversation—*methodical, epistemological*, and *ontological* (Chapter 2, Interviews in Three Conversations). They involve the interview as a specific conversational technique for obtaining knowledge of the subjects' lived worlds, the conversation as the ultimate context within which knowledge is understood, and finally men and women as dialogical beings through their words and actions in a material situation constituting the human world as a conversational reality. In this understanding, the use of conversations is not only an additional method of social science research, but conversations among researchers, and the public, provide the context for ascertaining the truth about and value of the knowledge produced by interview conversations about a conversational world.

Interview inquiry leads neither to a subjective relativity of interpretations, nor to an absolute objective knowledge, but to knowledge produced and tested intersubjectively through conversations. The question of the objectivity of the knowledge produced involves the issue of the nature of the social world studied. One meaning of *objectivity* is that an objective investigation reflects the nature of the object investigated, it "lets the object speak." This is literally the case in an interview inquiry where intersubjective knowledge is constructed in a conversation between the researcher and the "objects" investigated. With the "objects"—the interview subjects—giving voice to their understanding of an interpersonally negotiated social world, the qualitative research interview obtains a privileged position for creating objective knowledge of a conversational world.

References

Altheide, D. L., & Johnson, J. M. (1994). Criteria for assessing interpretive validity in qualitative research. In N. K. Denzin & Y. S. Lincoln (Eds.), *Handbook of qualitative research* (pp. 485-499). Thousand Oaks, CA: Sage.

American Psychological Association. (1981). Ethical principles of psychologists. *American Psychologist, 36,* 633-638.

American Psychological Association. (1989). *Publication manual* (3rd ed.). Washington, DC: Author.

Andersen, T. (1987). The reflecting team: Dialogue and meta-dialogue in clinical work. *Family Process, 26,* 415-428.

Anderson, W. T. (Ed.). (1995). *The truth about the truth: De-confusing and re-constructing the postmodern world.* New York: Tarcher/Putnam.

Becker, H. S. (1979). Do photographs tell the truth? In T. D. Cook & C. S. Reichardt (Eds.), *Qualitative and quantitative methods in evaluation research* (pp. 99-117). Beverly Hills, CA: Sage.

Becker-Schmidt, R. (1982). Modsætningsfyldt realitet og ambivalens: Kvinders arbejdserfaringer i fabrik og familie. *Udkast, 10,* 164-198.

Berg Sørensen, T. (1988). *Fænomenologisk mikrosociologi.* Aarhus, Denmark: Gestus.

Berger, P. L., & Luckmann, T. (1966). *The social construction of reality.* Garden City, NY: Doubleday.

Bernstein, R. J. (1983). *Beyond objectivism and relativism.* Philadelphia: University of Pennsylvania Press.

Bogdan, R., & Biklen, S. K. (1982). *Qualitative research for education.* Boston: Allyn & Bacon.

Borum, F., & Enderud, H. (1980). Organisationsforskeren som reporter. Om analyse og rapportering af interview. *Tidsskrift for Samfunnsforskning, 21,* 359-382.

Boss, M. (1963). *Psychoanalysis and Daseinsanalysis.* New York: Basic Books.

Bowles, S., & Gintis, H. (1976). *Schooling in capitalist America.* London: Routledge & Kegan Paul.

Brandt, L. W. (1973). The physics of the physicist and the physics of the psychologist. *International Journal of Psychology, 8,* 61-72.

Calder, B. J. (1977). Focus groups and the nature of qualitative market research. *Journal of Marketing Research, 14,* 353-364.

Carson, T. R. (1986). Closing the gap between research and practice: Conversation as a mode of doing research. *Phenomenology + Pedagogy, 4*(2), 73-85.

Cherryholmes, C. H. (1988). *Power and criticism: Poststructural investigations in education.* New York: Teachers College Press.

Cornforth, M. (1971). *Materialism and dialectical method.* New York: International Publishers.

Cortazzi, M. (1993). *Narrative analysis.* London: Falmer.

Cronbach, L. J. (1971). Test validation. In R. L. Thorndike (Ed.), *Educational measurement* (pp. 442-507). Washington, DC: American Council of Education.

Cronbach, L. J. (1980). Validity on parole: How can we go straight? *New Directions for Testing and Measurement, 5,* 99-108.

Cronbach, L. J., & Meehl, P. E. (1955). Construct validity in psychological tests. *Psychological Bulletin, 52,* 281-302.

Dean, J. P., & Whyte, W. F. (1969). How do you know if the informant is telling the truth? In G. J. McCall & J. L. Simmons (Eds.), *Issues in participant observation* (pp. 105-115). London: Addison-Wesley.

Denzin, N. K., & Lincoln, Y. S. (Eds.). (1994). *Handbook of qualitative research.* Thousand Oaks, CA: Sage.

Dichter, E. (1960). *The strategy of desire.* Garden City, NY: Doubleday.

Donmoyer, R. (1990). Generalizability and the single-case study. In E. W. Eisner & A. Peshkin (Eds.), *Qualitative inquiry in education* (pp. 175-200). New York: Teachers College Press.

Dreyfus, H. L., & Dreyfus, S. E. (1986). *Mind over machine.* New York: Free Press.

Dreyfus, H. L., & Dreyfus, S. E. (1990). What is morality? A phenomenological account of the development of ethical expertise. In D. Rasmussen (Ed.), *Universalism vs. communitarism: Contemporary debates in ethics* (pp. 237-263). Cambridge: MIT Press.

Eco, U. (1984). *The name of the rose.* New York: Harcourt Brace.

Eco, U. (1989). *Foucault's pendulum.* London: Secker & Warburg.

Eco, U. (1990). *The limits of interpretation.* Bloomingtown: Indiana University Press.

Eco, U. (Ed.). (1992). *Interpretation and overinterpretation.* Cambridge, UK: Cambridge University Press.

Eisner, E. W. (1991). *The enlightened eye.* New York: Macmillan.

Eisner, E. W. (1993). Forms of understanding and the future of educational research. *Educational Researcher, 22*(7), 5-11.

Eisner, E. W., & Peshkin, A. (Eds.). (1990). *Qualitative inquiry in education.* New York: Teachers College Press.

Fischer, C., & Wertz, F. (1979). Empirical phenomenological analyses of being criminally victimized. In A. Giorgi, R. Knowles, & D. L. Smith (Eds.), *Duquesne studies in phenomenological psychology, III* (pp. 135-158). Pittsburgh, PA: Duquesne University Press.

Fisher, S., & Greenberg, R. P. (1977). *The scientific credibility of Freud's theories and therapy.* New York: Basic Books.

Flick, U., v. Kardoff, E., Keupp, H., v. Rosenstiel, L., & Wolff, S. (Eds.). (1991). *Handbuch qualitative Sozialforschung.* München: Psychologie Verlag Union.

Fog, J. (1992). Den moralske grund i det kvalitative forskningsinterview. *Nordisk Psykologi, 44,* 212-229.

Freud, S. (1963). *Therapy and technique.* New York: Collier.

Gadamer, H. G. (1975). *Truth and method.* New York: Seabury Press.

Gergen, K. J. (1992). Toward a postmodern psychology. In S. Kvale (Ed.), *Psychology and postmodernism* (pp. 17-30). London: Sage.

Gergen, K. J. (1994). *Realities and relationships. Soundings in social constructionism.* Cambridge, MA: Harvard University Press.

Giorgi, A. (1970). *Psychology as a human science.* New York: Harper & Row.

Giorgi, A. (1975). An application of phenomenological method in psychology. In A. Giorgi, C. Fischer, & E. Murray (Eds.), *Duquesne studies in phenomenological psychology, II* (pp. 82-103). Pittsburgh, PA: Duquesne University Press.

Giorgi, A. (1985). The phenomenological psychology of learning and the verbal learning tradition. In A. Giorgi (Ed.), *Phenomenology and psychological research* (pp. 23-85). Pittsburgh, PA: Duquesne University Press.

Giorgi, A. (1992). Description versus interpretation: Competing alternative strategies for qualitative research. *Journal of Phenomenological Psychology, 23,* 119-135.

Giorgi, A. (1994). A phenomenological perspective on certain qualitative research methods. *Journal of Phenomenological Psychology, 25,* 190-220.

Giorgi, A., Fischer, C., & Murray, E. (Eds.). (1975). *Duquesne studies in phenomenological psychology, II* (pp. 82-103). Pittsburgh, PA: Duquesne University Press.

Glaser, B. G., & Strauss, A. M. (1967). *The discovery of grounded theory: Strategies for qualitative research.* New York: Aldine.

Glesne, C., & Peshkin, A. (1992). *Becoming qualitative researchers: An introduction.* White Plains, NY: Longman.

Guidelines for the protection of human subjects. (1992). Berkeley: University of California Press.

Habermas, J. (1971). *Knowledge and human interests.* Boston: Beacon.

Hagan, T. (1986). Interviewing the downtrodden. In P. D. Ashworth, A. Giorgi, & A. de Koening (Eds.), *Qualitative research in psychology* (pp. 332-360). Pittsburgh, PA: Duquesne University Press.

Harel, I., & Papert, S. (Eds.). (1991). *Constructionism.* Norwood, NJ: Ablex.

Haug, F. (1978). Dialektische Theorie und empirische Methodik. In *Das Argument, Berlin,* 111, 9/10.

Hertz, R., & Imber, J. B. (Eds.). (1995). *Studying elites using qualitative methods.* Thousand Oaks, CA: Sage.

Hillman, J. (1984). *Inter views.* New York: Harper.

Holbrook, M. B. (1995). *Consumer research.* Thousand Oaks, CA: Sage.

House, E. R. (1980). *Evaluating with validity.* Beverly Hills, CA: Sage.

Hvolbøl, C., & Kristensen, O. S. (1983). Bivirkninger ved karaktergivning. *Psychological Reports Aarhus, 8*(1). Aarhus, Denmark: Aarhus Universitet.

Jacobsen, B. (1981). *De højere uddannelser mellem teknologi og humanisme.* København: Rhodos.

Jensen, K. B. (1989). Discourses of interviewing: Validating qualitative research findings through textual analysis. In S. Kvale (Ed.), *Issues of validity in qualitative research* (pp. 93-108). Lund, Sweden: Studentlitteratur.

Kennedy, M. M. (1979). Generalizing from single case studies. *Evaluation Quarterly, 3,* 661-678.

Kerlinger, F. N. (1973). *Foundations of behavioral research.* New York: Holt, Rinehart & Winston.

Kerlinger, F. N. (1979). *Behavioral research.* New York: Holt, Rhinehart, & Winston.

Kimmel, A. J. (1988). *Ethics and values in applied social science research.* Newbury Park, CA: Sage.

Kirk, J., & Miller, M. L. (1986). *Reliability and validity in qualitative research.* Beverly Hills, CA: Sage.

Koch, S. (1959). Epilogue. In S. Koch (Ed.), *Psychology: A study of a science, III* (pp. 729-802). New York: McGraw-Hill.

Kvale, S. (1972). *Prüfung und Herrschaft.* Weinheim, Germany: Beltz.

Kvale, S. (1976a). Meanings as data and human technology. *Scandinavian Journal of Psychology, 17,* 171-180.

Kvale, S. (1976b). The psychology of learning as ideology and technology. *Behaviorism, 4,* 97-116.

Kvale, S. (1980). *Spillet om karakterer i gymnasiet—Elevinterviews om bivirkninger af adgangsbegrænsning.* Copenhagen: Munksgaard.

Kvale, S. (1992). A postmodern psychology—A contradiction in terms? In S. Kvale (Ed.), *Psychology and postmodernism* (pp. 31-57). London: Sage.

Kvale, S. (1993a). En pædagogisk rehabilitering af mesterlæren? [An educational rehabilitation of apprenticeship?] *Dansk pædagogisk Tidsskrift, 41,* 9-18

Kvale, S. (1993b). Examinations re-examined—Certification of students or of knowledge? In S. Chaiklin & J. Lave (Eds.), *Understanding practice* (pp. 215-240). Cambridge, UK: Cambridge University Press.

Kvale, S., & Grenness, C. E. (1967). Skinner and Sartre: Towards a radical phenomenology of behavior? *Review of Existential Psychology and Psychiatry, 7,* 128-150.

Laing, R. (1962). *The self and others.* London: Tavistock.

Lather, P. (1991). *Getting smart: Feminist research and pedagogy with/in the postmodern.* New York: Routledge & Kegan Paul.

Lather, P. (1992). Critical frames in educational research: Feminist and poststructural perspectives. *Theory Into Practice, 31*(2), 2-13.

Lather, P. (1995). The validity of angels: Interpretive and textual strategies in researching the lives of women with HIV/AIDS. *Qualitative Inquiry, 1,* 41-68.

Lave, J., & Kvale, S. (1995). What is anthropological research? An interview with Jean Lave by Steinar Kvale. *Qualitative Studies in Education, 8,* 219-228.

Lave, J., & Wenger, E. (1991). *Situated learning: Legitimate peripheral participation.* Cambridge, UK: Cambridge University Press.

Lazarsfeld, P. L. (1944). The controversy over detailed interviews—An offer for negotiation. *Public Opinion Quarterly, 8,* 38-60.

Lewis, O. (1964). *The children of Sanchez.* Harmondsworth, UK: Penguin.

Lincoln, Y. S. (1990). Toward a categorical imperative for qualitative research. In E. W. Eisner & A. Peskin (Eds.), *Qualitative inquiry in education* (pp. 277-295). New York: Teachers College Press.

Lincoln, Y. S., & Guba, E. (1985). *Naturalistic inquiry.* Beverly Hills, CA: Sage.

Loftus, E. L., & Palmer, J. C. (1974). Reconstruction of automobile destruction: An example of the interaction between language and memory. *Journal of Verbal Learning and Verbal Behavior, 13,* 585-589.

Løvlie, L. (1993). Of rules, skills, and examples in moral education. *Nordisk Pedagogik, 13,* 76-91.

Lund, N. O. (1990). *Collage architecture.* Berlin: Ernst.

Lundgren, E. (1985). *I Herrens vold.* Oslo: Cappelen.

Lyotard, J. F. (1984). *The postmodern condition: A report on knowledge.* Manchester, UK: Manchester University Press.

Lyotard, J. F. (1991). *Phenomenology.* Albany: SUNY Press.

Madison, G. B. (1990). *The hermeneutics of postmodernity.* Bloomington: Indiana University Press.

Mandler, G., & Kessen, W. (1959). *The language of psychology.* New York: John Wiley.

Marshall, C., & Rossman, G. B. (1995). *Designing qualitative research.* Thousand Oaks, CA: Sage.

Marton, F. (1981). Phenomenography—Describing conceptions of the world around us. *Instructional Science, 10,* 177-200.

Mathison, S., Ross, E. W., & Cornett, J. W. (1993). *A casebook for teaching about ethical issues in qualitative research.* Washington, DC: American Educational Research Association, Qualitative Research SIG.

May, R., Angel, E., & Ellenberger, H. F. (Eds.). (1958). *Existence—A new dimension in psychiatry and psychology.* New York: Basic Books.

Maykut, P., & Morehouse, R. (1994). *Beginning qualitative research.* London: Falmer.

Mayring, P. (1983). *Qualitative Inhaltsanalyse.* Weinheim, Germany: Beltz.

Merleau-Ponty, M. (1962). *Phenomenology of perception.* London: Routledge & Kegan Paul.

Messer, S. B., Sass, L. A., & Woolfolk, R. L. (Eds.). (1988). *Hermeneutics and psychological theory.* New Brunswick, NJ: Rutgers University Press.

Miles, M. B., & Huberman, A. M. (1984). *Qualitative data analysis: A sourcebook of new methods.* Beverly Hills, CA: Sage.

Miles, M. B., & Huberman, A. M. (1994). *Qualitative data analysis: An expanded sourcebook.* London: Sage.

Mishler, E. G. (1986). *Research interviewing—Context and narrative.* Cambridge, MA: Harvard University Press.

Mishler, E. G. (1990). Validation in inquiry-guided research: The role of exemplars in narrative studies. *Harvard Educational Review, 60,* 415-442.

Mishler, E. G. (1991). Representing discourse: The rhetoric of transcription. *Journal of Narrative and Life History, 1,* 255-280.

Morgan, D. L. (1988). *Focus groups as qualitative research.* Newbury Park, CA: Sage.

Morse, J. M., & Field, P. A. (1995). *Qualitative research methods for professionals.* Thousand Oaks, CA: Sage.

Moustakas, C. (1994). *Phenomenological research methods.* Thousand Oaks, CA: Sage.

Mussen, P. H., Conger, J. J., & Kagan, J. (1977). *Child development and personality.* New York: Harper & Row.

O'Hara, M. (1995). Constructing emancipatory realities. In W. T. Andersen (Ed.), *The truth about the truth: De-confusing and re-constructing the postmodern world.* New York: Harper/Putnam.

Olesen, V. (1994). Feminisms and models of qualitative research. In N. K. Denzin & Y. S. Lincoln (Eds.), *Handbook of qualitative research* (pp. 158-174). Thousand Oaks, CA: Sage.

Ong, W. J. (1982). *Orality and literacy—The technologizing of the word.* London: Methuen.

Osiatinsky, A. (1976). Tillämpning av psykologiska kundskaper i näringslivet. In J. Arent & A. Friman (Eds.), *Industriel marknadsföring* (pp. 47-59). Stockholm: Liber.

Packer, A. L., & Addison, R. B. (1989). *Entering the circle—Hermeneutic investigation in psychology.* Albany: SUNY Press.

Palmer, R. E. (1969). *Hermeneutics.* Evanston, IL: Northwestern University Press.

Patton, M. Q. (1980). *Qualitative evaluation methods.* Beverly Hills, CA: Sage.

Pervin, L. A. (1984). *Personality.* New York: John Wiley.

Plato. (1953). *V. Lysis, Symposion, Gorgias* (W.R.M. Lamb, Trans.). Cambridge, MA: Harvard University Press.

Poland, B. D. (1995). Transcription quality as an aspect of rigour in qualitative research. *Qualitative Inquiry, 1,* 290-310.

Polkinghorne, D. E. (1983). *Methodology for the human sciences.* Albany: SUNY Press.

Polkinghorne, D. E. (1988). *Narrative knowing and the human sciences.* Albany: SUNY Press.

Polkinghorne, D. E. (1989). Changing conversations about human science. In S. Kvale (Ed.), *Issues of validity in qualitative research* (pp. 13-45). Lund, Sweden: Studentlitteratur.

Polkinghorne, D. E. (1992). Postmodern epistemology of practice. In S. Kvale (Ed.), *Psychology and postmodernism* (pp. 146-165). London: Sage.

Potter, J., & Wetherell, M. (1987). *Discourse and social psychology.* London: Sage.

Radnitzky, G. (1970). *Contemporary schools of metascience.* Gothenburg, Sweden: Akademiforlaget.

Rapaport, D. (1959). The structure of psychoanalytic theory: A systematizing attempt. In S. Koch (Ed.), *Psychology: A study of a science, III* (pp. 55-183). New York: McGraw-Hill.

Reason, P. (1994). Three approaches to participatory inquiry. In N. K. Denzin & Y. S. Lincoln (Eds.), *Handbook of qualitative research* (pp. 324-349). Thousand Oaks, CA: Sage.

Reichardt, C. S., & Cook, T. D. (1979). Beyond qualitative versus quantitative methods. In T. D. Cook & C. S. Reichardt (Eds.), *Qualitative and quantitative methods in evaluation research* (pp. 7-32). Beverly Hills, CA: Sage.

Richardson, L. (1990). *Writing strategies.* Newbury Park, CA: Sage.

Richardson, L. (1994). Writing: A method of inquiry. In N. K. Denzin & Y. S. Lincoln (Eds.), *Handbook of qualitative research* (pp. 516-529). Thousand Oaks, CA: Sage.

Richer, P. (1992). An introduction to deconstructionist psychology. In S. Kvale (Ed.), *Psychology and postmodernism* (pp. 110-118). London: Sage.

Ricoeur, P. (1970). *Freud and philosophy: An essay on interpretation.* New Haven, CT: Yale University Press.

Ricoeur, P. (1971). The model of the text: Meaningful action considered as a text. *Social Research, 38,* 529-562.

Riegel, K. F. (Ed.). (1975). *The development of dialectical operations.* Basel: Karger.

Rogers, C. R. (1965). *Client-centered therapy.* Cambridge, MA: Houghton Mifflin.

Rorty, R. (1979). *Philosophy and the mirror of nature.* Princeton, NJ: Princeton University Press.

Rorty, R. (1992). The pragmatist's progress. In U. Eco (Ed.), *Interpretation and overinterpretation* (pp. 89-108). Cambridge, UK: Cambridge University Press.

Rosenau, M. P. (1992). *Postmodernism and the social sciences.* Princeton, NJ: Princeton University Press.

Rubin, H. J., & Rubin, I. S. (1995). *Qualitative interviewing.* Thousand Oaks, CA: Sage.

Ryan, M. (1992). *Marxism and deconstruction.* Baltimore, MD: Johns Hopkins University Press.

Runyan, W. M. (1981). Why did van Gogh cut off his ear? The problem of alternative explanations in psychobiography. *Journal of Personality and Social Psychology, 40,* 1070-1077.

Salner, M. (1989). Validity in human science research. In S. Kvale (Ed.), *Issues of validity in qualitative research* (pp. 47-72). Lund, Sweden: Studentlitteratur.

Sartre, J.-P. (1963). *The problem of method.* London: Methuen.

Scheflen, A. E. (1978). Susan smiled: On explanations in family therapy. *Family Proceedings, 17,* 59-68.

Scheurich, J. J. (1995). A postmodernist critique of research interviewing. *Qualitative Studies in Education, 8,* 239-252.

Schofield, J. W. (1990). Increasing the generalizability of qualitative research. In E. W. Eisner & A. Peshkin (Eds.), *Qualitative inquiry in education* (pp. 201-232). New York: Teachers College Press.

Scott, S. (1985). Feminist research and qualitative methods: A discussion of some of the issues. In P. Burgess (Ed.), *Issues in educational research: Qualitative methods* (pp. 67-85). Philadelphia: Falmer Press.

Scriven, M. (1972). Objectivity and subjectivity in educational research. In L. G. Thomas (Ed.), *Philosophical redirection of educational research* (pp. 94-142). Chicago: Chicago University Press.

Seidman, I. E. (1991). *Interviewing as qualitative research.* New York: Teachers College Press.

Shakespeare, W. (1951). *Collected works.* London: Collins.

Shepherd, L. J. (1993). *Lifting the veil: The feminine side of science.* Boston: Shambala.

Shotter, J. (1993). *Conversational realities.* Thousand Oaks, CA: Sage.

Siegel, S. (1956). *Nonparametric statistics for the behavioral sciences.* New York: McGraw-Hill.

Silverman, D. (1993). *Interpreting qualitative data.* Thousand Oaks, CA: Sage.

Simons, H. W. (Ed.). (1989). *Rhetoric in the human sciences.* Beverly Hills, CA: Sage.

Skinner, B. F. (1961). A case history in scientific method. In B. F. Skinner (Ed.), *Cumulative record* (pp. 76-99). New York: Methuen.

Skou, C. V. (1996). *Qualitative interview and therapy analysis (KIT)* [computer program developed by Carl Verner Skou at the Center of Qualitative Research at the University of Aarhus, Aarhus, Denmark].

Smith, J. K., & Heshusius, L. (1986). Closing down the conversation: The end of the quantitative-qualitative debate among educational researchers. *Educational Researcher, 15*(1), 4-12.

Smith, L. M. (1990). Ethics in qualitative field research: An individual perspective. In E. W. Eisner & A. Peskin (Eds.), *Qualitative inquiry in education* (pp. 258-276). New York: Teachers College Press.

Spence, D. P. (1982). *Narrative truth and historical truth. Meaning and interpretation in psychoanalysis.* New York: Norton.

Spiegelberg, H. (1960). *The phenomenological movement, Vol. II.* The Hague, The Netherlands: Martinus Nijhoff.

Spradley, J. (1979). *The ethnographic interview.* New York: Holt, Rinehart & Winston.

Stake, R. E. (1994). Case studies. In N. K. Denzin & Y. S. Lincoln (Eds.), *Handbook of qualitative research* (pp. 236-247). Thousand Oaks, CA: Sage.

Strauss, A. (1995). Notes on the nature and development of general theories. *Journal of Phenomenological Psychology, 25,* 190-220.

Strauss, A. M., & Corbin, J. (1990). *Basics of qualitative research.* Newbury Park, CA: Sage.

Sullivan, H. S. (1954). *The psychiatric interview*. New York: Norton.

Tannen, D. (1990). Ordinary conversation and literary discourse: Coherence and the poetics of repetition. *Annals of the New York Academy of Sciences, 583*, 15-32.

Taylor, S. J., & Bogdan, R. (1984). *Introduction to qualitative research—The search for meanings*. New York: John Wiley.

Tedlock, D. (1983). *The spoken word and the work of interpretation*. Philadelphia: University of Pennsylvania Press.

Tesch, R. (1990). *Qualitative research: Analysis types and software tools*. London: Falmer.

Tschudi, F. (1989). Do qualitative and quantitative methods require different approaches to validity? In S. Kvale (Ed.), *Issues of validity in qualitative research* (pp. 109-134). Lund, Sweden: Studentlitteratur.

van Kaam, A. (1959). Phenomenal analysis: Exemplified by a study of the experience of "really feeling understood." *Journal of Individual Psychology, 15*, 66-72.

Van Maanen, J. (1988). *Tales of the field*. Chicago: University of Chicago Press.

Weber, S. J. (1986). The nature of interviewing. *Phenomenology + Pedagogy, 4*(2), 65-72.

Webster's Seventh New Collegiate Dictionary. (1967). Springfield, MA: Merriam Webster.

Weitzman, E. A., & Miles, M. B. (1995). *Computer programs for qualitative data analysis*. Thousand Oaks, CA: Sage.

Wolcott, H. F. (1990). *Writing up qualitative research*. Newbury Park, CA: Sage.

Wolcott, H. F. (1994). *Transforming qualitative data*. Thousand Oaks, CA: Sage.

Yin, R. K. (1994). *Case study research*. Newbury Park, CA: Sage.

Yow, V. R. (1994). *Recording oral history*. Thousand Oaks, CA: Sage.

Author Index

Subject Index

About the Author

Steinar Kvale is Professor of Educational Psychology and Director of the Centre of Qualitative Research at the University of Aarhus, Denmark, and adjunct faculty at Saybrook Institute, San Francisco. He was born in Norway and graduated from the University of Oslo. He continued his studies at the University of Heidelberg with an Alexander von Humboldt scholarship, and has been a visiting professor at Duquesne University and at West Georgia College, Carrolton. He is consulting editor on the *Journal of Phenomenological Psychology, Qualitative Inquiry, Qualitative Studies in Education,* and *Theory of Psychology.*

His long-term concern is with the implications of such continental philosophies as phenomenology, hermeneutics, and dialectics for psychology and education. He has studied examinations and grading, and is the author of *Prüfung und Herrschaft* (1972). His current interests are in evaluation as constituting the knowledge of a discipline, and in addressing the potentialities of apprenticeship as an educational form. He has written extensively on qualitative research, including editing the volume *Issues of Validity in Qualitative Research.* In *Psychology and Postmodernism,* which he also edited, he argues that psychology is a discipline so entrenched in modernity that it can hardly grasp human relations in a postmodern age.